MOJO
WORKIN'

MOJO WORKIN'

THE OLD AFRICAN AMERICAN HOODOO SYSTEM

KATRINA HAZZARD-DONALD

UNIVERSITY OF ILLINOIS PRESS

Urbana, Chicago, and Springfield

∞ This book is printed on acid-free paper.

Library of Congress Cataloging-in-Publication Data
Hazzard-Donald, Katrina, 1948–
Mojo workin' : the old African American Hoodoo system /
Katrina Hazzard-Donald.
p.   cm.
Includes bibliographical references and index.
ISBN 978-0-252-03729-0 (cloth : alk. paper)
ISBN 978-0-252-07876-7 (pbk. : alk. paper)
ISBN 978-0-252-09446-0 (e-book)
1. Hoodoo (Cult) 2. Voodooism—United States.
3. African American magic. 4. Medicine, Magic, mystic, and spagiric—
United States. 5. African Americans—Religion. 6. African Americans—Folklore.
I. Title.
BL2490.H39   2013
133.4308996073—dc23   2012020649

*To my late husband, Lathan Lee Donald, tried in battle;
and to my daughter, Jameka, who is on her way to becoming a skilled Hoodoo. To daddy, Stonewall Hazzard, child
of freedmen, who regaled me and my childhood friends with
Hoodoo tales of ghost horses, High John roots, haints, lodestone, and powerful Hoodoos from Alabama. To mamma,
Susie Isaac Hazzard, who treated our "chest colds" with
coal oil and white sugar, who dropped keys down our backs
to stop nose bleeds, who wrapped minor cuts in cobwebs,
who treated our swellings with mullein leaves, who dug the
roots, healed the sick, transformed negative energies into
positive using sardine oil and "greasy fat meat." To those
who treated the crack epidemic of the 1990s with Hoodoo
medicine, who still scold and praise the children, who
chew the root for all those unjustly incarcerated in Ronald
Reagan's attack on the African American community disguised as the "War on Drugs."*

*To all those born of black women who came walking in
the spirit of our African ancestors. And for those African
American "race men and race women" yet to be born.*

Contents

Acknowledgments

All work, whether monumental or modest, is never the result of a solitary effort. I owe thanks to people too numerous to name who supported and assisted me in the production of this work. I thank the American Council of Learned Societies who supplied me with a fellowship that allowed me to take a year from teaching in order to travel to various locations to examine resources and interview informants; without the support of the ACLS fellowship program, this work might never have been undertaken. I thank Robert Farris Thompson, who agreed to read an early draft of this work. I am indebted to Marquetta Goodwine, known to the residents of St. Helena Island, South Carolina, as Queen Quet, Queen of the Gullah people. I thank my generous informants Ms. Mary; Arthur Flowers; Brother Gregory; Papa Ce; Dancingtree Moonwater; Hougan Vincent, known to some as Papa Cosmos; Phoenix Savage; and Djenra Windwalker, who fight to maintain the old tradition, to keep African American Hoodoo alive, and who serve the African American community in the names of our ancestors. I give special thanks and honor to Mama Zogbe, chief Hounon-Amengansie of West African Mami Wata Vodoun. Thank you for keeping the faith. I thank Professor James Turner of the Africana Studies and Research Center at Cornell University, who told me the story of his aunt's potential arm amputation by white medical doctors and her healing encounter with Hoodoo medicine. I thank all the African Americans who told Hoodoo stories and renewed the moribund faith in us even as the tradition was facing transformation by marketeers and confronting impending death.

I owe special thanks to all the reference librarians and archivists, from Mr. Willie Maryland of the Montgomery state archives in Montgomery, Alabama, to Catherine C. Khan, the archivist at the old Touro Infirmary in New

Orleans, who allowed me to examine the original admission logbooks and records from 1855 to 1861 in search of information on Hoodoo and slave health care. I owe thanks to both Grace Cordial in special collections at the Beaufort, South Carolina, public library, who was helpful in directing me to vertical file materials on local Hoodoo, and the librarian in the Cleveland, Ohio, public library, who allowed me to examine several uncataloged boxes of Newbell Niles Puckett materials. The librarians at the Tallahassee, Florida, state archives pointed me to several boxes of interview materials from both Zora Neale Hurston and the Works Progress Administration writers. I offer a special thank-you to the library staff at the Amistad collection in pre-Katrina New Orleans, who directed me to copies of missionary records as well as public health interviews from the 1930s conducted with informants on the street about their healing practices and beliefs in "Hoodoo medicine." And a special thank-you to the border control agent in Laredo, Texas, William Graves, who sent me a dozen High John roots. To Professor Mark Leone of the University of Maryland, College Park, who allowed me to examine and to photograph the artifacts from an antebellum slave conjurer's cache, circa the 1820s, uncovered in an archaeological dig in southern Virginia: Thank you for the afternoon.

Last but not least, I thank my family and my dear late husband, Lathan Donald, who supported me when I became ill and had to stop working on the manuscript. He nursed me, fed me in bed, and encouraged me to return to work whenever I became discouraged. Above all, I thank God, known to me as Olodumare, but who is called by many names. I thank my ancestors, who always "had my back," and my personal orisha father, Ogun, and mother, Oshun, for the will to keep fighting and for the wisdom to know when to change tack in the battle. Finally, I thank all those African American believers and practitioners of the Old Black Belt Hoodoo tradition for holding on until we could arrive.

African Traditional Religions

African · Religion · Complex

- water immersion
- spirit possession
- principle of sacrifice
- belief in spiritual cause of malady
- divination
- counterclockwise sacred circle dancing
- ancestor reverence
- naturopathic medicine

The Old Hoodoo Religion

Ring Shout

Conjure/Hoodoo/Root Work

The Black Church

- The Sanctified Church
- A. M. E. Church
- The Baptist Church

Holy Dance/Shouting

Marketeered Hoodoo/curios

Secular Dance Forms

Theatrical Dance

- Alvin Ailey
- Katherine Dunham
- Pearl Primus
- Hemsley Wingfield

Social/Folk/Vernacular Form

- the stroll
- snake hips
- wringin' and twistin'
- slop
- shimmy
- dog
- Texas Tommy

African traditional religion chart.

The Old Tradition "Black Belt" Hoodoo Complex

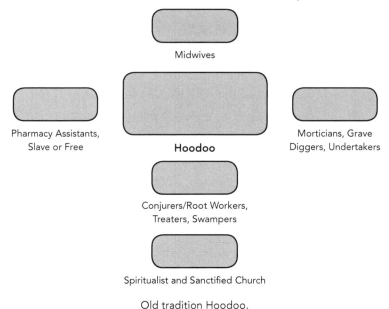

Midwives

Pharmacy Assistants,
Slave or Free

Hoodoo

Morticians, Grave
Diggers, Undertakers

Conjurers/Root Workers,
Treaters, Swampers

Spiritualist and Sanctified Church

Old tradition Hoodoo.

Modern/Contemporary Hoodoo Complex

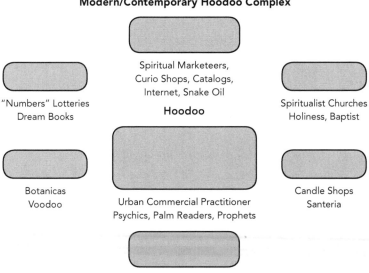

Spiritual Marketeers,
Curio Shops, Catalogs,
Internet, Snake Oil

"Numbers" Lotteries
Dream Books

Hoodoo

Spiritualist Churches
Holiness, Baptist

Botanicas
Voodoo

Urban Commercial Practitioner
Psychics, Palm Readers, Prophets

Candle Shops
Santeria

Old Tradition Practitioners
Conjurers, Root Doctors, Treaters

Modern marketeered Hoodoo.

PRESCRIPT

On October 7, 1994, then nationally known talk show host Phil Donahue featured a segment highlighting a terrifying and bizarre incident that occurred in Dallas, Texas. The incident involved a young African American woman, a school teacher named Myra Obasi, who allegedly had been taken to a "hoodooist"[1] who had confirmed that she was possessed by an evil spirit. Obasi, two of her sisters, and five of their children had fled Arcadia, Louisiana, and ended up in Dallas at the church and home of Mattie Bradfield; there Obasi had been allegedly blinded by the removal of her eyeballs. She appeared on *Donahue* in the company of two of her sisters, two attorneys, and a psychotherapist. Though Obasi and her family members repeatedly confirmed their belief in and adherence to Christian doctrine, they also asserted their belief in demonic possession, malevolent magic, and spiritual realities beyond everyday comprehension.

Throughout the televised segment, the terms *hoodoo* and *voodoo* were used interchangeably to plumb the mysteries of such an incident; in the process, the observer was left with a reinforced feeling of dread, confusion, and fear already associated with those two terms. Professor David Otto, also a guest on the show and by no means an expert on African-derived religion or African traditional religions (ATRs), when asked whether such an incident was possible inside Hoodoo practice, replied that he had never heard of such a thing in Hoodoo, but that in Voodoo it could have occurred. He further defined Hoodoo as largely a rural, folk, herbal-based, health care system used primarily by blacks who have little access to mainstream medical care. Otto's incomplete definition revealed that his understanding of Hoodoo was more closely related to the now invisible folk religion of the old black belt Hoodoo tradition.

The occurrence of this bizarre event and its media association with the terms *Voodoo* and *Hoodoo* signaled and confirmed for this writer the distance between African American cultural reality and mainstream America's unsympathetic misunderstanding of that reality. The apparent invisibility of Hoodoo practice to much of the American mainstream might lead one to conclude that if Hoodoo exists and functions at all, it has little relevance for younger African Americans and is only an insignificant remnant of useless superstition still clung to by older, uneducated blacks. Certainly the context of Hoodoo practice has evolved and been modified by a range of factors; nevertheless, certain seminal or core Hoodoo practices, informing principles, paradigms, and values have persisted with extraordinary sociocultural tenacity.

Asking "what is Hoodoo?" invites a range of interesting responses, not excluding a straightforward working definition that Hoodoo is the folk, spiritual controlling, and healing tradition originating among and practiced primarily, but not exclusively, by captive African Americans and their descendants primarily in the southern United States. If one were to ask a randomly selected group of African Americans that same question, a variety of answers would be forthcoming, ranging from "I don't know," to emotional testimonials whispered through secretive tones. Some respondents would openly dismiss Hoodoo as a remnant of African primitivism and superstition; others would attest to its efficacy. The answers would all be influenced by demographic variables and possibilities, such as the age of the respondents and the region of the country in which they grew up and currently reside as well as their socioeconomic status. Hoodoo, like other aspects of African American culture, is class sensitive, though not always class specific.

Hoodoo has endured numerous definitions. More than twenty-five years ago, Ralph R. Kuna defined Hoodoo as the indigenous medicine and psychiatry of the black American.[2] Like its predecessors, the traditional African religions transported to America, Hoodoo made no separation of its medicinal and spiritual function. Because of its evolving nature as well as its invisible and frequently secretive presence, it is difficult to pin down a satisfactory definition of Hoodoo that conveys its totality. Such an elusive topic and task can even be somewhat challenging to a well-focused examination of how Hoodoo functions and what difficulties or problems it addresses. Hoodoo is no longer a religion; it is the view here that Hoodoo is the reorganized remnants of what must have been, albeit short-lived, a full-blown syncretized African-based religion among African American bondsmen. The syncretic quality was unlike that found occurring under Roman Catholicism; it was far less apparent and achieved a less direct as well as a lesser degree of syncretic penetration. Only a few religious figures would achieve something resembling syncretic transfer. The case of High John the Conquer and its correlation with John the prophet was the best known. But other syncretic possibilities existed in the quasi-religious folktales, religious stories, and jokes. And like many West and Central West African traditional religions, the Hoodoo religion involved spirit possession, ancestor reverence, water immersion, herbal medicine, sacred music, circle dancing, and shaman priests who functioned in a variety of roles, including that of leader in religious activity such as role model in the sacred ritual of the Ring Shout.[3]

The assertion that Hoodoo could possibly have been a religion to bondsmen may surprise and even offend some readers. It is generally agreed in both scholarly and public discourse that African American slaves could not possibly have had a real religion, especially since their African predecessors were viewed as idol worshipers by both Christians and Muslims alike. The contention that early Hoodoo could not have assumed the status of a religion is in part informed by prejudicial notions that Africans, in their "primitive" state, did not have "true" or "real" religion but something less; or that slavery destroyed all vestiges of African religions and spiritual activity. Thus they needed Christian missionaries or Muslim proselytizers to "save" them and teach them "the way." Definitions are fraught with both political content and intention. Defining African religious and spiritual and supernatural practices as outside of "religion" in part justified the invasion, oppression, exploitation, and conversion of Africans to Christianity.

In the transitional loss of the old gods, Africans in the United States, in their own process of interethnic assimilation separate from whites, initially maintained characteristics and practices common to many West and Central West African religious traditions. Belief in a single god and its ability to intercede on mankind's behalf was a tenet in that belief system. For the purposes of this study, religion is defined as a coherent personal or institutionalized system of spiritual belief and practice. The old Hoodoo religion contained those African elements that would later give birth to numerous religious practices that would be labeled "superstition" because they were outside of acceptable mainstream Christian practice. It would also give birth to numerous practices that would become secularized and move into African American popular culture, particularly in music and dance, but into other areas and into the black church as well.

The function of any belief system is to make sense of experience and reality. A historic view of Hoodoo as a system of spiritual belief and explanation reveals that it appears to address every problem that African Americans have confronted, past or present. Those problems include obtaining freedom and protection while resisting or running away from slavery; harming the master, his family, or his property; protecting a loved one about to be sold; preventing beatings and other forms of harsh punishment; returning a loved one; healing a malady; addressing issues of mental, sexual, and public health; and protecting against curses or witchcraft. Issues of family uncertainty, employment and financial difficulties, legal issues involving current or future possible incarceration, as well as health problems would dominate later Hoodoo. In addition to specific individual problems, Hoodoo specialists have treated, and continue to treat, the general condition of "luck" or lack thereof. This treatment of "bad luck," though apparently unfocused, is particularly significant in that it addresses a general spiritual condition believed to influence overall aspects of an individual's existence. This is often expressed in contemporary Hoodoo belief as "jinx removing," though the term probably has its origin outside of African American culture. Today one can purchase a range of products aimed at jinx removing; these products include jinx-removing oil, jinx-removing air freshener, house blessing spray, jinx-removing bath powders and soaps, jinx-removing floor wash, jinx-removing incense, and jinx-removing candles, to mention only a few. This range of products is sometimes marketed under the label "good luck" candles or "luck-drawing oil," "personal blessing oil," or other similar names.

For the purposes of this study, Hoodoo is the indigenous, herbal, healing, and supernatural-controlling spiritual folk tradition of the African American in the United States. Hoodoo has endured numerous labels, among them black magic, witchcraft, devil's work, and superstition, though other less pejorative names include spirit work, root work, conjure, spiritualism, psychic work, or simply "the work." Similar to some missionary treatment of African traditional religion as evil, the conceptualization of Hoodoo as the devil's work is not new; this long-standing conceptualization of conjure as evil sometimes leads contemporary informants to refer to conjure as witchcraft and to view it as a force opposing Christianity.

Essentially, Hoodoo, for African Americans, is embodied historical memory linking them back through time to previous generations and ultimately to their African past. It is also a paradigm for approaching both the world and all areas of social life. Among contemporary African Americans, certain retained aspects of Hoodoo were learned from parents, grandparents, and great-grandparents who passed tales, information, beliefs, practices, and paradigms to their descendants, sometime inadvertently.[4] And more recently, marketeered hoodoo supplies and paraphernalia have made their appearance in Internet catalogs and Web sites, supermarkets, botanicas, spiritual supply houses, drugstores, as well as revitalized curio shops, the place turned to most often by the uninformed for Hoodoo supplies and sometimes services. Because certain practices found in early Hoodoo successfully found their way into a new life in the African American church, postemancipation Hoodoo tradition is not completely separate from black Christian church tradition, but rather it is entwined with it, either as a complement or a challenge to church power. This is especially true for the Spiritualist, Sanctified, and Baptist churches where old tradition black belt Hoodoo ritual is often a complement to sacred church activity.

While significant effort has been made since the 1970s in rethinking African American historical and cultural development, until recently little effort has been given to rethinking African American Hoodoo. Other aspects of African American cultural and religious life, especially music and literature, receive more enlightened attention. Like African American music, dance, and literature, Hoodoo is ever changing, evolving, and responding to the sociocultural environment as well as undergoing modification by its practitioners. Until recently, especially in public discourse, Hoodoo was neither discussed nor understood in terms of religion or legitimate spiritual practice. Nor was African American spirituality understood or much discussed outside of the discourse on American Protestantism.[5] An underlying intent of this work, then, is to reinforce the study of African American Hoodoo within the dialogue on African religion in the New World as well as to reveal certain hidden and previously unconsidered aspects of this tradition; this has not always been the direction of previous Hoodoo studies. Hoodoo has been conceptualized and explained by some as a derivative of a syncretized Spanish or French Catholic expression, such as in Haitian Vodun or Santeria, rather than having its own independent developmental path. It continues to be viewed today by some African Americans as merely a collection of foolish superstitions with little meaning, little if any cultural history, and no redeeming social significance; few perspectives could be less accurate. Framing some of this reaction is a fear as well as a failure to separate the practices and outline of the old plantation Hoodoo from contemporary commercially marketeered and "snake oil" Hoodoo.

Growing up in a community of first- and second-generation southern African American migrants from the Montgomery, Alabama, black belt into the urban, industrial Midwest, this writer had been exposed to some aspects of Hoodoo but took it for granted and never gave it serious thought until I began studying traditional West African dance. I became interested in Hoodoo as a result of my involvement with African and African-derived dancing. Moving from dance to Hoodoo may appear a rather circuitous path; it was not. As scholar John S. Mbiti states "African religion is found in music and dance."[6] So as I studied more of the African-derived dance forms of the New World, I was introduced to the African religions that had given rise to a majority of the dances. In the process of becoming more involved in both practicing and investigating West African religion, I observed subtle but apparent similarities between it and both black church ritual and the Hoodoo I had seen and heard of in my childhood and teen years; this stimulated my further interest in Hoodoo.

When considering the relationship between Hoodoo and the Ring Shout, my work as a dance researcher informs my perspective. Researching this work has encouraged me to reexamine the African American sacred dance ritual known as the Ring Shout and its function in the African American community, slave and free, in light of historical old tradition black belt Hoodoo practice. As I raised questions about the nature of the Ring Shout ritual, I could only conclude that a religion other than Christianity was the context for its emergence and continued existence. Searching for that religion, I could only conclude that Hoodoo had to have been that religion, albeit briefly, and the Ring Shout was its sacred dance.

As someone whose past work has involved the search for continuities and preexisting African influences as a way to understand contemporary African American core culture dancing,[7] understanding the sociocultural movement of Hoodoo in terms of its continuities with African religion seemed reasonable to me as I searched for ways to approach the topic. The notion of continuities is certainly not novel and is part of a well-established tradition. Like African American dancing and music making, African American folk spirituality, as Hoodoo, demonstrates strong continuities with African spirituality elsewhere both in the New World and in Africa; yet Hoodoo is its own unique cultural manifestation. And in that posture it has been affected by a range of demographic, ethnic, marketing, and technological influences that have impacted African Americans.

Throughout my investigation of conjure, another name for Hoodoo, I have tried to remain sensitive to possible comparisons with other New World, African-derived religious systems as a way to possibly shed light on the origin, development, and function of African American Hoodoo; preceding writers have done this. I found this approach most useful when I noted similarities with the cultural continuities with preexisting or "parent" traditions as well as with the developmental uniqueness of Hoodoo. Where similarities are noted, there are two possible explanations, either that Hoodoo practice is similar because it is influenced by a collateral practice from another system such as Santeria, New Orleans Voodoo, or Haitian Vodun, the most com-

6

mon position, or that the similarity exists because Hoodoo an̸
systems have common religiocultural ancestors and great-gra̸
and stand as third cousins with separate lines of developme̸
acknowledge possible influences from other systems in the eaɪ̠,
of Hoodoo, I tend to favor the latter perspective on Hoodoo developɴ̠.
I limit the discussion of cross-cultural similarities primarily to those New
World African and traditional African religious practices and themes that
are noted most frequently in the U.S. literature and are most familiar.

The earliest transformation of African religion into Hoodoo likely involved significant components of cultural exchange with other groups, Europeans or white American settlers and especially the Native Americans.
Though the full complement of contributions by Native Americans to old
tradition Hoodoo may never be recounted, the herbal healing aspect of
Hoodoo is probably heavily influenced by Native American custom, knowledge, and tradition. The belief that Native American practice contributed
directly to Hoodoo development is widespread, but little evidence is offered to support that assertion. I offer a small amount of evidence and
several possibilities. Mixing with traditional African, European, and Native
American herbal knowledge, African American Hoodoo could very well
have analogues in Native American and European practices. Certainly Native Americans were the most familiar with the continent's flora and fauna,
and they had established centuries-long knowledge of local plants and their
properties. Black Indians or African Native Americans, who often stood
in both Native American and African American communities, could have
accessed both traditions and may have been influential in the transfer of
information, knowledge, customs, and practices into Hoodoo. Native Americans also encountered African Americans at historically black colleges and
universities such as Hampton in Virginia.

In this work, Hoodoo's development is more precisely conceptualized as
a series of overlapping progressions and regressions of intertwined strands
for which accurate description ranges far beyond one approach. Nevertheless, here the movement of Hoodoo through time is conceptualized
in three broad stages with overlapping demarcations and subsets. Because
Hoodoo movement cannot be neatly packaged in three clean-cut linear
historical packages, I have partially demarcated the stages based on changes
in Hoodoo and located them in time, temporally correlating them with a
changing historical backdrop of major mainstream influences on black
life and culture.

As a sociocultural phenomenon, Hoodoo's movement is governed by
unique cycles of stimuli that have varied in duration and social location.

Much of what we today conceptualize as African American culture may have entered African American cultural space as sacred reenactments; for example, practices such as the eating of animal intestines may have begun on southern plantations as a clandestine sacred observance reminiscent of practices performed in traditional African ritual. This practice would gradually secularize and become known simply as eating chitterlings. These types of ritual reenactments supported the shape and social formulation of the early though short-lived Hoodoo religion.

Though much of the data for this study is not new and is used by other researchers, this study intends to present a new look at Hoodoo development and a reinterpretative glimpse at contemporary as well as preexisting Hoodoo practice. Much of this work is speculative, particularly the discussion of the most sacred root in Hoodoo practice, High John the Conquer root. Hoodoo has been of interest to a wide diversity of observers, from law enforcement officials to marketeers. Researchers from anthropological to medical and psychiatric have expressed scholarly interest in the subject for at least the past century. Few have discussed the topic in such a way as to reveal the meaning, fluctuating legitimacy, and place of Hoodoo to those who believe in and utilize it. Hopefully I will avoid the same pitfalls and will both contribute to and complement the research that has preceded my own small effort.

As with all investigative manuscripts, this one has its weaknesses; since no one has offered data indicating that Hoodoo was unknown to a significant number of African Americans, I operate on the assumption that Hoodoo was known to all members of core culture black communities. I have never asked an African American about "roots" or "Hoodoo" who had not heard of it. I have chosen for a number of reasons not to emphasize "race," as one critic has suggested. That is the subject of another study. Though "race" is of bedrock significance in both U.S. history and African American life, it is not the only dimension that lends understanding to interpretations of black life and culture and need not be included as a dominant theme in all research on African Americans. There is a rapidly emerging new body of scholarship, such as that of psychiatrist Frances Cress Welsing and labor historian David R. Roediger, that challenges previous scholarship on "race" in the United States and is too vast and ideologically challenging to be included here without obscuring the subject of this study. I have chosen not to utilize postdeconstructionist language or paradigms as a way to approach Hoodoo's movement. The two seemed incompatible, and their use risks giving the subject an academic faddish overlay that would either obscure or possibly skew many of the points that I wished to make.

This is not to say that Hoodoo is uncontested. Indeed it is by those who see Hoodoo as a national African American cultural product and those who are outsiders to the African American community and who claim their right to sell it for income. Cultural contestation is not new and can be found in places throughout the Western Hemisphere wherever African derived culture is manifest on a national level, as in Cuba or Brazil.

In a number of places, I make explicit an idea that underpins and informs the approach and to some degree the conclusions here. The idea that African Americans have formed a "nation within a nation" with their own territory, common ancestry, unique aesthetic in music, dance, literature, food, clothing, and religion, and not simply a segregated group in American life, is an old idea with a history of vigorous debate on both the left and the right.

Some of the cultural practices discussed here have been the focus of earlier examinations, but these examinations rarely have contextualized the practice in a wider religious framework. Studies of African American folklore, folk medicine, folk magic, dance, and music have all been approached as separate entities with no common overarching umbrella under which they all at one time fit. Most previous studies have not connected the elements of music, dance, medicine, midwifery, spirit possession, and water immersion. This study both asserts and assumes that the old Hoodoo religion was the African American "sacred canopy" and that certain aspects of black culture were once part of the old African American Hoodoo system, a system of folk religion that precedes both the black Christian church and the process of secularization of aspects of the culture, such as music and dance. But other aspects of African American culture such as traditional proverbs, "sacred voice" and "sacred signs" were also part of the old Hoodoo tradition. This work sees many of those practices related to one another in a "Hoodoo complex" that either has been previously overlooked or presumed to be nonexistent.

The earliest examinations of conjure, as Hoodoo was also known, was in periodicals, particularly the *Southern Workman* and the *Journal of American Folklore,* which published Leonora Herron and Alice M. Bacon's 1878 work for the Hampton Virginia Folklore Society, with other articles occasionally appearing in journals such as *Century Magazine* or *American Mercury.* Since the 1960s, a range of specialists has used interdisciplinary approaches to the study of Hoodoo. Physicians such as Roland Steiner, psychologists, medical anthropologists, and social workers have generated a body of literature that examines the role of belief in supernatural healing and harming among African Americans. Regional studies and specialized vertical file materials have provided the Hoodoo researcher with a source of materials and have contributed significantly to the literature on Hoodoo during the 1930s, '40s, and '50s.

Beginning with Melville Herskovits, a number of scholars have addressed some of the implicit cultural issues leading to the misunderstanding that surrounds the reception and interpretation of African American culture in the United States. Certainly Harry Middleton Hyatt's five-volume work *Hoodoo-Conjuration-Witchcraft-Rootwork*,[8] which completed publication in 1978, is a landmark collection. Hyatt has provided those interested in Hoodoo with an extensive body of texts, dates, locations, and interview data gathered over several decades. Traveling extensively, he interviewed self-identified Hoodoo practitioners and believers from Baltimore, Maryland, to Jacksonville, Florida, from Brunswick, Georgia, to Little Rock, Arkansas. He collected the words and practices of his informants and made few attempts to interpret his vastly fertile material. Though some of his data may be questionable and problematic, Hyatt nevertheless created the single most impressive repository of Hoodoo interviews and observations. Hyatt's two primary flaws are, first, that he began collecting his data after the "golden age" of Hoodoo had passed. The Hoodoo that he collected was different from that of the old black belt system. By the time Hyatt began collecting his data, Hoodoo marketeering had altered the old system in favor of fabrications that permeated Hoodoo nationally and had transformed it. Hyatt's data collection could have one other significant flaw, that known as "interviewer effect." Working with tape recording technology, and as a "white man" outsider and representative of the American mainstream, Hyatt's professional presentation of self may have influenced the answers he received from his primarily black informant pool.

Probably the second most extensive examination of Hoodoo and perhaps the first full-scale examination is Newbell Niles Puckett's work that culminated in the publication of *Folk Beliefs of the Southern Negro*.[9] His examination raised significant questions and opened an important view of the scope of Hoodoo practice. Including both the medicinal and spiritual components of Hoodoo in his examination, Puckett demonstrates the richness, scope, and tenacity of the Hoodoo tradition as it was practiced by Hoodoo contemporaries of his day. He also highlights numerous similarities between African American Hoodoo practices in healing, burial, and conjuring and various West African traditional practices.

One cannot think of Hoodoo studies without the work of Zora Neale Hurston coming to mind. Several of her works give insight into the Hoodoo tradition, including her works "High John De Conquer," *Mules and Men,* and "Hoodoo in America."[10] Unlike earlier researchers on the subject, Hurston is said to have undergone several Hoodoo initiations to become a practitioner and insider. Some writers have challenged this claim. Her participant observation would have given her access to Hoodoo on a level that was closed to most scholars interested in the topic. This author's personal experience as a participant observer verifies this.

I found that searching out data and writing about Hoodoo required me to become sensitized to Hoodoo's hiding places and secret locations. One place that Hoodoo data hides is in the literature on help-seeking behaviors, particularly medical concerns. The works of Loudell F. Snow, Faith Mitchell, Wanda Fontenot, and most recently Phoenix Savage focus their investigations here.[11] Gilbert Cooley, who also writes under the name Elon Kulii, focused his work on Hoodoo in Indiana in the mid-1970s and provides important ethnographic data in the form of conversations and collected Hoodoo tales.[12] I later concluded that Cooley did not interview any old tradition Hoodoo workers. I examined two studies of black healing and conjure that focused on the period preceding emancipation, namely Jean Robinson's and Yvonne Chireau's dissertations completed in 1979 and 1994, respectively; they provide useful historical information.[13] In addition, Chireau extends her work by examining the relationship between Hoodoo and the African American church.[14] But Chireau stops short of distinguishing between the old African American Hoodoo system, the folk form, and the marketeered version found at Web sites like Luckymojo.com. Because she had no contact with old tradition Hoodoo workers, Chireau's subsequent work, *Black Magic*, demonstrates a fundamental shortcoming in that she turns to Santeria to explain Hoodoo and that she appears not to know that the old system even exists.

Cassandra Wimbs's master's thesis on candle shops examines the intersection of several alternative spiritual traditions, notably Hoodoo, Voodoo, and Santeria, as they present themselves in her primary research site, the candle shop. Her work allows us to further chart the movement and influence of Hoodoo in its metamorphic balance between sustaining old traditions and intersecting with previously unencountered ones.

The work of Michael Edward Bell in its analysis and interpretation of Harry Middleton Hyatt's data brings an organized legitimating analysis to the vast uninterpreted collection of Hoodoo informants' interviews in Hyatt's five volumes. Bell outlines structure and function in Hoodoo practice and makes one of the great contributions to a fuller understanding of Hoodoo.[15]

I examined a master's thesis on what the author called "the Gullah church," and this work came closest to my own observation on the uniqueness of the Ring Shout context. This same author also touches on the relationship between the Gullah church and root work but falls short of calling ly expressions of this church what it was, the Hoodoo church. This ...usal directly reflects the fear and negativity associated with that term.

Finally, Jeffery Anderson's work *Conjure in African American Society*[16] was published just as I was completing a first draft of this work. Anderson attempts to construct a theory of Hoodoo development using a cultural dichotomy dividing Africans enslaved by "Latins" versus Africans enslaved by English speakers. This sociocultural dichotomy, which uses the culture of the "slave master" to chart the development of Hoodoo, is, by itself, thin and neglects an important element considered by this text. Certainly, the dominant European ethnicity in the area would exert influence on slave cultural development, but how deeply influential would it be? And could there be any other equally influential presence impacting upon macrocultural development as well as microsocial elements of slave life and culture? I contend that there were at least two; one was the slaves' ethnicity, and the other was the slaves' labor. Anderson envisions two primary cultural areas as he constructs a model to explain certain aspects of Hoodoo practice, but he completely neglects the contribution by the regional and labor determinants of the material culture of the various slave regions. He also neglects the influence of the various African ethnic groups on Hoodoo's development. Unlike Anderson, this author uses a "tricotomy" based on region of the country, primary crop, and material culture as well as the culture of both the slave master and the ethnicity of Africans in considering Hoodoo's origin and development. I also contend, but do not explore, that some of the European-based outsider contributions to Hoodoo were imposed on Hoodoo by the later marketeers and were not the sociocultural heritage of the plantation.

The model of culture, whether it was in cotton culture, or in tobacco of the upper South, or in sugarcane of the Gulf Coast, or in rice and indigo of the Gullah Coast, was supported by labor and a derivative material culture, all of which impacted Hoodoo. Although I personally believe that Native American spiritual tradition and healing influenced early Hoodoo development, I found little evidence to support this, so I did not pursue that trajectory of investigation.

As I was beginning to formulate my first ideas about Hoodoo, I was initiated into one of the traditional New World African religious systems. I did not choose Orisha reverence through the Yoruba/Lukumi tradition; it chose me. One evening in August 1995 in Sewanee County, Florida, I was bathed in the hot waters of the Sewanee River and taken to a railroad track where part of my initiation to Ogun, Lord of Iron, warrior Orisha, would take place. The initiation into the mysteries of Orisha have provided me with an additional backdrop against which I can view Hoodoo practice. By familiarizing me from the inside out with a West African religious system and its syncretic New World variant, the Orisha tradition broadened my basis for comparison, suggested alternative avenues of interpretation, and gave me an additional set of spiritual grips with which to handle Hoodoo.

In July 1993, two years prior to my initiation as an Olorisha, I had received my Egungun cloth and ancestral pot and sacred protective necklace known as *eleke*. Next came Esu/Elegba and the accompanying warriors, Ogun and Ochosi, as well as the red and black *eleke* for Esu, principle of uncertainty, often and popularly known as the trickster deity. Next came the full set of *elekes* or *collares*, including Oshun, Yemoja, Shango, and Obatala. I now had a full set of *elekes*, including one for Ogun, received with my Orisha, and one for Agaju, the Volcano, which I received in Havana, Cuba, in the summer of 1990. In addition, after my initiation I received my Ede de Ogun, a green and black bracelet indicating my status as an initiated Olorisha of Ogun. One year later, I would receive the "first hand of Ifa" (*mano de ifa*), including the sixteen Ikin nuts, a green and reddish orange *ede* (bracelet), and a green and reddish orange *eleke* for Orumila, divinatory Orisha. I found that entry into one of the African, syncretic, New World traditions, whether it was Vodun, Candomble, Regla de Orisha (also known as Lukumi, Santeria, and Yoruba), Palo Monte/Mayombe, or Akan, gave me a certain degree of access to all African traditional religions that was extended as a courtesy to initiates of other systems. I found this fluidity of acceptance helpful in conversing with devotees of African religious traditions different than my own, but more important it sensitized me to possible sites of exchange and to invisible cultural process. Through the initiation process and Orisha practice, I broadened my basis for comparison when viewing Hoodoo. Initiation into the worship system of a major West African religion has suggested additional avenues of interpretation to me and hopefully has provided me with an additional vantage point from which to view early Hoodoo practice as described in the existing literature.

Penetrating and understanding the world of Hoodoo has never been, and is not today, an unchallenging task; Hoodoo has undergone numerous changes since its birth under American slavery. After about a year of attempting to discuss Hoodoo with a range of informants with diverse vested interest in it, I found it necessary to adopt multiple personas, fashioned to meet the expectations of my widely ranging informant pool. Except for two stores that I visited in New Orleans in April 2003, some owners of curio shops that sell Hoodoo paraphernalia were often the least cooperative, some responded with controlled hostility when questioned and appeared to be annoyed and sometime threatened by my inquiries. This was especially true of three Internet sources I contacted.[17] Contrary to my assumptions that my insider status would make them more cooperative, my insider status seemed to increase their defensiveness, particularly of one merchant in Philadelphia. I could only conclude that my insider status was threatening because I could potentially challenge the authenticity of their services and "spells."

An unanticipated response to discussing my research has been convincing members of my potential audience that I was not mispronouncing the term *Voodoo*. The exchange usually went something like this: "What did you say you were researching, Voodoo?" "No, Hoodoo." "Did you say Voodoo? You mean Voodoo, don't you?" "No, I mean Hoodoo with an *H*, I'm not mispronouncing Voodoo." Usually after several minutes they realized that Hoodoo and Voodoo are not exactly the same phenomenon and that I was not simply mispronouncing Vodun. I usually went on to explain that the two traditions were linked as distant cousins.

Although it is not as overwhelmingly significant and visible today as it once was for African Americans, Hoodoo in the not-too-distant past has been as significant as music and dance in shaping and revealing African American psychology and ethnic identity as well as outsider portrayals of blacks. African American deep spirituality, extending beyond accepted Christian practice, has been part of many comic portrayals, and these portrayals have been part of a wider campaign of "public dishonor" heaped upon African Americans. In the past, belief in Hoodoo was viewed by white Americans as part of African American national character and identity. African American celebrities no less than Lincoln "Stepin Fetchit" Perry, Mantan Moreland, Willie Bess, and more recently Whoopi Goldberg have all given widely viewed comic portrayals whose effectiveness is underpinned by a marginalized, subtly ridiculing, and negatively stereotyped understanding and misinterpretation of African American deep spirituality.[18] This deep spirituality extends beyond Christian practice acknowledging a world of spirits, haints, witches, and malevolent as well as beneficial forces that can be accessed and harnessed by humans with either the gift or the training to do so.

How has Hoodoo practice been able to survive and persist? How has it changed over the years? Unlike African American music, which has been highly visible, Hoodoo has not proved to be universally marketable, so we must exclude marketability and cultural appeal as the only significant factors in its longevity. Unlike food, it is not consumed daily, resulting in conditioned tastes, thus explaining its persistence and longevity. Hoodoo had achieved a high level of functionality and must have served, and for some continues to serve, a community of believers and practitioners whose needs are somehow met by it. The adherence to Hoodoo represents a hopeful refusal by African American bondsmen and their descendants to completely relinquish either African-style deep spirituality or their own spiritual agency in daily slave life, thus preserving elements of their African identity. Enslaved Africans and their descendants held on and believed in themselves.

In the process of this research, I discovered the existence of two Hoodoos. One that I designated as "old tradition black belt Hoodoo" includes the original short-lived Hoodoo folk religion and, later, when Hoodoo as a religion became unsustainable, the Hoodoo spiritual tradition that continued to be developed by African and African American captives on southern U.S. plantations. The second I labeled "marketeered" or "snake-oil Hoodoo." None of the authors writing on the topic have drawn this significant distinction, pointing out that dichotomy is a unique feature of this small effort. There are distinctive, though not always apparent, differences between the two Hoodoos. In my examination, I tried to stand as far back as possible in an attempt to view Hoodoo in both its broadest expression and movement. And the broad brush strokes with which I paint this portrayal can be considered an additional weakness of this manuscript. The broad strokes are made at watershed points in African American cultural development and reveal a view that microexamination overlooks.

Old tradition black belt Hoodoo is a long-standing indigenous folk spiritual belief, medicinal, and controlling system created by African slave descendants, originating on American slave plantations in the black belt South, with a significant number of primary practices that resemble traditional West and Central West African spiritual practices. As Hoodoo developed, it was known to all in the slave community and was a part of the psychic structure of every individual enslaved there. It was a glue that held the slave community together. It included folk wisdom and advice. It addressed the needs of the slave community and, later, the free African American community; it integrated psychological support, spiritual direction, physical strength, and medicinal treatment. It helped to define the cultural uniqueness of the old black belt nation, its members, and their descendants. Characteristically, old tradition Hoodoo was frequently passed down in families, often through the ritual of "being called"[19]; it was often associated with an African American church in which spirit possession could be experienced; it used freshly obtained ingredients, circumventing the interference of "spiritual marketeers" and their supply line whenever possible; and it addressed the medicinal, psychological, physical, and spiritual needs of the slave community and, later, the community of free African Americans.

As with numerous other native traditions and customs, there was resistance by purists, arbiters, cultural gatekeepers, established authorities, and traditionalists. Others resisted, not because they wanted to preserve traditionality or resist hybridization, but rather because they saw the incursion of outsiders who would sell them their own traditions as further demonstration of their own powerlessness in a world dominated by both wealth and a "whiteness" hierarchy. The existence of the old system stands as a testament to a number of potential conclusions, not the least of which is the staying power of culture under the harshest conditions and the ability of an oppressed and economically exploited people to sustain their cultural identity and uniqueness. The existence of the old system contradicts much of the negative assessment of African American culture and demonstrates the positive attributes of institution building and the passing on of positive community values, all while developing strategies that resist commercialization and standardization. The work of both Yvonne Chireau and Jeffery Anderson neglect this important aspect in much the same way that some music and social dance research neglects the role of the folk form, the "core culture,"[20] within its own sociocultural context in the production of mainstream music and dance.

Created by outsiders, marketeered Hoodoo exhibits none of the aforementioned characteristics exhibited by the old tradition. Marketeered Hoodoo was created around the turn of the twentieth century but does not achieve peak penetration in northern urban black communities until the, 1930s, '40s, and '50s, concomitant with black migration northward and black displacement from old, rural, black belt community traditions. Marketeers distorted old tradition Hoodoo into a profitable business for themselves. Some marketeers purchased Hoodoo information from blacks who frequently were not conjurers and who often distorted information and gave incomplete or incorrect recipes. Other marketeers simply created their own "spells," packets, and baths with no basis in old tradition Hoodoo. They renamed ritual practices and supplies, distorting what was apparently fragments of old tradition Hoodoo into a poorly designed caricature of its authentic self. It inundated the Hoodoo market with unauthentic supplies and spells that they often created to financially exploit African Americans and the old black belt Hoodoo belief system.

It is important that the southern, black belt, African American origins of Hoodoo not be obscured in contemporary descriptive phrasing. Terms such as *southern origins* or *southern style* evade the mention of the socioethnic impact of African slave laborers on the development of their own traditions. It is not enough to merely say that Hoodoo is southern; African captives did indeed engage in the process of creating both culture and community, and the black belt Hoodoo tradition is evidence of that. The Hoodoo marketeers are totally disconnected from the communities they exploit or loosely connected through their commercial supply line. They do not perform the all-important "community sanction" function of conjurers; they treat no physical, psychological, or behavioral maladies; they do little traditional Hoodoo work; and they issue the disclaimer "sold as a curio only" on many, perhaps most, products that they sell.

Chapter 1 briefly discusses the major manifestations of African traditional religion in the New World. It examines and outlines significant general principles and practices carried to the Western Hemisphere by captive Africans from two regions, which inform West and Central West African religious practices as well as the major New World African religious manifestations establishing where Hoodoo fits in vis-à-vis the other New World syncretic religious forms.

Chapter 2 considers the movement and recoalescing of eight essential elements into the African Religion Complex, or ARC, thus enabling the Hoodoo religion to emerge briefly. Here the manuscript discusses the "mechanism" that lays the groundwork for Hoodoo's birth. This mechanism consists of eight distinct cultural characteristics familiar to all the African ethnic groups landed in the American South. This idea has not been explored in any other work on Hoodoo and is entirely new. This is the first manuscript to identify and conceptualize the movement of Hoodoo against a series of watershed changes in the American cultural landscape.

Chapter 3 discusses the most powerful and best-known root in Hoodoo practice, High John the Conquer root and addresses the intriguing question of "how did a root that is native only to Xalapa, Mexico, become so significant to African American Hoodoo practice, particularly in places like Virginia or other locales thousands of miles away?" With the exception of Zora Neale Hurston, all previous authors, including Anderson and Chireau, have totally overlooked the possible sociocultural origins and movement of this long-standing and empowering spiritual myth and its representative plant. The chapter explores these issues.

Chapter 4 charts the transformation of Hoodoo as it moves from the plantation environment and encounters both "snake oil" Hoodoo and the spiritual marketplace of the urban environment.

Chapter 5 extends chapter 4 and introduces an overlapping discourse on the merging of Hoodoo, dream interpretation, sign interpretation, the relationship between Hoodoo and the numbers, the rise of candle shops, and the domination of the Hoodoo marketplace by commercial sites and supply houses. This chapter also discusses Hoodoo's best-known conjurer, Stephaney Robinson, known as Dr. Buzzard.

Chapter 6 examines Hoodoo as health care and includes an aspect totally overlooked in the research literature on Hoodoo practice: the role of the African American midwife in the old tradition black belt Hoodoo complex.

Chapter 7 looks at Hoodoo's movement during the post–World War II years and draws a portrait of several contemporary root practitioners working in the old tradition. The book concludes with a postscript.

I have chosen to capitalize *Hoodoo* wherever I have used it, even though I would like to have used the lowercased *hoodoo* when designating marketeered Hoodoo practice; that task became time-consuming and cumbersome. It is my hope that this reinterpretive glance will make a small contribution to a greater understanding of African American culture and tradition and ultimately American life and culture.

TRADITIONAL RELIGION IN WEST AFRICA AND IN THE NEW WORLD
A Thematic Overview

Though some scholarship of the past four decades on African religion and culture has been fairer, broader, more objective, and more accurate in its examination and presentation than many earlier works, overall much traditional African and African-derived life and culture continue to be misinterpreted and misunderstood. Nowhere is the mischaracterization of West and Central West African tradition more discordant with reality than in numerous early portrayals and interpretations of African traditional religion. As both the product of and the producer of pejorative misrepresentations of African traditional cultural life, some of the materials that degrade and misinterpret the religious core of traditional African society can be found in the private journals and other accounts by missionaries, traders, explorers, settlers, and agents of the Crown used as primary sources. Though this scholarship has often been racist and pejorative, it is still possible, however, to glean comparative factual information concerning traditional African religious practices that would carry over into the New World.

With the apparent exception of Kongo, where early conversion of the Kongolese nobility to Catholicism appears to have been voluntary, or at least without colonial pressure,[1] the dual notions of Christianizing and civilizing "African savages" complemented each other; in some instances, the two processes, generally accompanied by colonialism, were one and the same, as a quote from a prayer by Rev. T. Muller, chaplain to the 1841 expedition up the Niger, illustrates:

> Our help is in thee, O God! Who hast made heaven and earth. Undertake Thou for us, and *bless Thou the work of our hands.* Give success to our endeavours to introduce civilization and Christianity into this benighted country. Thou hast promised, *Ethiopia shall soon stretch out her hands unto God:* make us, we pray thee, instrumental in fulfilling this Thy promise.[2]

Similar attitudes would confront traditional African religious practice in the Americas and Hoodoo in the United States.

Of all the harmful labels attached to traditional West African religion, the labels *idol worship* and *superstition* and their association with evil or "dark" forces have been long-standing. The notions that the Christian god was the one "true God" and that West African spiritual practice was founded solely on ignorance and fear accompanied the numerous and influential outsiders entering Africa. African scholar John S. Mbiti, an astute observer on the attitude of both early and contemporary scholarship toward traditional African life and culture, speaking in 1990 of the early scholarship on African traditional religion, had this comment:

> One of the dominating attitudes in this early period was the assumption that African beliefs, cultural characteristics and even foods, were all borrowed from the outside world. German scholars pushed this assumption to the extreme, and have not all abandoned it completely to this day. All kinds of theories and explanations were put forward on how the different religious traits had reached African societies from the Middle East or Europe. . . . These earlier descriptions and studies of African religions left us with terms which are inadequate, derogatory and prejudicial.[3]

Even in the twenty-first century, unfounded prejudice, misrepresentation, and misunderstanding of traditional African religion, though challenged and somewhat abated, still continue. Unfortunately, contemporary popular images, with unlimited power to capture the psyche and imagination of the youthful observer through special effects and fantastic animation, have continued to be one of the most powerful tools in reinforcing the older misrepresentations. Where these images would be contested and challenged, the African as the human element is simply excluded from the portrayal, as with Disney's 1999 animated version of Tarzan. This full-length cartoon fantasy, which continues the insidious legacy of pejorative portrayals, may be even more harmful than earlier misrepresentations because it completely eliminates the African from his homeland and, through exclusion, silences and renders him invisible and inferior in his own environment. Because these types of misportrayals encourage a denial and erasure of African culture, the ideological implications of this vicious manipulation are potentially far reaching for those of African heritage as they further contribute to the already existing self-loathing.

The African slave trade to the New World would not only be an enterprise that extended nearly four centuries but would also deposit large populations of Africans in North America, the Caribbean, Mexico, and Central and South America. One result of this massive involuntary population transfer would be the reestablishment of traditional African religion in the new environments. Beginning in the late sixteenth century and continuing until the late nineteenth, Spain, England, Portugal, Holland, and France would establish slavery as the dominant labor relationship producing the New World crops of sugarcane, pineapple, tobacco, indigo, rice, and cotton. In addition, slave labor would be used in mining gold, silver, coal, and saltpeter and would be used in quarries, lumber camps, and later in industries such as the production of liquor and iron. Nearly all forms of work, skilled and unskilled, domestic and professional, were performed by slave labor.[4]

Of the African ethnic groups transported to the Americas, all believed in a supreme being. Traditional West and Central West African religion encompassed the totality of African existence; it was the medium through which explanation for all events was sought and given. It framed and gave meaning to daily occurrence as well as to events across the life cycle; it was the bonding agent that held the universe together, and it assured universal balance, the ultimate governing principle. Birth, puberty, marriage and family, death, illness and health, planting and harvest, herd size, and interpersonal relationship were all framed by, underpinned by, influenced by, and integrated into religious practice. Whenever illness plagued the individual or misfortune overwhelmed the community, an explanation and a solution was sought in sacred ritual, which restored both spiritual and physical balance. For the traditional African, there was no clear separation between sacred and secular as one finds in contemporary European and American society. This would also be true for the early practitioners of Hoodoo religion.

In addition to containing a socially penetrating and well-integrated religious philosophy, traditional life in West Africa was ordered around a rigid status hierarchy based on, among other allotment principles, age or seniority, exceptional personal accomplishments, and possession of needed skills. Many of the Africans brought to the North American mainland, like the Bambara, Akhan, Temne, Bakongo, Igbo, and Yoruba, came from highly organized, well-developed, and widely spread empires and kingdoms; they knew, firsthand, the power, durability, and importance of religious and ancestral tradition such as the secret societies. New World African captives came from these highly ordered societies that were structured to include a variety of both institutions and organizational principles.[5] In traditional West African societies, status could be inherited, ascribed, or achieved, but however it was attained, the status hierarchy was expressed and reinforced in numerous symbolic forms, including clothing, body adornment, gesture, dance, as well as other indicators of status such as birthmarks.[6] Life in West Africa was so governed by symbolic representation that the smallest feather, seemingly insignificant scarification, special hairdo,[7] or simple bead might be the indicator of power or status in the social structure. West African social life was negotiated and ordered through a complex system of multilayered symbols that linked members to the society and formed the basis of ethnic consciousness. "Each color, each band of cloth, each design and pattern of textile, each article of clothing, each ornament, each number has religious significance. There is thus, no separation between artisanship, artistic creation and religious observance."[8]

Significant numbers of traditional West African religions contained their own divination system or system of direct communication between humans and spiritual forces such as deity and ancestral spirits.[9] Recognized as the only vehicle through which one can obtain information about one's destiny, divination governed all important decisions. Such a communication system is seen in the example of Ifa divination. Practiced by the Yoruba of Nigeria as well as others in the region, Ifa is seen as the superior form of communication with God and destiny. With this system, the diviner uses sacred Ikin nuts, kola nuts (specifically Obi abata), or cowry shells, known as the Meridillogun.[10] Among traditional Yoruba, and among traditional West Africans generally, no serious decisions such as marriage or major financial dealings are undertaken without consulting a diviner to read the oracle. The inner workings of traditional West and Central West African cultures were negotiated within a sacred and highly symbolic universe imbued with spiritual significance; there was no secular realm and no atheism. Like village society, the universe was seen as ordered in a status hierarchy that arranged humans, ancestors, spirits, aspects of God, and intermediary forces according to a position between God and humankind. The use of such conceptualization enabled the adherents to move through life meaningfully while addressing challenges to universal order, balance, and survival while engaging God's direct intervention.

The traditional African religious world is populated by a variety of manipulable spiritual forces and spiritual beings capable of beneficial as well as malevolent actions that can be directed at any earthly entity, including plants, minerals, animals, or humans. Within the realm of spirits, there are different categories of supernatural existence. One such category of intermediary forces, what John Mbiti refers to as divinities, is a hallmark of many of the traditional African religions:

> Divinities are on the whole thought to have been created by God, in the ontological category of the spirits. They are associated with Him, and often stand for His activities or manifestations either as personification or as the spiritual beings in charge of these major objects or phenomena of nature. Some of them are national heroes who have been elevated and deified, but this is rare, and when it does happen the heroes become associated with some function or form of nature.[11]

Known by different appellations, these divinities are regarded as vehicles for or manifestations of God itself. Among the Ashanti, some are referred to as Abosom; among the Fon, Vodu; among the Yoruba, they are called Orisha. Divinities govern, guard, reward, and protect humans in their endeavors; they are similar in some respect to angels or saints. Among the areas of existence relegated to control by divinities are war, harvest, fertility and motherhood, smallpox, health, love relationships, wealth, rivers, oceans, volcanoes, farming, thunderstorms, and lightening; the proliferation may be elaborate, as in this observation made among the Fantee of Cape-Coast town: "[A]ll the fetishes of the place are mentioned by name, which, as in the case of Cape-Coast town, where there are seventy-seven guardian-deities, is sometimes a tedious enumeration."[12] The traditional African divinities are petitioned for protection, healing, and favors; they are also propitiated or "fed" their favorite offerings. Speaking of the area now known as Ghana, one 1830s observer had this comment:

> These deities are identified with many of the most striking objects of nature. They are suppose to inhabit rivers. The river Tando is a favorite fetish among the Ashantees. . . . Lakes as well as rivers, have a share of the public veneration. . . . Remarkable mountains and rocks are also regarded with religious veneration. . . . The animate creation, moreover, furnishes other objects of superstitious veneration. Some animals (as leopards, panthers,

and wolves) and dangerous reptiles (as serpents) are believed to be the messengers of the gods; and others are worshiped as the living incarnations of certain deities.[13]

Similar practices would find their way into Hoodoo.

The spirit world of the various African traditional religions has the commonality of being both multilayered and varied. Everything in nature, including plants, animals, and inanimate objects, is believed to have a spirit or soul or governing principle and a function in addition to a certain level of spiritual power. Some plants, because of their particular level within the hierarchical order in the universe, are believed to contain spirits, spiritual power, or governing principles that can influence, harm, or heal. The Bambara, for example, believe that plants as well as animals have souls and that herbal medicine derives its power from the soul force of the plant.[14] The Yoruba of Nigeria refer to this soul force as *ashe* and, like the Bambara, believe it can be found in plants as well as animals. The people of the Kongo believe in the power and soul force of certain plants, such as the root of the munkwiza plant, which was ritually chewed to release power and the juice spit all around for protection from enemies. Centuries later, African Americans would witness a startlingly similar ritual practice in what would become a major part of Hoodoo's courtroom ritual. This notion of governing spirit or governing principle is often extended to inanimate objects as well. The use of designated plants, animals, and inanimate objects as flashpoints for harnessing supernatural power would continue in the Americas as part of the syncretic religious traditions of the African diaspora. These spirits or flashpoints are entities that enable the individual and the group to focus on, tap into, and use God's power, which can be found in individual personal effects as well as in hair, dead skin, saliva, bodily secretions, fingernail clippings, and clothing. Among some traditional practitioners, items such as hair or fingernail clippings are carefully guarded and disposed of lest they be obtained by an enemy and used against the owner, causing misfortune, sickness, or death, a tradition that would carry over into the twenty-first century among African Americans. Rev. Robert Hamill Nassau leaves this account from the nineteenth century:

> If it be desired to obtain power over some one else, the oganga must be given by the applicant, to be mixed in the sacred compound, either crumbs from the food, or clippings of finger nails or hair or (most powerful) even a drop of blood of the person over whom influence is sought. These represent the life or body of that person. So fearful are natives of power being thus obtained over them, that they have their hair cut only

by a friend; and even then they carefully burn it or cast in into a river. If one accidently cuts himself, he stamps out what blood has dropped on the ground, or cuts out from wood the part saturated with blood.[15]

Speaking in the nineteenth century of the Mpongwe of the Gabon, Robert H. Milligan made this observation:

> Sickness and death, they believe, may be caused by fetish medicine, which need not be administered to the victim, but is usually laid beside the path where he is about to pass. Others may pass and it will do them no harm. The pairing of finger-nails, the hair of the victim and such things are powerful ingredients in these "medicines." An Mpongwe, after having his hair cut, gathers up every hair most carefully and burns it lest an enemy should secure it and use it to his injury.[16]

The same observer had this comment concerning the uses and power of hair, fingernails, and saliva among the Fang people of the Gabon: "A man who possesses a fetish-skull usually invokes its aid to prevent secret unfaithfulness on the part of his wife. He compounds a certain fetish the ingredients of which include a lock of his wife's hair, cuttings of her nails, or her saliva. . . . It seems to be a fact that this fetish frequently proves effective without the aid of poison; that is to say, the woman dies."[17] Among the Bambara, hair is believed to contain an important aspect of the soul.[18] Saliva is believed to be spiritually potent and is used in making both talismans and amulets.[19] Interestingly, we now know that both hair and fingernail clippings as well as bodily secretions contain the individual's DNA, the unique genetic key or "life code."

The spirits of the departed or the ancestors are universally honored among West and Central West African religious traditionalists. Performed in a variety of ways involving both the individual and the community, reverence toward the departed is a continuation of the relationship between family members. Conceptualized as having a full range of human motives and desires, including misdeeds, anger, and revenge, ancestors are remembered, honored, and spoken of so that the familial continuity is strengthened. Ancestral spiritual power is consulted and invoked as it was when the elders were in their earthly existence. This passage from the 1841 journals of Rev. James Frederick Schon and Samuel Crowther illustrates several points:

> The first thing which the Natives usually ask for, is their favourite rum; . . . But before he put it to his lips, he took care to pour out a few drops on deck, showing his attention to the superstitious notions of his heart . . . this custom prevails among many of the tribes of Africa, and is observed

with religious punctuality. Its origin or intention is uncertain; but I am inclined to think that the Sherbro People have given me the most satisfactory solution of it. In observing this ceremony, they generally say "Koo bana!" ("To the old people!") meaning their ancestors, now in another world. . . . They are in the habit of carrying rice and other eatables to the graves of their departed friends; and frequently, in cold or wet nights, they will light a fire on them.[20]

Though ceremonies for the ancestors are held in which the community participates, individuals can personalize their gestures toward the departed by leaving food or drink on ancestor shrines or at grave sites. This, as well as a range of significant gestures, often outlines and exhibits the relationship with the ancestor. John Beecham, who lived from 1787 to 1856, made this observation of the Ashanti and Fantee people while he was living on the Gold Coast of what is now Ghana: "The people believe that the spirits of their departed relatives exercise a guardian care over them; and they will frequently stand over the graves of their deceased friends and invoke their spirits to protect them and their children from harm. . . . Elderly women are often heard to offer a kind of prayer to the spirit of a departed parent, begging it either to go to its rest, or, at least, to protect the family, by keeping off evil spirits, instead of injuring the children or other members of the family by its touch."[21] Through ancestor reverence, the individual is able to seize the power and memory of his ancestors for support, direction, and protection. Speaking of the Fang and other interior ethnic groups of the Gabon, an observer had this to say: "In most tribes offerings of food and drink are placed beside the grave. As the drink evaporates and the food wastes they say the spirit is consuming it. Fire-wood is left on the grave that the body may be kept warm."[22]

The previously cited passage from the journal of Schon and Crowther gives a subjective snapshot of ancestor reverence, presenting a single gesture in a richly endowed, deeply imbedded, and highly significant aspect of the traditional African spiritual universe. The practice of honoring one's ancestors, seizing the power of the departed, is universal in West and Central West Africa and would carry over into the Americas in a variety of forms, including grave site decoration and the magical use of internment soil, known in Hoodoo as graveyard dirt. When Africans honor and commune with their progenitors, they are framing their own existence and substantiating who they are while both focusing ancestral energies and directing them toward a positive end, not simply engaging in "worshiping the dead," as it has often been mischaracterized. Traditional Africans reaffirm their familial privilege to request spiritual assistance as well as their familial responsibility for other family members. Powerful ancestors like the founders of the nation or significant political or cultural heroes are sometimes deified and moved into the realm of divinities.

Regarded as a sacred occurrence, spirit possession by a deity, spirit, or ancestor is universal among West and Central West African religious traditionalists and is an incredibly powerful experience even for the observer. Its occurrence announces the arrival of beings from the spirit realm while demonstrating the possibilities for human communion with the direct representatives of God. During the journey through possession, the devotee loses full consciousness and slips into a semiconscious state in which the physical appearance is transformed, the individual becomes oblivious to the world around him, and he is believed to become the temporary vessel for the spiritual entity. Sometimes the possessed both experiences and demonstrates fantastic effects of personality, physical strength, endurance, and pain tolerance. John Beecham leaves us this description: "The order of fetishmen is further augmented by persons who declare, that the fetish has suddenly seized, or come upon, them. A series of convulsive and unnatural bodily distortions establishes their claims."[23] This practice of spirit possession, like other traditional African practices, would be observed in sacred contexts among African Americans in the United States in the twenty-first century.

Within the context of African traditional religion, herbal and naturopathic healing were dependent upon spiritual forces for efficacy. The medicoreligious process from diagnosis to treatment was carried out in the spiritual realm. The traditional practice of medicine was intertwined with both the practice of religion and spiritual power. Indeed the ongoing use of shaman, medicine men, and later African American conjurers as well as other traditional practitioners was tied to religious belief in their ability to harness and utilize spiritual power to treat physical and mental malady.

In both traditional African society as well as in old plantation Hoodoo, diagnosis of physical or mental illness was often through divination alone or in combination with other diagnostic methods. In divination, a range of objects served as the oracle: stones, bones, shells, pods, seeds, sand, animals, animal entrails, and sticks were all used.[24] In addition, the traditional healer would use his or her senses or the responses of natural creatures such as insects to help with the diagnosis.[25] Ants, for example, have been used as a diagnostic tool in traditional African medicine in testing for diabetes. The patient is instructed to urinate on the ground; if within an hour the spot is infested with ants, then the patient probably has sugar in his urine.[26]

In cases such as broken bones, burns, cuts, or obvious physical injury, divination was not necessary to discover the source of the discomfort. Treatment could proceed using the traditional herbal/spiritual procedure or remedy. In some cases, specialists, such as bonesetters, who often used birds as para-sympathetic healing models, were consulted to facilitate the healing. Since the spoken word was believed to embody spiritual potency, sacred remarks in the form of incantations and prayers were a significant component in African traditional medicine and would later perform a similar function in Hoodoo. The healing specialists used these spiritual methods in combination with physical methods such as applying splints and herbal supports in the form of herbal packs and medicinal juices to stimulate circulation, aid healing, reduce swelling, and prevent infection. Prayers accompanied the mixing of medicines as well as the tying of sacred string for healing and strength. Imbedded within the religion was a code associated with speaking that extended beyond medicine to daily life; words were power. According to Mbiti:

> There is a mystical power in words, especially those of a senior person to a junior one, in terms of age, social status or office position. The words of parents for example, carry "power" when spoken to children: they "cause" good fortune, curse, success, peace, sorrows or blessings, especially when spoken in moments of crisis. The words of the medicine-man work through the medicine he gives, and it is this, perhaps more than the actual herb, which is thought to cause the cure or prevent misfortunes. Therefore, formal "curses" and "blessings" are extremely potent; and people may travel long distances to receive formal blessings, and all are extra careful to avoid formal curses.[27]

This would also be true in old plantation Hoodoo religion. Phrases such as "put the bad mouth on" or "burn bread on" attest to the power and longevity of words in the Hoodoo belief system.

The use of string and knot tying in the traditional healing process is found throughout West and Central West Africa as well as throughout the African diaspora; it would appear throughout the black belt South as well as in northern urban black communities until the mid-twentieth century. In earlier times in Africa, the strings were made from either leather, special plants, or the vines of sacred climbing plants. Strings were tied on various body parts, including the neck, wrist, ankle, and groin-waist area for spiritual-physical health and strength. String was used in the old Kongo kingdom to hold in spiritual power[28] and was used throughout the Gabon tied around the waist for health.[29] In Ghana, among the Ashanti people, strings rubbed with vegetable dressings were used.[30] Finally, concerning the use of string for sacred healing, Robert Hamill Nassau, forty years a missionary in the Gabon district of Kongo-Français had this to say: "Some kinds, worn on a bracelet or necklace, are to ward off sickness. The new born infant has a health-knot tied about its neck, wrist, or loins. Down to the day of oldest age, every one keeps on multiplying or renewing or altering these life talismans."[31]

In addition to noninvasive healing techniques, traditional medicine encompassed surgery, including circumcision, cesarean delivery and the cutting of the umbilical cord, uvulectomy, scarification, piercing of ears and other body parts, as well as complicated and delicate procedures such as drilling into the skull to repair fractured bone or to relieve severe and persistent headaches.[32]

Among some traditionalists, herbal knowledge was secretly guarded and was passed on only through long apprenticeships, often, but not exclusively, limited to family or clan members. The traditional priest, healer, or shaman often entered into an extensive study period and training process that began in childhood and lasted for many years. Beecham made the following observation in nineteenth-century Ghana: "The fetishmen apply themselves, moreover, to the study of medicine; and the knowledge which they acquire of the properties of herbs and plants it will be seen hereafter, powerfully contributes to strengthen their influence with the people."[33]

A division of labor, which was sometimes diversified according to specialty, often informed the acquisition of herbal knowledge; midwives, for example, would know best which plants to use for treatment of childbirth-associated problems and concerns. Other practitioners had a general knowledge of herbal and naturopathic medicines. The most mystical and feared aspect of naturopathic and herbal healing was the knowledge of poisonous and otherwise harmful plants and substances. In Africa, possession of herbal knowledge gave an individual both power and unique status within his social group and oftentimes resulted in the acquisition of material gain. In the United States, the conjurer with knowledge of poisons was feared. Both the knowledge and the fear associated with herbal acumen would attend Hoodoo practice.

Traditional African ethnopsychologists used narcotic, stimulant, and hallucinogenic plants to treat mental and emotional problems. Herbal and naturopathic practitioners mixed and administered herbal medications that calmed, aided sleep, stimulated the nervous system, dulled pain, and produced antibacterial and antifungal action. Numerous African ethnic groups had complete medicinal systems integrated thoroughly into the religious complex. Within the Yoruba religion, for example, each Orisha or divinity force not only governs a part of the human body but also has a list of medicinal herbs and naturopathic substances assigned to it and over which it has dominion. The herbs of a particular Orisha are said to treat ailments of the part of the body governed by that aspect of God. The Orisha Oshun, for example, is said to govern the bloodstream; various disorders connected to the blood such as diabetes and anemia are said to be governed by her and can be treated by her sacred herbs.

Water immersion in the form of either baptism or ritual bath for medicinal or initiatory purposes, the practices of guarding discarded hair and fingernail clippings as well as other personal effects, the "feeding" of spirits, pouring libations, as well as belief in spiritual causation for malady were part of traditional West African religious practice. Spirit possession, divination, belief in sacred words and words of power, use of string in healing, herbal and naturopathic medicine, as well as the basic philosophical principles on which these practices were constructed and sustained would come to the New World with each shipload of captive Africans.

Cuba, after centuries of importing Africans as slave laborers, would abolish slavery in 1886. Brazil would begin importing Africans as slave labor in the mid-sixteenth century and continue its use until the abolition of slavery more than three centuries later in 1888. Haiti was somewhat different than either Cuba or Brazil because the Haitian revolution in the last decade of the eighteenth century preceded the abolition of slavery elsewhere in the New World by nearly a century. The Republic of Haiti was the second independent republic in the New World and the first to outlaw chattel slavery. During the history of all three nations, Cuba, Brazil, and Haiti, the traditional African religious beliefs and practices would mix with aspects of Native American religion and Catholicism. The syncretic strategy of identifying African divinities with Catholic saints would both protect, stabilize, and expand African religion while allowing it to sustain its own existence under enslavement.

The major pockets of African religious expression, in Haiti, the Dominican Republic, Puerto Rico, Cuba, Brazil, Trinidad, Jamaica, and the United States black belt South, were drawn both directly and indirectly from numerous and diverse African cultures, including but not limited to Igbo, Mandingo, Bambara, Kongo, Yoruba, Fon, and Ashanti sources and would yield syncretized religious expressions such as Vodun, Santeria, Lucumi, Candomble, GaGa, Shango Baptist, Palo Mayombe (Palo Monte), Obeah, and Hoodoo. In some instances, particular practices can be readily identified as with either Bakongo, Yoruba, or Fon in Cuba, Brazil, and Haiti; in other instances, a particular practice may have existed in all or a majority of the parent African cultures as well as among the settling Europeans and the native populations, making the process of identifying a point of origin

CHAPTER 1

tenuous. An example of this can be seen in beliefs anʳ
saliva or "spit." The Yoruba believe that spit contaiʳ
to create action. Spit also contains special spirituⱥ
Bambara, Igbo, and numerous other African ethniⱡ
to America. Spit also has magical significance in both Eu.
or witchcraft and for Native Americans.

The most widely known, sustained, and practiced New Woₓ
religious traditions appear to be from the Yoruba of Nigeria, witʜ
traditions second. Yoruba influences can be observed in Haitian Voduₓ
Cuba, where the religion is known as Lucumi and Regla de Ocha; in Brazₓ
as Candomble; in Puerto Rico as Santeria; and in Trinidad as Shango Baptist. This tradition draws directly from the Yoruba and Fon and celebrates
traditional African divinities known as Orishas. The priests and priestesses
are known as Babalorisha and Iyalorisha, respectively, with higher-order
priests and priestesses known as Babalawo and Iyanfa, respectively. A commonly used term for the Yoruba/Lucumi clergy is *santero* for a man and
santera for a woman. The liturgical language of prayer and praise song is
Yoruba, and the sacred Bata drum trio from Nigeria is used in worship.

In Haiti, Brazil, Cuba, as well as other places, African religion mixed
with both Native American beliefs and Catholicism while reestablishing
elaborate and complex levels of orthodoxy, including initiation rites, systems of divination, types of worship, and religious mythology. The Yoruba
Orisha tradition would come to not only peacefully co-exist with, but also
complement other African religious fragments, particularly the dominant
New World Kongo religious expression known as Palo as well as Obeah,
which resembles African American Hoodoo perhaps more than any other
syncretized religious tradition in the New World.

Palo, Palo Monte, or Palo Mayombe as it is known is directly related to
Kongo religious tradition, and its influences can be observed in Cuba, Haiti,
Brazil, and the southern United States. Known as Paleros, the mostly male
priesthood works with old Kongo spirits and with spirits of the deceased. Uti-
lizing internment soil (graveyard dirt), magical sticks from sacred spiritual
trees, plants and roots, stones, and animal parts, Palo harnesses the power
of potentially dangerous explosive spirits. Kongo religious philosophy con-
ceptualizes the world as expressed in the Kongo cosmogram, emphasizing
the continuity between the land of the living and the spirit realms where
the dead reside. And today in contemporary Cuba, though the traditions
are separate, Palo and Lucumi are often engaged simultaneously, particularly when the concern for which they are being sought involves serious
problem solving.

oeah, another African-derived religious tradition, is more closely associ-
d and identified with Jamaica but exists in other places in the Caribbean
, well as in Central and South America. Believed by some scholars to be
of Ashanti derivation, Jamaican Obeah, perhaps more than any African-
derived syncretic New World spiritual tradition, resembles African American
Hoodoo.[34] The resemblance is twofold, both in content and in structure.
Like Hoodoo, Obeah is not openly connected with a church or regularly
meeting ritual and ceremony, and like Hoodoo it is often identified as "evil."
Further, like Hoodoo, Obeah's syncretic development occurred under English Protestant slave masters. Both traditions once probably were connected
to an African deity but experienced the loss of the African gods similar to
that described by Albert Raboteau in his landmark work, *Slave Religion*.[35]

Obeah and Hoodoo are similar in other respects, and they have evoked
strikingly similar descriptions by both white observers and slave masters.
As in Ghana where Anansi is revered and his stories are used as a teaching
device, both Obeah and Hoodoo traditions hold spiders sacred, and Anancy
in Jamaica is held in high regard in a fashion strikingly similar to "Aunt
Nancy" the spider in the sea islands off the Georgia and South Carolina
coasts. Traditionally, spiders are used for divination in the West African
country of what is now Cameroon as well as other places in West Africa.[36]

In addition to Orisha worship, the Cuban Lucumi engage in ancestor
reverence, as do the Brazilians. Known as the Egun, ancestors are revered
and petitioned by believers whenever spiritual assistance of a particular type
is needed. The widely circulated adage that "the Orisha walk in front of you,
but the Egun have your back" demonstrates the surrounding bulwark of
protection provided through the dual forces of Orisha and Egun. Though
obscured in Christian practices, Egun worship as ancestor reverence would
be sustained in the Mother's Day ceremonies and rituals still found in many
modern-day African American churches. These rituals include the wearing
of a red or white flower to signify whether one's mother is living or dead;
saluting or honoring the church's elder mothers in which the youth of the
church file past, embracing or shaking the hands of the deacon board mothers and other church mothers; trips to the local burial site of the ancestor
mothers; special baptismal ceremonies as well as special dinners and special
foods prepared for the ancestor; and the placing of that food on the grave;
all reflect African American ancestor reverence.

The survival of African religious tradition in the United States would take
a noticeably different path than it did in the large plantation societies of the
Caribbean and Latin America. Known by several names, including Hoodoo,
conjure, Juju, and root work, African traditional religion in the United States

would have a shorter life span as a completely sustainable religious system than those African religious forms in Cuba, Haiti, or Brazil. In the United States, partly because of demographic differences in African, white, and Amerindian population ratios and density and partly because of cultural factors such as religious differences, especially those differences attributable to Catholicism in Haiti, Cuba, and Brazil and Protestantism in mainland North America, its origins would be nearly completely lost. Under Protestantism, there were few syncretic possibilities, so Hoodoo development would follow a unique path different from its Caribbean and Latin American counterparts. With similar cultural material, Africans in the North American colonies and in the United States would face different circumstances and would produce an alternative belief system of spiritual and medicinal knowledge that could serve and sustain them. Highly organized, Hoodoo would evolve a flexible system, logic, and structure and maintain practices observed in West and Central West Africa, the Caribbean, and Latin America while replacing its sacred African backdrop with nature deity, Protestant prayers and imagery, as well as newly created mythology.

*This church was not at first by any means Christian
nor definitely organized: rather it was an adaptation
and mingling of heathen rites among the members of
each plantation, and roughly designated as Voodooism.*
—W. E. B. DUBOIS, *The Souls of Black Folk*

DISRUPTIVE INTERSECTION
Slavery and the African Background
in the Making of Hoodoo

The improbability of precisely locating when and where Hoodoo emerged
has not precluded this author from including this as a subtextual concern.
Throughout this inquiry, this author questions the common and popular
understanding that, like jazz, "Hoodoo came from New Orleans." Although
New Orleans has its significance, wherever there was a sizable African population, African naturalistic religious practices that would contribute to
Hoodoo were there also. Something resembling Hoodoo undoubtedly developed among the first generation of culturally diverse Africans born in the
North American colonies. Enslaved Africans undoubtedly manifest a range
of responses to contact with both enslavement and Christian worship. Some
bondsmen eagerly accepted Christianity and modified it to their needs,
others flatly refused to participate, still others participated both in worship
organized on behalf of the masters as well as in clandestinely organized
slave worship services. But whenever they worshipped, these children of
Africa expressed spiritual emotion in bodily patterns inherited from African
traditional religion.

The primary African components from which Hoodoo would be con-
stituted were drawn from a range of different African ethnic cultures that
stretched from the area now known as Senegal down the West African coast

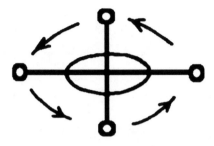

Kongo cosmogram. The symbol represents the Bakongo people's view of the universe and the place of humankind in that universe. Among other qualities, it symbolizes the movement from the otherworld of the ancestors as they travel in a dynamic cycle of life, death, and rebirth.

to the Democratic Republic of the Congo. Because it concerned the transformation of a variety of traditional African religions into one spiritual tradition, Hoodoo must have involved a major confrontation of spiritual forces. The early disintegration process included a great reduction in ability not only to ritualize across the life cycle, but also to engage openly in significant events, which would help to stabilize and enrich the psychocultural continuity in the slave community. Though enslavement was a powerful deterrent to African cultural survival and maintenance, its power was not enough to force enslaved Africans to completely relinquish all their traditional spiritual and worship practices, thus significant traditional practices persisted through the conflict and tension necessary for Hoodoo's emergence as a dynamic spiritual form functioning at the boundaries of slavery's power; there are numerous examples of African traditional practices retained by Africans and their descendants in North America. In order for African religious traditions to contest or be combined with Christianity, they had to remain alive and viable on their own, outside of the supports of Christian practice; and they did. Further supporting that process were the numerous aspects of Christianity that resonated with certain African cultural traditions. The most sacred of Christian symbols, the cross, resonated both with African notions of the crossroads as a supernatural site and with the sacred cross of the Kongo Yowa cosmogram. The Old Testament reference to animal sacrifice and the use of ritual water immersion would certainly have been familiar to many traditional Africans, including those enslaved in North America.

Enslaved Africans in the United States and early colonies apparently retained aspects of traditional African religious practice with ferocity and created a place for its safe existence. In that safe space, Hoodoo was born and maintained. Neither uniformly located nor uniform in their parameters, those safe spaces sustained a regrouping of regional fragments that would later come together and contribute to a new whole. In addition to both a variety of African religious fragments and Protestantism, Native American belief undoubtedly impacted on the formation of African American New World spiritual belief. Africans and Native Americans were often in close contact with one another as slaves, held by either white American or European settlers. Additional cultural contact occurred when Native Americans both held African slaves themselves and hid runaway slaves from patrollers. Native Americans and Africans have a long history of intermarriage, tribal adoption, and shifting identities that make it difficult in some instances to locate where one community ends and the other begins.[1] With this in mind, it is safe to say that Native American spiritual belief remained comparatively intact when encountering fragmented African spiritual belief disrupted by insufficiently concentrated numbers in the enslaved African ethnic groups as well as by removal from the African homeland. There existed certain cultural elective affinities between Africans and Native Americans in their spiritual reverence for nature, the wind, the moon, the rivers, the ocean, the forest, as well as living creatures. These cultural affinities would ease the use of substitutions and facilitate any possible exchange between African and Native American spiritual beliefs. For a period of time, intact Native American spiritual belief systems could have been a somewhat secure backdrop that contributed to and supported the retention of African spiritual belief.

In spite of conditions under enslavement that inhibited and circumscribed Hoodoo's growth toward institutionalization, by either the late-eighteenth or early-nineteenth century three firmly established southern regional Hoodoo traditions existed that, after the coming of cotton, would cross-fertilize one another against a backdrop process of regional and cultural homogenization. The African spiritual and cultural influences were especially significant in the formation of early African American culture, particularly Hoodoo.[2]

This tricotomy of regional Hoodoo clusters, the location of their major cities and financial centers, to some extent reflects the regional organization of slave labor around such crops as rice, indigo, tobacco, pineapple, sugarcane, and later cotton and around nationally known slave markets and financial centers, including New Orleans, Richmond, and Charleston/ Savannah. This tricotomy also roughly parallels certain African ethnic concentrations and influences as well as European ethnic settlement patterns and regional Native American ethnic populations. Certain Hoodoo practices would be retained and disbursed from Virginia tobacco culture, other practices would be known to Gulf Coast bondsmen, while other regional traditions would center in the Florida, Georgia, and South Carolina Sea Island Gullah culture of the Atlantic coast.

In no particular order, area one, the Southwest Hoodoo region, was centered in the Gulf Coast/New Orleans/Mobile area; this area would include the western Florida panhandle, Alabama, Louisiana, and Mississippi and extend westward into eastern Texas and northward to Missouri and Tennessee. The ethnic mix and cultural influences from the various enslaved and imported African ethnic groups ebbed and flowed over time, its profile modified with each major importation. In this region, the Senegambian, Mande speakers, particularly the Bambara in Louisiana, would leave a fortified cultural legacy that recognizably contributed directly to Hoodoo development. The Bambara in particular were concentrated in such numbers there, that a Bambara interpreter was installed in the New Orleans court system. Their best-known and documented contribution to Hoodoo may be in the fabrication of protective amulets known by a variety of Mande labels, including *gerregery* (gris-gris), *wanga,* and *zinzin.*[3] Other groups in area one include those from the Yoruba, Fon, and Ewe cultural complex as well as from Central West Africa or the Kongo-Angola-Zaire area.

Area number two, the Southeast region, included the Sea Island/central and coastal Georgia/Florida area centered in and around Savannah, Georgia, and Charleston, South Carolina, extending northward to North Carolina and southward into Florida. Several African ethnic groups would exercise a formative influence on Hoodoo's development in area two. Captives from Sierra Leone, enslaved Igbo, and those from Central West Africa or Kongo-Angola would achieve cultural influence in this area's development during different historical periods.[4] In ritual context in the African homeland, the counterclockwise circle would be familiar to them all, further supporting chances for continuity, retention, and survival. It appears that the Central West African contributions from Kongo culture would be both long-standing and spread far and wide. The counterclockwise sacred dance circle is believed by some scholars to represent a full cycle of life through the phases of birth, childhood, adulthood, death, and rebirth[5] as represented by the Kongo cosmogram and that the Ring Shout traced the circle of the Kongo cosmogram on the ground. Indeed, information that the Ring Shout traced this cosmogram could possibly answer why bondsmen in America convened the sacred circle during death rituals.[6]

Area number three, the Northeast Hoodoo region included Maryland-Chesapeake, Virginia, eastern Tennessee/North Carolina and was centered around Richmond and extended westward. In this area, the Akan and Gold Coast slaves as well as those from the Bight of Biafra were particularly significant.

When cotton enveloped the South after 1807, cultural leveling and homogenization would exert itself as a continual backdrop process to the developing national consciousness as well as to African American cultural formation. Prior to that time, regional and African ethnic differences would reveal themselves more recognizably in the daily life of the enslaved. The tobacco-centered culture of the Virginia Hoodoo cluster was different from the culture of either South Carolina low-country rice and indigo of area two or Gulf Coast basin sugarcane and pineapple of area one. The contours of life, including African ethnic population, population density, landscape, diet, type and organization of labor, and level of technology, were all somewhat varied in the different regions. Commenting on the differences between rice and tobacco culture, Philip D. Morgan gives us this analysis:

> Apart from the availability of the soils required for tobacco and rice, the type of supervision required of the two crops also dictated differing unit sizes. Because tobacco cultivation required close attention from planting through processing, it was most efficiently grown on a small scale. . . . In short, a tobacco plantation could be set up with no slaves at all, or with one or two, and certainly with no more than ten, whereas a rice plantation required at least thirty workers.[7]

Though not always obvious, the differences in climate, dress patterns, and slave quarter organization had an impact on Hoodoo development and practice as they did other aspects of slave life. An example can be observed in the prevalence of shoes—or items functioning as shoes—among captives in the colder northern regions of slave territory, which certainly impacted on the Hoodoo practice of "track gathering"[8] in that region. Once again Morgan comments: "Foot and head coverings showed little uniformity. Shoes were either imported . . . or locally made. . . . In spite of this varied footwear, many slaves, particularly field hands, went barefoot—a practice that might well have been more common in the Low country than in the Chesapeake."[9] The difference in climate meant also that local plants that composed the local Hoodoo pharmacopeia, as well as the landscape, were different. Certain plants that could possibly grow or be transplanted to the tropical or semitropical climate of the coastal Deep South regions would be unavailable except through import in places like Virginia, Tennessee, or Delaware.

Influenced by myriad factors, including the demand for slave labor, African ethnicity, black population density in a particular locale, and work patterns, neither the content, the rate, nor the process of Hoodoo's development was necessarily the same in all three regional clusters. Hoodoo's proliferation ebbed and flowed as the regional and national contexts for its development changed. Certainly the Senegambian influence from the 1720s as well as an influx of Haitian and Cuban blacks after 1795 would impact upon the profile and durability of Hoodoo in the New Orleans, Louisiana, and Gulf Coast basins where Hoodoo and New Orleans Voodoo would come to be viewed as indistinguishable in many respects by outsiders and believers alike.[10] Similarly, the isolation of Africans in the South Carolina and Georgia Sea Islands and Atlantic coastal regions supported the unique Kongo-influenced profile of that region's Hoodoo after 1720.

Hoodoo's emergence and early development under enslavement covered an extended period of time and involved a multilayered process. The fragmentation and breakdown of the West African religious systems, "the death of the Gods" to use Albert Raboteau's phrase,[11] were first in that process. What W. E. B. DuBois described as a "terrific social revolution,"[12] the religious disintegration-transformation process, was sometimes subtle and gradual, sometimes directly overt and immediate; and for the slave, the process involved sorting out which African religious and cultural fragments could be salvaged. The creation and perpetuation of Hoodoo among bondsmen depended on their ability to sustain and transfer historic memory, memory of life as seen in the traditional African village. African captives in a seeming condition of cultural abandonment not only would certainly look for the familiar in the new environment but also would consciously strive to re-create as high a degree of familiarity as possible via perception. The enslaved Africans' encounters with new plants and animals, as well as new cultural patterns and work practices, would result in comparison and search for analogous forms that captives had known in the African homeland and were now carried in their living memories. In this process, Africans undoubtedly depended, to some degree, on information from Native Americans whose familiarity with the plants and animals of the North American environment could verify the sacred and spiritual uses of plants and animals unfamiliar to them. It is indeed possible that a picture of life in Africa carried in the memory of first-generation captives began to acquire a new quasi-mythic quality in subsequent generations as Hoodoo emerged to sustain the enslaved psyche. Stories of very real occurrences in Africa, now impossible or unlikely in America, entered the newly forming Hoodoo religion as part of its belief system and sacred enactments.

The period between 1740 and 1780 may be especially significant in contemplating when Hoodoo was likely to have emerged. Numerous sources agree that nearly half of all Africans arriving in America did so during this period. Slavery in all three regional Hoodoo clusters had existed for at least a century prior to the intensive influx of Africans during this period. Something of an indigenous and regionally distinct African American culture developed among early slave descendants. The captives that had been in North American colonies for two generations had, at varying times, lost their traditional gods, a process supported by ethnic heterogeneity in the slave population. The process of loss was neither rapid nor abrupt, but it involved transference and investment directly into aspects of nature associated with African higher spiritual reality. This included the river, the ocean, certain trees, bushes, plants, animals, rain, and wind. These all became intermediary forms in the transference process, thus sustaining, salvaging, and transferring essential aspects of old belief into new, yet familiar, and intermediary African naturalistic spirituality.

In the same process, eight common and essential components of traditional African religion, which I have labeled the African Religion Complex (ARC), were so potent in each of the culturally varied regions that, after the coming of cotton, they would partially coalesce across regions and remain a supporting foundation for further magical, spiritual, and religious development. The eight components in all probability were shared by all the African ethnic groups in the American slave population. Linking the New World to the Old, the African Religion Complex included:

1. counterclockwise sacred circle dancing,[13]
2. spirit possession,
3. the principle of sacrifice,
4. ritual water immersion,
5. divination,
6. ancestor reverence,
7. belief in spiritual cause of malady, and
8. herbal and naturopathic medicine.

Within each of the eight components, the elective compatibilities and transethnic similarities further supported the social construction of a new and essentially Pan-African spiritual tradition that would become the basis for the African contribution to Hoodoo. An example of such similarities can be seen in the structural fabrication as well as the contents of amulets from different African ethnic groups. Most West and Central West African traditionalists use and prescribe charms that are strikingly similar in their construction, content, and function. Similar charms and amulets appear across cultures in the African diaspora. Whether the charm is constructed from leather, from a tiny gourd encased in raffia, from an animal skin, or from a piece of cloth, the similarities of bags, from the African American mojo bag to the Kongo *nkisi,* are undeniable.[14]

The half century preceding 1740 is the period of Hoodoo's germination and dormancy. Though the "death of the Gods" had occurred, slave worship retained enough familiar elements that newly arriving African captives would certainly be familiar with similar practices in the homeland and possibly recognize them. By 1740 some bondsmen had been in the American colonies for three generations or more. Both the 1740–80 influx and the increase from 1790 to 1799 deepened the cultural complexity of the slave community by adding a significant number of newly imported Africans to the already developing African American culture. Bondsmen in regions with a significant-size homogeneous ethnic group, such as the Bambara in Louisiana, could possibly sustain more African traditional practices for a longer period. According to author Michael Gomez,[15] simply because of their longevity, longer-standing practices bore an increased chance either of being disbursed or of cross-fertilizing other practices. The simmering Hoodoo pot was constantly being stirred.

Though occurring across a span of time and through different social, economic, and political eras, legal importation of African slaves served to shore up, and to strengthen, many of the surviving African cultural elements, particularly those eight from the ARC. The continuing illegal importation and smuggling of continental Africans, though dwindling after 1807,[16] further supported the establishment of a new, unique, and transferable African-based culture among American-born slaves.[17] A product of the ARC, the religiophilosophical cornerstone for that new culture would be the emerging Hoodoo religion.

Certain African religious and cultural practices were doomed to extinction under enslavement. Major religious and psychic adjustments affected every facet of the captive's daily existence. Africans, in making this adjustment, availed themselves of every limited option to respond to enslavement's cultural disruption, but they would soon realize that they could neither recreate nor save everything they had known in the homeland. For example, essential elements in family life were irretrievably transformed for some African captives once the religious aspects of traditional African ancestor reverence were destroyed, and neither the ancestor institution nor other institutions were fully sustainable if, at the slave owner's will, one could be sold away from one's family and community at any time, including infancy.

Nor could traditional social institutions be permanently and openly sustained where legal, social, and economic structures and practices successfully limited or barred their existence as they did under American slavery.

Continual interethnic assimilation and cross-fertilization between Africans from different ethnic groups further informed the complex, multilayered process of cultural transformation and salvaging. Though the Africans in a particular region or locale might sometimes exhibit a culturally dominant and identifiable ethnic strain, like the Bambara in Louisiana, African bondsmen were brought into the American colonies and the United States, from the late seventeenth through the early nineteenth century, from numerous African as well as West Indian sources.[18] The "death of the Gods" and disruption of traditional spiritual continuity was concurrent with interethnic assimilation among the captive Africans themselves. The dual social processes of cultural disintegration and interethnic assimilation were neither straight-line[19] nor separate, but occurred under widespread overarching cultural commonalities shared by a significant percentage of the enslaved Africans. Indeed for some of them, the interethnic assimilation process had begun in Africa and would continue in the New World.[20] The two processes interplayed with each other, both limiting and expanding possibilities for cultural retention as they occurred.

Yet an additional process would begin to intercede after 1807—further homogenization—resulting from the coming of cotton. King Cotton would blanket the South while modifying the material culture of crop production. As a result, slave labor in some regions was totally reorganized and the lives of those who had previously been involved in the production of sugarcane, rice, indigo, pineapple, and tobacco were changed by cotton culture. With a now widespread and somewhat common material culture across the black belt South, the lives of slaves in different regions became more similar and uniform with respect to tools, vocabulary, planting and harvesting techniques, and schedules. Though ethnic and cultural differences remained and overlapped, the nearly universal movement to cotton culture further homogenized the three regional differences and further stirred the Hoodoo melting pot.

Given the necessity for expedience, in all probability the modifications forced on African religious practice, mandated by adjustment to enslavement, involved, in part, conscious decisions by religious specialists and elders. This possibility existed for all the New World manifestations of African religious tradition. Through the prism of enslavement, the traditional priests and religious leaders consciously moved to preserve, modify, and extend the possibilities for African religious survival. Cuba demonstrates the classic expression of this type of agency and conscious decision making among slaves. In order to preserve African religious tradition, slaves in Cuba learned the mysteries of many divinities known as Orisha rather than of only one Orisha, as had been done in the African homeland, thus enabling the Orisha tradition to increase its chances for survival under the system of slavery. Though the demographics in North America were different than in Cuba, there is no evidence to indicate that a similar or analogous process of conscious decision making did not begin to take place and influence the emergence of Hoodoo in what would become the United States.

Early on in the American slave experience, in the seventeenth and eighteenth centuries, Africans, Native Americans, and Europeans probably experienced a more visible exchange of cultural folkways. The exchanges could and did occur in areas where plantations were both large and small, as well as in urban centers. For Africans, the Americanization process was no mere straightforward discarding of African religious traditions and embracing of European folk superstitions or Christianity. In the slave quarter, there were certain practices that slaves would have been at liberty to openly discuss, retain, and pass on. Child rearing practices, certain religious beliefs, healing, and burial practices were all areas of slave life in which bondsmen could and did exercise some limited agency. The cultural exchange between the three groups would encourage and support a greater diversity in the developing Hoodoo practice across regions and with respect to treatment of individual problems and maladies. This diversity would remain the case and would be modified with the coming of cotton, which expanded national cultural boundaries and promoted an intensified cultural homogenization across regions among Americans both slave and free and again when Hoodoo becomes commercially viable, as it does after Reconstruction.

Without implying a reductionist model to either the variety of cultures included here or to the interethnic assimilation process, one more important feature, shared by a significant number of the enslaved ethnic groups, allowed and supported a unified new spiritual tradition to emerge from a variety of West and Central West African religions. This feature, though not directly derived from religious content as were the components of ARC, along with interethnic assimilation, enabled enslaved Africans to find a commonly shared basis on which to salvage religiocultural essentials while constructing a new tradition. Openness or the inclusive-integrative principle,[21] which also marks West African religion generally, is the other characteristic. This feature allows Africans to integrate aspects of external beliefs and practices into their religion as well as to make substitutions of required ritual items while maintaining religious vitality, validity, and integrity.

The eight components of the ARC would become the foundation elements in the new Hoodoo religion; the inclusiveness principle would imprint on the process. Retaining many of the particular practices of African traditional religion, Hoodoo, like Vodun, Lucumi, and Candoble, would have its sacred dance as well as its herbal medicinal practice. At its most fully developed point, the Hoodoo religion would contain not only African supernaturalism but a corpus of orally transferred religious wisdom that contained advice on issues from selecting an acceptable spouse to community relations, from advice on treating illness to relationships with slave owners and other whites. These vessels of traditional religiocultural components sometimes took the form of stories, riddles, folk tales, proverbs, or dance plays. It is likely that some of them were even linked with dance plays similar to the "Buzzard Lope," which Lydia Parrish observed still in existence in the Georgia Sea Islands in the 1930s.[22] The dance known as the Ring Shout certainly imitated actions from the work routine that extended meaning into daily life. The gesture known as "picking up or harvesting leaves" made visible the work ethic and advised one to harvest while the season is ripe lest you do without during winter. Some traditional African dance acted out miniature pantomimes of deity in their daily activities. And much African-derived African American social dance includes mimetic gestures that comment on life's daily issues. In addition to rendering advice and intervening on life cycle issues, personal concerns, and issues of public and private conduct, Hoodoo would celebrate its divinities, such as High John the Conquer. It would protect against feared as well as negative supernatural forces such as Plat-eye, Robination Horse, haints, hags, and curses, and it would revere and use the elements of nature such as lightening, rain, the river, and other natural phenomena. Early Hoodoo religion would have its sacred locations and power sites such as the crossroads, the cemetery, the threshold, railroad tracks, and special clearings in the woods. Initially it would contend with Christianity for control of the souls of black folks and for religious hegemony in the slave community. Bondsmen would resolve the contestation by integrating their version of Christianity into conjure and vice versa.

The size of the plantation community as well as black, white, and Native American population ratios, population density, whether the slavery existed in an urban or rural setting, and fluidity of the slave population resulting from mortality, sale, or transportation to another region[23] were all additional factors promoting or inhibiting either the breakdown or the retention of African religious traditions. Add to the cultural development process the intensity of interactive exchange of folk religious and cultural influences from Native Americans and at least several European ethnic groups, and you have quite a complex cultural context. Under these influences, bondsmen engaged in the process of reconstructing and maintaining an African-based culture, including religion, for themselves. Though enslaved, they appear to have freely substituted intellectual frameworks as well as external customs from Native Americans and whites while modifying and inventing new ones wherever necessary and possible.

With its pantheon of saints, Catholicism would easily serve as a vehicle for syncretic transfer between African deity and Catholic saints, as it did in relevant parts of the West Indies and Latin America. But the stringent minimalism of North American Protestantism provided few points for syncretic transfer of African deity. North American Protestantism had few if any syncretizable saints, so that any transfer, syncretism, or combining of African religion with Protestantism had to either occur within a unique paradigm or achieve the impossible and remain totally autonomous. On the level of content and practice more so than structure, the cultural transformation process necessary for Hoodoo's emergence occurred gradually, taking place over several generations, during which time cultural practices were continually adjusted and adapted. Though there was limited consistency, and no long-term, unmodified, sustainable traditional African institutional structures, certain practices survived long enough to take hold and become a breeding ground for new, transferable elements. Throughout this process, community physical and spiritual necessity called forth, influenced, and fulfilled corresponding and developing roles within the slave community.

An especially important component in the old Hoodoo religion was the sacred circle dance that would come to be known as the Ring Shout. This group religious dance was performed in a circle that moved counterclockwise. Scholars have not speculated about the relatedness of Hoodoo and the Ring Shout, but there is certainly enough evidence to associate both Hoodoo and conjure, in its broadest aspect, with the sacred dance circle. Early in Hoodoo's development, there had to have been the association with surviving African religious dance. It is not unreasonable to assert that conjure and the Ring Shout were components of a quickly evolving, uniquely African American adaptation of West and Central West African traditional religion to the Protestant environment of North American enslavement. And just as the syncretic religions of the Caribbean were danced, the Ring Shout was the sacred dance of the Hoodoo religion.

Sterling Stuckey asserts that the Ring Shout may have been the most important sociocultural occurrence in the slave community. "The Shout," as it would eventually come to be called, sometimes had white observers, though it was largely a private, often secret, occurrence among blacks. On such occasions, African religious values were reinforced as well as modified to respond to enslavement. And when outside observers, especially whites, were present, they rarely understood what they were seeing. Slaves privileged the Shout ritual over forms of dance so much that they refused to label "shoutin'" as a type of dancing. It is against the backdrop of the Shout that we see the primary cleavage between sacred and secular, not typical of African traditional religion and culture, drawn first on dancing. On sacred celebratory occasions, bondsmen were basically free from the dance performance expectations of both blacks and whites, which frequently influenced African American secular dancing. Unlike secular dancing, the sacred Ring Shout involved no personal competition, as was often found in plantation breakdowns. In the Shout, dance was neither for entertainment of the master, as in the contra dances, nor for rewards, as in the plantation cakewalks or jig contests.[24] The expectations in the Shout were those of the enslaved spiritual community.

Dance vocabularies and the motor muscle memory retention patterns of the various African ethnic groups could be quite different. The range and uses of movement were often dissimilar, though the general characteristics of West African and Central West African dance distinguish sub-Saharan African dancing generally and mark its uniqueness when compared with European or Asian dance forms. Dance scholars generally agree that delineation, articulation, and segmentation of body parts; angularity; asymmetry; polyrhythm; and mimicry are among those overarching, distinguishing qualities of traditional African dance.

Because the sacred counterclockwise circle was familiar to all the enslaved African ethnic groups in North America, each group could potentially participate in the sacred ring ritual. Each ethnic group would potentially bring a unique signatory contribution to the Ring Shout. Thus the Shout originally allowed a wide range of ethnic expression and dance vocabularies to prevail. These varied contributions seen as expressions of individual identity were encouraged as long as the circle was maintained.

As often as possible, the Shout itself, its location, was away from the eyes of outsiders, especially the slave master, who had the power to mete out punishment. The sacredness of the circle imparted a protection to participants that allowed them wide boundaries of personal and community expression—something unknown to them in their daily labors. The abandonment permitted in the movement of the Ring Shout submerged the individual shouter in a mother lode of sacred African values expressed as dance innovations. Shaped by labor and their African heritage, their bodies created and stabilized the early African American dance vocabulary in the Shout ritual. The most intense levels of movement innovations were in the threshold movements, those rhythmic gestures that immediately preceded spirit possession. These gestures would ultimately have a developmental effect on African American dance itself. Fundamental to the support of African American culture, especially dance, the Ring Shout, more than any other dance form, developed and sustained elements that would influence the development, vocabulary, movement quality, and organization principles of future sacred dance, secular social dance, and theatrical dance forms, including modern, jazz, and tap. In the circle, all Africans could contribute from their particular dance vocabulary and cultural motor muscle memory.

Dance supported the construction and coalescing of wider spiritual values. It allowed bondsmen to establish a spiritual continuity with their former homeland in West and Central West Africa. As dance was the oarsman of spirituality in the African religious ocean, the distant shore to which the Ring Shout boat was rowed was spirit possession, and the wider sea in which it traveled was the Hoodoo religion. Hoodoo was simultaneously both the context for the dances in the circle and the result of it. The relationship was gestational and mutually nourishing. At the new religion's birth, the incipient dances were influenced by and reflected the forces of nature, as do significant West African deity. The traditional African names of the gods would be lost, but the forces of nature that deity often represented were clearly recognizable to all. From the captive Africans' common consciousness of the sacred counterclockwise circle, the forces of nature, including lightening, rain, certain stones, rivers, oceans, and forests, were all reflected in the construction of the early Ring Shout. Without Hoodoo and its sacred dance that preserved much of the traditional African dance vocabulary, the African American dances would not have survived. In the assault that was American enslavement, a variety of African traditional religions, initially clustered by region, combined with other ethnic and religious influences, merged, and gradually metamorphosed into Hoodoo. The Hoodoo religion was born.

As the sacred dance of the old Hoodoo religion, the Ring Shout contained all the antecedent dramatic, mimetic, and stylistic elements of future African American sacred as well as secular dancing. The perspective of the Ring Shout as text inside the context of the old Hoodoo religion allows us to speculate on the dance's origins in Kongo cosmology. This view also allows us a vision of how one aspect of the old Hoodoo religion moved into African American Christian church practice and eventually into secular popular dance. The sacred circle was an essential vehicle in early black Christian conversion for both slaves and freedmen. Several scholars have commented on the possible cosmological significance of the use of circularity in this sacred dance, Sterling Stuckey among them. Seen as a possible tracing of the Kongo cosmogram, the sacred circle was the gateway to a broader spiritual experience, that of spirit possession.[25]

Dance was an important central repository for African values, including the distribution and allotment of intragroup status. In the context of the Ring Shout, slaves could and did assert a limited independence from slavery's pain as well as agency in forging their community, personality, and place. As worshippers circled, some of them fell into the spiritual vortex of the circle's center, where they were embraced by both the community and the supernatural spiritual forces. A hallmark of African spiritual values in worship, the Ring Shout emerged early on in the slave community and included both sacred dancing and spirit possession while being a vessel for the retention of foundation African spiritual values that informed individual and community relations.

In the process of spirit possession, the devotee was embracing the spirit, abandoning earthly control, and entrusting all to the spiritual community. The values of caring, secrecy, community obligation in work, and spiritual help were all conveyed in the sacred Shout ritual. The Shout was the central occasion in which community roles, statuses, values, and sanctions were played out, and it was a time to express spiritual individuality.

As a result of frequent participation in the sacred circle, a shouter could often be identified with a particular style of shouting or a special nuance or dance step. One can surmise that once Hoodoo emerged, its foundation values were sustained in the Ring Shout as the participants drew on the spiritual power of the circular Shout ritual to sustain themselves. And there were those who had spiritual power in the Shout.[26] The African priest, who would evolve into the plantation conjurer, and later the plantation's black preacher possessed spiritual power in the Shout. In addition, he was a likely individual who could seek out Native American spiritual knowledge to augment his and his community's own.

Additional similarities in role structuring and status attribution were shared by a significant number of the enslaved African ethnic groups. These similarities supported the interethnic assimilation process and eased the appearance and development of newly created and ever-changing roles, further supporting the possibility for this ethnically diverse group of slaves to develop limited but effective responses to immediate as well as long-term needs among the bondsmen and later among freed blacks. For example, in the African homelands, roles such as blacksmith, diviner, or herbalist were universally special status positions, even among the ethnically diverse. In the maelstrom of slavery and New World cultural re-creation, certain components of social structure were compatible enough for there to be an achievable interethnic syncretic settling among the ethnically diverse enslaved Africans when the actual process of restructuring the spiritual community began. Roles would quickly become institutionalized within Hoodoo practice. Among those roles were religiomagical practitioners such as conjurers and religiomedical specialists such as treaters, midwives, healers, and slave "doctors."

In the African homeland, certain special status individuals were sometimes insulated from enslavement and sale abroad; that notwithstanding, it is near certain that tens of thousands of African priests and other spiritual specialists such as diviners, musicians, herbalists, bonesetters, bronze casters, and blacksmiths from different ethnic groups were transported to the New World during the slave trade. They carried their religions with them, and their spiritual work would not cease with their enslavement and displacement to American shores.[27] Upon arrival in the new environment, slave priests, shamans, and other religious specialists were confronted with major cultural trauma. If African religion were to survive at all in North America, it would have to make major adaptations; many of those adaptations were forced, but other adaptations were arrived at through rational decision by using age-old principles to modify the religious conventions. The nature of the "peculiar institution" and its attendant restrictions and instabilities required it.

Enslaved Africans carried with them to the New World traditional African modes of understanding and responding that were both informed by and developed in conjunction with other elements of African village social structure and economy. These included norms, values, and beliefs functional in and tailored to their respective cultural environments. Well suited to and formed in cultures bound together by tradition and ritual that were responsive to societal needs, the remaining elements of African social structure would continue developing through centuries of practical experience.

The African American Hoodoo priest and other religiomedical functionaries were focal points in which the difficulties of sociocultural restructuring under the harsh conditions of bondage were partly resolved. More than a mere spiritual representative, the Hoodoo priest was embodied hope. Like his African counterpart, he was a regulator of community; in West and Central West Africa, the priest's regulatory influence sometimes extended to state affairs. He was essential to community harmony and survival, political stability, as well as personal prosperity. He was a major player in the slave community and was perhaps the most serious potential challenge, by an individual slave, to the slaveocracy's power; within the circumscribed context of enslavement, plantation conjurers were powerful and influential. An observer notes: "On every large plantation of Negroes there is one among them who holds great sway over the minds and opinions of the rest; to him they look as the oracle—and this same oracle is, in ninety-nine cases the most consummate villain and hypocrite on the premise. . . . The influence of such a negro is incalculable."[28]

Concerning the conjure priest as African American shaman, folklorist Julien A. Hall, made this observation: "They firmly believe that certain ones amongst them are able to conjure or trick those they have a grudge against, and when one is supposed to be possessed of this ability he is called a 'conjure doctor,' and is looked up to by the others with the profoundest awe and dread. The conjure doctor's word is law, and he can generally live without working, as he frightens his companions into contributing freely to his support."[29]

Though Hoodoo's scope and content would be modified and tailored after emancipation, Hoodoo's functions in the slave community included supernatural controlling and community regulation, protecting individuals from harm, and stimulating or drawing good fortune; but its most widely accepted and least threatening function was herbal healing and medicine. Members of both the slave and free population relied heavily on homemade herbal medicinal treatments. The atmosphere of mutual codependence encountered in frontier, colonial, and plantation communities encouraged exchanges of traditional information, approaches, prescriptions, remedies, formulas, herbal, magical, and curative knowledge. The African healing tradition via Hoodoo was so widely accepted among African American slaves that those who practiced it effectively enjoyed enviable reputations and high status among bondsmen, among free blacks, and often among whites.[30] One such slave was named Cesar, who was given state emancipation by the South Carolina General Assembly and 100 pounds per year for the remainder of his life. His ability to cure rattlesnake envenomation as well as poisoning from ingestion of mercury earned him great acclaim as well as his freedom.[31] Cesar's snakebite cure could possibly have been derived from information and knowledge mutually shared by African and American indigenous communities. Certainly with the large number of venomous snakes in Africa, Africans were familiar with natural treatments for snakebite in their homeland.

The West and Central West African ancestors of African Americans had a highly diversified and centuries-long tradition of healing and healing specialists. John Beecham, born in 1787, leaves us this account of Ashantee: "The fetishmen apply themselves, moreover, to the study of medicine; and the knowledge which they acquire of the properties of herbs and plants, it will be seen hereafter, powerfully contributes to strengthen their influence with the people."[32] Beecham continues:

> In case of bodily affliction, a medical preparation is ordered for the patient. It has already been noticed, that the fetish men and women apply themselves assiduously to the study of the healing art, and acquire such a knowledge of the properties of herbs and plants as enables them to effect the cure of many complaints. . . . It is backed, moreover, during the healing process, by occasional fetish practices; such as the binding of strings round the knees and other joints of the patient, the ends of the strings which hang down after the knots are tied being covered with red vegetable application.[33]

E. J. Glave leaves us another glimpse of the Hoodoo conjure man's highly skilled spiritual ancestor, the Nganga or Congo traditional priest:

> To his religious functions the Nganga unites those of surgeon and the physician, and however his pretensions in the one calling may be, his skill in the other is more than considerable . . . In skirmishes of intertribal warfare natives are often badly wounded: . . . The slugs used are rough pieces of copper, brass wire. . . . In the extractions of these rude bullets the fetish-man displays great surgical skill . . . several of my men received wounds from enemy's overcharged flintlocks. I called in a native charm doctor who was renowned for surgical skill.[34]

These statements indicate that among American bondsmen's West African progenitors, healing and spiritual beliefs were thoroughly comingled; and because success at healing was tied to religious belief, the most proficient healers were frequently spiritual leaders as well. In addition to surgical skill, Africans possessed a highly developed knowledge of herbal medicines and other naturopathic treatments. Cotton Mather, for example, learned of smallpox inoculation from his West African servant, Onesimus: "I was first instructed in it by a Guaramantee servant of my own long before I knew that any Europeans or Asiatics had the least acquaintance with it."[35]

Using government money, Lieutenant Governor William Gooch, during his first year as lieutenant governor of Virginia, purchased a slave's freedom. This slave had provided him with information on plants, roots, and herbs that would cure venereal distempers. Gooch's explanation for expending government funds was that the information the slave provided was valuable to mankind.[36]

It was from the healing facet of the Hoodoo tradition that African Americans derive the term most frequently used for a conjurer: root doctor. There is some distinction between the concepts of conjurer and root doctor; although in some of the literature on Hoodoo as well as in common usage, that distinction is often confusing and unclear.[37] The interchangeable use of both terms indicates a time when there was an indistinguishable division of labor between the two; nevertheless, it is from this facet of the Hoodoo tradition that U.S. blacks derive the use of herbs and roots to affect supernatural occurrences as well as natural cures.

Partly from necessity, the herb and root tradition was strong on the southern plantation. White medical doctors were costly and often inaccessible, so circumstances encouraged the use of home remedies by both slave and free persons.[38] Evidence indicates that Africans and Native Americans exchanged knowledge and beliefs. John P. Reynolds, a black healer, gained much of his knowledge of medicine and treatment of patients from a Native American physician.[39] Bondsmen often acknowledged the use of herbal remedies that they learned from Native Americans.[40] Native Americans and Africans were more familiar with the subtropical and tropical flora and fauna of the Deep South than were European settlers, so it is not surprising that early white settlers made extensive use of the root and herbal traditions of both Native Americans and Africans.[41] Considering this, it is not surprising to find that novels depicting nineteenth-century life included descriptions of root doctors or that slave doctors treated whites as well as blacks. This began to change after legislation passed in Virginia in 1748.[42]

The constant appearance of slave doctors, treaters, and conjurers was seen by certain segments of the white population as such a problem that some municipalities enacted legislation against the transmission of the very information these practitioners needed to continue their work.[43] This reaction against slave expertise in both healing and herbalism was at least in part from fear of the slaves' knowledge of poison plants, but also from fear of the power that root doctors, conjurers, and healers could wield over some bondsmen. Each success in physical healing or spiritual controlling potentially served to strengthen and validate not only the reputation and power of the slave priest-healer, but also the complete storehouse of slave community folk knowledge. Each visible success confirmed for the slave that his tradition-bound view of the world was both functional and correct in the face of what threatened to become all-encompassing enslavement and oppression.

Early in American history, there was tension between the practice of prohibiting slaves from acquiring medicinal herbal knowledge and the medical needs of the frontier and colonial communities. There was inconsistency in both the legal and the social treatment of slaves with herbal knowledge and healing skills. On one hand, they were needed and utilized; on the other hand, they were feared and regarded with suspicion, and rightfully so because slave owners in many parts of the New World lived in fear of being poisoned by their slaves.[44] Though a slave would have to pay dearly for attempting a poisoning, there is ample evidence to justify the fears that whites held of being poisoned by a captive laborer. In their homeland, many of the Africans had mastered the knowledge of poisonous plants and substances for both medicinal purposes and dealing with enemies. Once in the Americas, they continued the practice throughout the eighteenth and nineteenth century, enabling the lore as well as the practice of poisoning to remain fairly well developed among bondsmen. Consider the following statement published in November 1749: "The horrid practice of poisoning white people by the Negroes, has lately become so common, that within a few days past, several executions have taken place in different parts of the country, by burning, gibbeting, hanging, &."[45] A newspaper account from Charleston, South Carolina, dated October 30, 1749, and found in the *Pennsylvania Gazette* leaves the following:

> Wednesday last, a Negro Wench, about sixteen Years old, Slave to an Apothecary in this Town, was committed to Goal for poisoning a Child of her Master, about 11 Months old, by putting Arsenick, or Ratsbane, several times into what it drank. The Child continued in great Misery till Thursday Morning, and then died. The Wretch has not only acknowledged the poisoning of this Child, but also another of the same Family, about 15 Months old, some Time before.[46]

From Maryland, two similar reports:

> On Friday last, William Stratton, Negro Toney the Poison Doctor, and Negro Jemmy, were all executed at Port Tobacco, in Charles County, pursuant to their Sentence, for the poisoning the late Mr. Chase, and the Bodies were all hung in Chains the same Day, in different Parts of the County.
>
> At the same Time and on the same Gallows, Were executed, Negro Jack, for attempting to poison Mr. Francis Clements, His Master.[47]

As emancipation ended slavery and dispelled the fears of such poisoning, the public discourse on—and the white concern with—its practice diminished in magnitude and eventually vanished. Poisoning as a method of dealing with an enemy, or exacting revenge, would continue in the African American community, its greatest adherents being emancipated slaves, their children, and their grandchildren. The root doctor, conjurer, or two-head remained the link with the past; an element in his African legacy included his mastery of poisonous substances as part of his command of a complete medicinal system. In support of this, esteemed African American author Charles W. Chesnutt leaves us his observations in 1901: "Some of the more gruesome phases of the belief in conjuration suggest possible poisoning, a knowledge of which baleful art was once suppose to be widespread among the imported Negroes of the olden time. The blood or venom of snakes, spiders, and lizards is supposed to be employed for this purpose."[48] In many locales, the cultural environment in the postemancipation, pre–World War I black community was scarcely different than it had been under enslavement, so even after emancipation, poisonings among blacks continued to take their toll. One of the most famous examples was the poisoning of bluesman Robert Johnson. Johnson was allegedly poisoned by a rival over a woman. He died not long after he had drunk from an open bottle of liquor given to him at a southern jook.[49]

The strength of the herb and root aspect of Hoodoo not only resulted from its clearly defined functionality, but also was due, in part, to the African slaves' cultural tenacity and familiarity with their own healing, controlling, and spiritual paradigms and traditions. That Hoodoo could be sustained through slavery speaks to the effective tenacity of the paradigm of silence, a highly valued and well-understood posture in the slave community and one necessary for Hoodoo's existence and development. Couched in a Hoodoo presentation of self, the paradigm of silence served blacks in their relationships with whites, while being the primary vehicle in which secrecy was expressed, modified, and further defined. The silence paradigm was made visible in a variety of ways; for example, in the African secret societies, in the pursed lips of the elders demonstrating an intentional closing of the mouth, as well as in the poetry of Paul Laurence Dunbar's "We Wear the Mask."

At least one other factor promoted Hoodoo's development and survival during slavery: its high level of adaptability. This previously mentioned quality is expressed in more than a few West and Central West African religions. Inclusive adaptability enabled the required substitutions of both specific plants and conventions of preparation to be successfully made and applied as nondisruptively as possible. This quality would serve Hoodoo development well as Hoodoo struggled to stabilize and sustain itself.

From an examination of Hoodoo artifacts uncovered in an archaeological dig in southern Virginia and dated circa 1820–30, it is clear that by the late

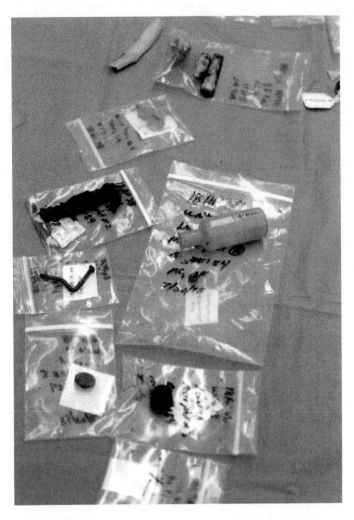

Conjurer's cache. Items uncovered in an archaeological dig
in Virginia. Items pictured here include rib bones and
a small blue-green bottle. This bottle was probably the
conjurer's "walking boy" divination device.

eighteenth or early nineteenth century Hoodoo was fully functioning in the
slave community, completely self-sufficient with its own supply lines, networks, and ritual procedures as well as substitutions. The "Hoodoo clergy,"
conjurers, root workers, and Hoodoo priests had developed acceptable
substitutions that could be obtained and sanctified. An early nineteenth-
century Hoodoo priest's storehouse of supplies would contain his divination

devices, such as a set of rib bones or the walking boy made from a tiny blue bottle suspended from a cord, or he kept a "frizzly chicken" as a divination device. Later Hoodoo workers would use a deck of regular playing cards, dominoes, or even dice to read a situation and diagnose the concern. He would also have a supply of dried peach pits that, used for spiritual work only, he could substitute for the more difficult to obtain High John the Conquer root. He would also have broken pieces of ceramic pottery or china, four hole buttons, nails, pins, metal buttons, beads, small wooden sticks (some from spent matches), small ceramic doll's head, arms and legs, crab claws, various types of seeds, pods, shells, crystals, dried herbs, pieces of leather and cloth scraps, and lodestone.[50] Some of these items were similar to those given to this author as part of the divinatory implements following my first-level initiation as an olorisha of Ogun. The doll's head, piece of broken white ceramic pottery, large seed, and black stone found in the dig were remarkably like those same items given to this author at initiation.

Contained within traditional West and Central West African religion was an approach to health and healing as well as approaches to addressing all of humankind's major problems. Included were rituals, detailed procedures, and avenues to invoke protection from malicious intent such as poisoning[51] as well as protective objects that repelled harmful forces. There were also commonly known and engaged in protective behaviors, which included avoidance procedures.[52] Learned in both the family and the community, these avoidance behaviors were designed to limit one's vulnerability and might include something as simple as not eating or drinking in potentially unfriendly or unfamiliar circumstances or environments or not allowing intimate personal objects such as clothing to fall into the hands of potential enemies. Half a century after the end of slavery, bluesman Robert Johnson knew the warnings against drinking from an opened bottle, a bottle of liquor that had the seal already broken; he ignored the traditional folk wisdom, and it cost him his life.[53]

Traditional African religions view the human state as part of a continuum in which life on earth is a duty-bound stop, as is time in the realm of the ancestors. Though time on earth is predestined within certain boundaries, mankind can affect change within those limits. In traditional West African religions, physical malady and illness, even misfortunes, are seen as spiritual in origin. Maladies are believed to be caused by a dissatisfied ancestor or a malcontent's wandering spirit that was captured and redirected. In other instances, the soul, essence, or *ashe* of an individual could be affected by supernatural means. These concepts varied somewhat in their overt and detail manifestations, but the principle was significantly similar among the people of the slave-plundered regions of West and Central West Africa.[54] This general tenet, that physical malady, illness, and misfortune can have a spiritual origin, was carried over into the syncretized spiritual traditions of the New World, where, encountering similar or compatible principles held by Native American traditionalists and in European folk belief, it became widespread and fused with vibrant longevity.

In a significant number of traditional West African religions, the religious leader was, and remains today, also a diviner, healer, and manipulator of worldly and spiritual events. The roles he or she fills are multifaceted.[55] With this fact in mind, it is not surprising to find that in the slave communities of the United States, the traditional social roles of healer, diviner, and conjurer were often occupied by one person, as they had been in West Africa. W. E. B. DuBois attests to the multifunctionality of the slave conjurer's role. According to him, the loss of traditional West African religion among American bondsmen was a:

> . . . terrific social revolution, and yet some traces were retained of the former group life, and the chief remaining institution was the Priest or Medicine-man. He early appeared on the plantation and found his function as the healer of the sick, the interpreter of the Unknown, the comforter of the sorrowing, the supernatural avenger of wrong, and the one who rudely but picturesquely expressed the longing, disappointment, and resentment of a stolen and oppressed people. Thus as bard, physician, judge, and priest, within the narrow limits allowed by the slave system rose the Negro preacher, and under him the first Afro-American institution, the Negro church.[56]

This "terrific social revolution" occurred under the influence of internal cultural tension resulting partly from the heterogeneity of bondsmen. Consciously or otherwise, these ethnically diverse groups contended somewhat with one another over which traditional elements could and would be preserved. The cultural-religious tensions thus generated would resolve themselves in a range of patterns, but always under the direct pressure and limitations imposed by slavery. Certainly elements familiar to nearly all enslaved Africans, such as spirit possession, ancestor reverence, animal sacrifice, and certain dance elements, would be more likely candidates for survival in the new environment of slavery, which mandated a protracted reconfiguring of traditional African religious beliefs.

Hoodoo religion did not emerge simultaneously and uniformly in every locale, but in certain concentrated plantation environments that exhibited the necessary and sufficient conditions that would nourish Hoodoo's germination and materialization. These core plantations were large by American standards, exhibiting high African population density, inadvertently allowing enslaved Africans some degree of autonomy or unhampered religio-cultural space. At least one of these core culture plantations existed within proximity to nearly every major urban locale and exercised influence on the model of culture that emerged in that region. At gatherings such as corn shuckings, plantation dances, Shout worship services, and at clandestine, illegal public gatherings bondsmen from the core plantations exchanged cultural and spiritual information with Native Americans as well as with slaves from other plantations. An account from the *South Carolina Gazette* describes what appears to be such an exchange. "They also had their private committees; whole deliberations were carried on in too low voice, and with much caution, as not to be overheard by the others. . . . The members of this secret council had much the appearance of Doctors in deep and solemn consultation upon life or *death* which indeed might have been the scope of their meditations at the time."[57] The dismal act of slave trading was inadvertently culturally significant in that it provided both regional and national reshuffling and exchange of African cultural and spiritual practices. The trader's infamous slave pens of New Orleans are noteworthy here. Slaves from every region of the country as well as some from Africa, the West Indies, and Mexico could spend as much as one to three months there waiting to be sold. During that time, slaves were exposed to cultural and spiritual knowledge from a variety of regions.[58]

The slave community's cultural leaders, conjurers, blacksmiths, priests and priestesses, proficient singers, musicians, and excellent dancers initially came from a variety of different African ethnic traditions. But familiarity with, or commonly shared knowledge about, a particular transethnic practice like the counterclockwise dance circle may have been the most significant in a series of culturally leveling selection principles, used by enslaved Africans, in holding onto elements of traditional African culture. Much of what becomes Hoodoo exhibits continuities with a range of West African and Central West African religious traditions. Consider the similarity in the following two passages for example:

> [I]t was thought by many that he would not be able to find the buried poison, but as they were about to give up their pursuit, . . . Then the doctor ordered the man to dig quickly, for the "trickbag" was there. On the order being obeyed, the poison was found. It was rusty nails, finger and toe nails, hair and pins sewed up in a piece of red flannel. The "doctor" carried this to the patient, and convinced him that he had found the cause

of his illness, and that he would surely get well. Not many days elapsed before he was walking as well as ever.[59]

"Bring me a hoe," said Okagbue. When Ekwefi brought the hoe, he had already put aside his goatskin bag and his big cloth and was in his underwear. . . . He immediately set to work digging a pit where Ezinma had indicated. . . . Suddenly Okagbue sprang to the surface with the agility of a leopard. "It is very near now," he said. "I have felt it." . . . "Call your wife and child," he said to Okonkwo. After a few more hoe-fuls of earth he struck the iyi-uwa. He raised it carefully with the hoe and threw it to the surface . . . he went into his goatskin bag, took out two leaves and began to chew them. When he had swallowed them, he took up the rag with left hand and began to untie it. And then the smooth, shiny pebble fell out. . . . All this had happened more than a year ago and Ezinma had not been ill since.[60]

The first passage is from the Hampton Institute's *Southern Workman* from 1899. The second passage, written more than half a century later, is from Chinua Achebe's 1959 novel of traditional Igbo life in Nigeria, *Things Fall Apart*. Both the Ibo *iyi-uwa* and the African American trickbag contained items that were wrapped in cloth, buried in the ground, and believed to be the cause of illness. Both the *iyi-uwa* and the trickbag required unearthing and neutralization by a spiritual specialist. The apparent similarities in preparation, appearance, and handling indicate the use of similar operational conventions and principles and suggest a common cultural ancestry or religious paradigm for both practices.

The roles of Hoodoo doctor, conjurer, and plantation preacher were directly inherited from the traditional African priest, but the role of conjurer had been more long-standing than any social role to emerge from slavery and existed well before the appearance of the Negro preacher. Like the African priest, both the Hoodoo priest and the early slave preacher employed a complex system of symbols to raise client expectations of a successful outcome, thus to achieve success in their practices.[61] Slaves viewed conjurers as embodied spiritual power; these enslaved men of power apparently provided a rewarding and hopeful counterbalance to the powerlessness experienced by blacks because of enslavement. As part of a wider community response to social expectations for problem solving, the conjurer himself was a living symbol signifying deep levels of hope as well as access to alternative sources of support and assistance beyond the slave master's control. The slave community inherited and passed on to freedmen the availability of the Hoodoo priest's particular services.

It is likely that when and where Hoodoo functioned as a complete religion, it was a momentarily stable cultural plateau in the decline of an interethnic yet traditional African religious formation. As it existed under slavery, the Hoodoo religion was a short-lived, transitional, and shrinking religious form that stabilized briefly, fragmented and declined, evolved, and then expanded after emancipation. As with the African American jook and other African-based cultural forms, Hoodoo made adaptations necessary for its own survival.

In its early years, Hoodoo had its secret signs and gestures associated with the spiritual forces of nature, with power over individuals and situations as well as over the darker forces such as haints or witches. These signs were likely to have been composites of signs and gestures from traditional African secret societies modified through great cultural loss and the experience of slave labor; many of them became the short-lived secret sign system of conjurers and Hoodoo priests. These signs and gestures would eventually die within Hoodoo, but not before a few of them would move into the vocabulary of gestures and signs used by the fundamentalist African American preacher. The sign would form a link between the believer and the world of supernatural power. In a scene from the film *The Color Purple* adapted from the Alice Walker novel of the same name, as Celie, the protagonist, is leaving Mister, her abusive husband, he raises his hand to strike her and she rapidly extends her right arm with her first two fingers outstretched pointing into a Hoodoo-influenced horizontal *V* as if throwing a fix on him. With a sense of protected bravery, she prophetically utters, "All that you do to me already done to you." Mister stops as if frozen in place; Celie then confidently rides away.

Momentarily, though perhaps not in all regions, Hoodoo religion had its own deity and religiocultural heroes, its sacred dance (the Ring Shout), its healing practices, and its religious specialists. But the Hoodoo religion could not sustain itself. So the aspect known as conjure, later called Hoodoo, quickly and concurrently appeared independently even as the Hoodoo religion was dying. Conjure required no worship services, no formalized doctrine, and could be embodied in a single individual, the conjurer. Like the system of signs, certain other elements of the Hoodoo religion would yoke themselves to and be sustained within Africanized plantation Christianity. Other elements, because of their functionality, would be sustained independently and later become an integral part of conjure/Hoodoo practice.

While asserting influence in the creation of all subsequent secular dance among blacks, the Ring Shout maintained a sacred identity during slavery and, though its circularity would eventually be destroyed by the linear organization of church pews,[62] its spiritual essence successfully moved from clandestine Hoodoo ritual into the Africanized Christian sacred dance ritual known as shoutin'. Aspects of shoutin' would secularize and move into at least two African American popular social dances: the Big Apple, appearing in the 1920s, and the Shout, which would appear in the late 1950s. In the transformative process that propelled the Ring Shout into African American Christian worship, certain aspects of Hoodoo as a component of black Christian worship would eventually be relegated to a separately existing sphere, at least in surface appearance. But on a deeper level, some aspects of Hoodoo were taken into the black church while certain aspects of the conjurer's role were merged into some Christian ministers' functional capacity. This occurred while other clergy condemned and abandoned Hoodoo practice. DuBois had this comment concerning the movement of African religious practice, repeated here from the epigraph to this chapter: "This church was not at first by any means Christian nor definitely organized: rather it was an adaptation and mingling of heathen rites among the members of each plantation, and roughly designated as Voodooism."[63]

African captives and their descendants in America were often left alone by their masters to worship as they saw fit in unhampered social space. The Hoodoo religion could develop in this isolated space. It also enabled the slave religious leadership to consciously retain, merge, or discard elements from African traditional religion. The older traditions would transform into a transgenerational form, in which conjure and the sacred dancing of the Ring Shout both played a significant and unified role as part of the Hoodoo religious tradition. Both the Ring Shout and aspects of Hoodoo were eventually taken over into black Christian ritual, with aspects of conjure gradually being discarded from black Christian practice in most churches.[64] Plantation conjurers were instrumental in this process because they undoubtedly functioned in several closely associated roles, like that of Ring Shout leader or perhaps as arbiter guiding the direction of worship. It is not unreasonable to assume that plantation conjurers achieved special status in both clandestine and openly visible Ring Shouts as well as in other activities, such as death rituals, where the sacred circle was convened. Attending these ceremonies and rituals in a variety of capacities, conjurers, in their general role as comforter, spiritual leader, protector, and earthly contact with the supernatural, were entrenched in the overall life of the slave community and were thoroughly familiar with its African-derived rituals, including its sacred dance. Similarly, both religious leaders and chiefs in parts of Africa are often expected to be competent dancers. The plantation preachers who merged Hoodoo practice with their Christianity were competent if not outstanding shouters and more sympathetic to the Ring Shout, allowing, encouraging, even participating in it.

The services provided by the Hoodoo priest, two-head, or conjurer were in perfect alignment with the traditional African religious worldview. In practice, this spiritual and healing specialist was a generalist whose religio-science enabled him to approach the world as a seamless entity with little demarcation between sacred and secular, physical and spiritual, natural and supernatural. He was a religioscientific practitioner operating inside a paradigm that he inherited primarily from his African cultural past and that was continually evolving and modifying itself to meet the needs of his clients in the environment of North American enslavement.

Hoodoo was no static phenomenon; it had to have been a complex social process influencing multiple levels of plantation and slave society. As a primary requirement for successfully sustaining itself, Hoodoo had to be thoroughly enmeshed in the social interaction of the slave community. Supernatural solutions were not embraced by bondsmen simply because other forms of controlling and other centers of power were closed to them. From the very beginning, Hoodoo both was embedded within an immediate network of sanctions and supports and was able to engage in coercion and behavior shaping representing a source of power within the fragile and uncertain normative structure of the slave community. Hoodoo, more than any other aspect of slave cultural tradition, promised power beyond the brittle normative structure of the community of bondsmen. This promise could not always be fulfilled; but when it was, it strengthened Hoodoo belief and practice.

The conjurer, as a symbol of both resistance and defiance as well as a model of secrecy, was a cultural signpost, a living semiotic indicator of a functioning worldview held by African American bondsmen. He was an important arbiter sanctioning the transformations in Hoodoo procedures, paraphernalia, ritual objects, ceremonial content, and decorum necessitated by American slave life. In the slave community, the conjurer was both thoroughly integrated and aligned in every way; he was a significant source of tradition, meaning, community definition, and cohesion. Not until emancipation and the destruction of the slave quarter community did the unusual appearance, demeanor, and qualities associated with conjurers in the post-Reconstruction environment become more apparent and particularly significant. In some traditional African contexts, traditional priests are marked by some unusual physical characteristic, such as a deformity, birthmark, or unusual birth circumstances; when this occurs, it is seen as a sign or indicator of supernatural verification of priestly status. This belief, like numerous others, would continue among both enslaved and free blacks on the North American mainland.

Under slavery, the conjurer or root doctor was not able to disconnect his specialized spiritual labor from that of other slaves, and this affected him. As slaves, conjure doctors were still accountable to their owners for their labor output. Their physical labor in the fields embedded them in the fabric of slave social structure and provided the social conditions for them to be similar to other bondsmen in appearance, language, sentiments, and expectations. But following emancipation, the destruction of the slave quarter community and the reorganization of slave labor into the individu-alized rural labor form known as sharecropping, the conjurer could be and often was disconnected from the labor routines of the field, factory, or urban environment. This freedom of movement as individual and spiritual laborer, accompanied by isolation from the routine of sharecropped labor, allowed the conjurer freedom to behave in ways that sharecroppers, who answered to their white landlords, could not. Because the emancipated conjurer made his living serving primarily an African American clientele, he was not immediately answerable to whites or anyone for his livelihood and labor. Within certain limits imposed by American white supremacy rac-ism, he had the latitude and mandate to look and behave in an unorthodox fashion. Strange appearance or behavior is one of the hallmarks of the post-Reconstruction conjure doctors.[65]

African traditional rituals and beliefs were and are today part of a com-plex philosophy of universal existence and order designating a place and procedure for all of humankind's concerns and problems. Included here, for example, are all rituals, procedures, and acts aimed at maintaining balance.[66] The principle of universal balance, and the need to maintain it, gave rise and development to a complex of practices. These practices were modified by varying degrees in the New World, depending on the afore-mentioned specific conditions of enslavement such as plantation size and intensity and frequency of contact with whites and Native Americans.

African slaves in America were surrounded by a complex spiritual universe defying simple categorization. The conjurer, treater, Hoodoo, or two-head, as root doctors were also known, was the mediator between the slave com-munity and that wider spiritual reality. Even after the acceptance of Chris-tianity, African-style spirituality continued to inform the slave community's supernatural belief system.[67] But African religion could not survive intact under slavery in the United States or in the less fragmented forms, as one finds elsewhere in the New World. According to scholar W. E. B. DuBois, in the United States: "African religion . . . was transformed. Fetish survived in certain rites and even here and there in blood sacrifice, carried out secretly and at night; but more often in open celebration which gradually became transmuted into Catholic and Protestant Christian rites."[68]

Success at re-creating the familiar was essential in the religious transformation process. Thus, as in the Ring Shout, the sacred circle was invoked at early Christian worship and conversion services, even against the wishes of the presiding Christian reverend.[69] Even within the boundaries set by enslavement, familiar cultural practices that imparted a sense of comfort and security were carried wherever possible into the ever-changing religious and cultural life of slaves. The older familiar practices acted as an ever-moving anchor in stabilizing and giving acceptable form to the emergence of Hoodoo and establishing Hoodoo's marginal acceptability in some black Christian churches.

The varied uses of Hoodoo religion or conjure in the slave community ranged from healing to injuring, from attracting a spouse to protecting oneself or loved ones. The development and maintenance of Hoodoo rituals and practices were influenced by the total spiritual backdrop of slavery. Some slaves approached Hoodoo with an attitude that was both desperate and reaffirming. The white man's religion was often seen as inaccessible and unresponsive, particularly when Christianization efforts aimed at slaves were minimum. So the harshness of the American system of enslavement coupled with Christianity's limited responsiveness intensified the slave's need for additional supernatural African assistance.

Hoodoo exhibited numerous contradictions under slavery. On one hand, certain aspects of the tradition, such as herbal work, appeared efficacious and thus achieved some degree of validity and legitimation among whites, particularly in early America, and imparted a positive reputation to black Native American "doctors."[70] On the other hand, the spiritual controlling aspect of the tradition was severely maligned, denigrated, misunderstood, and sometimes feared by outsiders. Because of the apparent power it held over bondsmen to incite as well as to strengthen the spirit of rebellion and individual resistance, Hoodoo was approached cautiously by some whites. There is ample evidence that conjurers played an important role in slave rebellion and individual slave resistance.[71] Frederick Douglass was one of the better-known bondsmen who spoke of their encounters with conjure. In his book *The Life and Times of Frederick Douglass,* he tells the story of being given a packet of magical roots by an older African-born slave named Sandy. Though Douglass doubted the root pack's efficacy, its purpose was apparently fulfilled and Douglass was never whipped by any man ever again.[72]

The protective amulet or charm known as the mojo bag, mojo hand, Hoodoo bag, Hoodoo hand, juju bag, root bag, conjure pack, gopher bag, jack, toby, lucky hand, or package, mentioned by a considerable number of freedmen as significant in their life experience, was universally carried and understood in the slave community. Similarly, Louis Hughes, a slave in Tennessee, Mississippi, and Virginia, carried one type of protection, a small leather bag, to ward off whippings. The charm's "magic" or power was usually encased in several layers of either cloth or leather and wrapped with either leather cord, hemp string, or twine so as not to be exposed. Given to him by an older slave, Hughes's bag was probably similar to a thousand others carried by slaves throughout the South; we are left with this account:

Kongo *nkisi*. This medicine bag from the Congo resembles one type of African American mojo bag. (Drawing courtesy of the Laman Collection; Wyatt MacGaffey, trans. and ed., *Art and Healing of the Bakongo, Commented by Themselves: Minkisi from the Laman Collection*, Bloomington: Indiana University Press, 1991.)

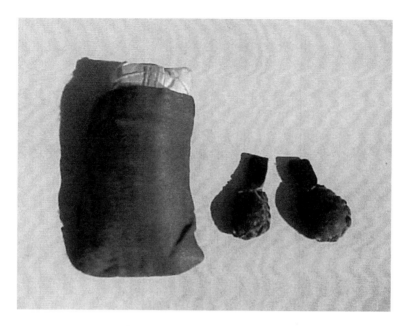

Mojo bags. African American package wrapped with thread and enclosed in a red silk bag and two Nigerian Yoruba medicine bags encased in leather.

It was the custom in those days for slaves to carry voo-doo bags. It was handed from generation to generation; and, though it was one of the superstitions of a barbarous ancestry, it was still very generally tenaciously held to by all classes. I carried a little bag, which I got from an old slaver who claimed that it had power to prevent any one who carried it from being whipped. It was made of leather, and contained roots, nuts, pins and some other things. . . . Many of the servants were thorough believers in it, . . . and carried these bags all the time.[73]

In traditional West and Central West African religion, the amulet, in addition to leather, could be housed in sacred cloth, seeds, insect pods, seashells, snail shells, woven raffia, animal horns, as well as small and large calabash gourds. In addition, the mojo might be a double or triple bag, that is two or three bags tied together and with other attachments such as bones, whistles, bells, thorns, or plant parts. Other types of protective fabrications, such as the type requiring the tying of knots directly on the body, would later retreat into isolated pockets and nearly disappear. The tying of knots and the making of protective packets were widespread religious practices in traditional West and Central West African religion and would become staples in African American black belt Hoodoo practice that would continue into the twenty-first century. Mary Alicia Owens in 1891 records a former slave conjure doctor's use of string and knots in making a "tricken bag" and "luck ball." Owens leaves us this observation:

> He broke off four lengths of yarn, each length measuring about forty-eight inches. These were doubled and re-doubled into skeins of four strands each and spread in a row before him. To each skein was added forty-eight inches of sewing-silk folded as the yarn was.
>
> "Dar now!" he said, "De silk am ter tie yo' frens unter yo' de yahn am ter tie down all the debbils. Des watch me tie de knots. Hole on dough!—dis fust!"
>
> The "fust" proceeding was to fill his mouth with whiskey. Then ensued a most surprising gurgling and mumbling, as he tied a knot near the end of the skein nearest him. As it was tightened, he spat about a teaspoonful of tobacco-perfumed saliva and whiskey upon it. "Dar now!" he said, "dat's er mighty good knot. Dey ain't no debbil kin git thu dat."[74]

Most authentic old tradition mojoes were baptized in liquid spirits and tailored to the client's specific needs; no two were exactly alike—there were no generic mojo bags as one would later find dominating the spiritual marketplace. In the construction of a protective mojo bag, for example, the conjurer-root doctor would consult with the client to understand his daily schedule, where he was likely to be, where he was likely to need protection, and from whom or what. Then the specifics of location, schedule, and personality would be fabricated into the amulet using the principles of physical power, speed, and territoriality. Specific instructions for the care, maintenance, and spiritual interaction with the mojo accompanied the amulet and were given to the client. And in latter-day Hoodoo-conjure, sometimes the client would be given something sacred to say, such as a Psalm.[75]

Emancipation would transform every aspect of African American life; Hoodoo in all its aspects was no exception. After emancipation, certain Hoodoo practices would find new life, others would die, still others would be engaged in selective adaptation that transformed them from their former state into something functionally new. In the area of folklore and myth, some beliefs would rapidly disappear, others would achieve prominence and functionality, as others faded, leaving the survivors in a stronger, more entrenched position within Hoodoo practice. The belief in High John the Conquer was one such myth that would be grounded in both a medicinal and magical reality; we now turn our attention to it.

I was accused of murder in the first degree
The judge's wife cried, "Let the man go free!"
I was rubbin' my root, my John the Conquer root
Aww, you know there ain't nothin' she can do, Lord,
I rub my John the Conquer root
—Willie Dixon, "My John the Conquer Root"

THE SEARCH FOR
HIGH JOHN THE CONQUER

Early in the North American slave experience, the conditions of bondage circumscribed African slave life and transformed the remotest aspects of slave psyche, mythology, and behavior. In response to this, resistance behaviors appeared in the slave population; rebellions, mutinies, and poisonings, along with subtler dissembling, creating a legacy of hope and support while providing models for further resistance. Since New World enslavement exacted a high price from both the slave's physical body and his spiritual apparatus, "hope" was indeed the tool that enabled the enslaved to salvage his own humanity. That vision of hope, resistance, rebellion, and triumph had no stronger expression in Hoodoo than in the sacred High John the Conquer myth.[1] The single most important root in contemporary Hoodoo practice, High John the Conquer root, a member of the morning glory family, has long been invested with magical and spiritual potency. Contemporary scholars of Hoodoo exhibit some confusion about what this root is and the source of its power. In her landmark research, scholar Yvonne Chireau incorrectly identifies High John as St. John's wart."[2] Others have stated that High John derives its power from the fact that it resembles a black man's testicle. The latter explanation reveals white supremacy's fear of, and fixation on, black sexuality, especially as it reflects black male sexual potency; neither is true.[3] Its power is derived from its relationship with enslavement and the spirit of rebellion and resistance.

Known also as bindweed and as jalap root, its botanical name *Ipomea jalapa* or *Ipomoea purga* indicates its kinship with the sweet potato, *Ipomoea patata*. It is sometimes classed as *convulvolacea jalapa*. Its most commonly known name, jalap, is derived from the region in Mexico—Xalapa, Veracruz—where this native plant grows in abundance and from where most of the stock used in Hoodoo has been imported. Jalap's other names include bindweed, *jalapa hembra, jalapa de Orizaba, brionia de las Indias, rubarbo de las Indias,* and *jalapa official;*[4] but the name *Mechoacan de guerrero* or *Michoacan de guerrero* indicates the Hispanicizing of a Nahuatl Indian name indicating a region with an abundance of fish. The Spanish term *guerrero* means "warrior." This linguistic combination points to a coastal area where warriors made a reputation, such as the coastal area of Veracruz, Mexico, where Xalapa is the capital city and jalap is said to be native to the area and can grow in abundance there. In fact, this region of Mexico is jalap's only native habitat.

The Xalapa region was inhabited by Teochichimecs, Totonocs, and Nahua-speaking peoples prior to an Aztec or Mexica conquest during the latter half of the fifteenth century. According to Patrick J. Carroll, the Aztecs modified the local economy, demanding greater production of "certain items such as *purga de Jalapa,* a medicinal herb that grew naturally in the area."[5] When the Spaniards arrived in Mexico in the fifteenth century, they discovered the plant in its native abundance. The roots exported to Europe by the Spaniards in the middle 1500s were collected from the extensive natural populations then growing in the region of Xalapa-Xico in the state of Veracruz.[6] The increased European demand eventually led to commercial cultivation. Between the mid-sixteenth and early seventeenth centuries, the plant was introduced into various European botanical gardens in France and England to attempt its cultivation. The British eventually introduced the species to Jamaica and India where it was cultivated. The demand for the root continued to increase, and between 1761 and 1851 the Xalapa-Xico region of Veracruz exported more than one and a half million tons of the root to Europe, where it was used in treatment of several maladies. Its most frequent use was as a purgative, laxative, and treatment for kidney disorders.[7]

Though it is only partly documented, there is evidence that a powerful culture of slave resistance developed in the American colonies and later in the United States. Examples of resistance culture included the use of song to facilitate escape, the use of quilts carrying messages aiding escapees, the use of conjure for protection in violating slaves codes and confounding patrollers, and folktales and myths that specifically nourished the seeds of resistance and hope. The story of High John the Conquer was one such myth.

Albeit enslavement demanded both mental isolation and some degree of individual loyalty, bondsmen created a community of resistance and support that constantly reminded them that both challenges to enslavement and triumph were indeed possible even when apparently unfavorable circumstances prevailed. Successful adjustment to enslavement stretched the limits of a slave's humanity and imprinted itself on every aspect of the person, marking the members of the slave community, predisposing them to a range of vulnerabilities, including early death. Hope was often all that bondsmen had.

Zora Neale Hurston describes High John the Conquer as "our hope bringer."[8] The picture she draws of him appears at first both ambiguous and contradictory yet all-encompassing. "There is no established picture of what sort of looking-man this John de Conquer was. To some, he was a big, physical-looking man like John Henry. To others, he was a little, hammered-down, low-built man like the Devil's doll baby. Some said that they never heard what he looked like. Nobody told them, but he lived on the plantation where their old folks were slaves."[9] Her examination and description in 1943 draws from history, literature, sociology, and folklore in presenting the scope of High John's domain. For Hurston, High John de Conquer is a cultural trope. He is the mythologized spirit of hope, resistance, and safekeeping. But equally important, he is a conveyor of significant values, particularly the values of justice and universal reciprocity. High John seems to take on the qualities of a savior, a personal protector for the enslaved, informing them that freedom was on its way, so they must persevere. "My mama told me, and I know that she wouldn't mislead me, how High John de Conquer helped us out. He had done teached the black folks so they knowed a hundred years ahead of time that freedom was coming. Long before the white folks knowed anything about it at all."[10] North American bondsmen clung to the belief that High John had preordained, predestined emancipation and freedom. They testified that it was the power of High John and not the American Civil War nor whites who brought them liberation from chattel slavery. The notion of High John as a liberating force as well as a "hope bringer" was intimately intertwined in the black popular imagination. "These young Negroes . . . talk about the war freeing the Negroes . . . 'course the war was a lot of help but how come the war took place? . . . John de Conquer had done put it into the white folks to give us our freedom, that's what. . . . Freedom just *had* to come. The time set aside for it was there. The war was just a sign and a symbol of the thing."[11]

The notion of High John also conveyed the spirit of kindness, humor, and morality while wrapping the embattled slave psyche in a protective package of functional values. Embedded in the concept of High John were many of the values extolled and esteemed in black popular folk discourse. The compilation of values posited a normative outline by which members of the slave community could sustain their sense of themselves. High John spread and remained viable because of the holistic model it represented. To African slaves encountering the Americanized story, there might be familiarity; to Americanized slaves, there would be identification and a source of esteem. Cassandra Wimbs asserts that High John, Jesus, and Shango are collateral or analogous spiritual forces.[12] High John was not merely a hope bringer, he also was an intermediary between man and God, a warrior martyr, dying for "us," a soul saver, a sustainer, and a virtual saint of the old Hoodoo religion. "Way over there where the sun rises a day ahead of time they say that Heaven arms with love and laughter those it does not wish to see destroyed. He who carries his heart in his sword must perish. So says the ultimate law. . . . John knew that it is written where it cannot be erased, that nothing shall live on human flesh and prosper."[13] Known among Santeria/Lukumi adherents as Juan el Conquistador, the idea of High John the Conquer is perhaps the most widely known non-Abrahamic folk spiritual figure in the black Atlantic New World.

Best and most potent if dug before September 21, the last day of summer,[14] High John is used in numerous types of Hoodoo work and has been the most utilized Hoodoo root. That was probably not always the case. Within the old black belt plantation tradition, High John's uses were probably more specific than in more recent usage. Across time, High John's uses appear to move from the specific to the general. Once used for only a few and very specific needs, High John eventually would be used as a substitute for increasing numbers of Hoodoo roots and plants. The specificity of High John's earlier uses was first tailored to the gender of the work to be done. Was the work predominantly male or female? Once determined, the High John root was selected based on its gender. The distinction between male and female High John was lost in the turn-of-the-century spiritual marketplace, as was the distinction between male and female mojoes.

With respect to its importance in the Hoodoo pharmacopeia, there are two perplexing questions: How did this legendary root, native only to the region around Xalapa, Mexico, become so significant to Hoodoo practice thousands of miles away in Tennessee, Virginia, Alabama, and the Carolinas where it does not grow? And how would bondsmen and later freedmen access this highly valued root?

In the 1950s, when someone asked "who was High John?" an elder would reply, "High John was an African prince, the son of an African king, who was kidnapped and sold into slavery. He was never to be a slave. He could not be broken by the slave breaker and he disobeyed the slave master at every opportunity. He was a troublemaker for the white man. He ran away, stole food, destroyed property, and led a band of rebels in many slave rebellions. Finally he was captured and publicly executed for all the slaves to witness. But before he died, he told the crowd of slaves looking on that before his spirit flew back to Africa he would leave a bit of it in the root of a certain plant. That whenever they needed hope or whenever they wanted to rebel and needed the spirit of protection to help them, to get that root and they would have a bit of his spirit." That root was known to nearly all black Americans as High John the Conquer root. A very similar version of that story was recited to this author by her Yoruba religion godfather, a Nigerian-initiated American Babalawo from Georgia, where, as a child growing up in the 1940s and 1950s, he heard the same story retold.[15]

Growing up in Cleveland, Ohio, in the 1950s and early 1960s, this author heard the High John story from the elders, those over sixty years old, most of whom were from central Alabama. These often lofty monologues of the elders were complemented by the "Niggah John" jokes and tales told mostly by the younger adults, those well below the age of sixty. I would later come to realize that by the time I encountered these "Niggah John" jokes, they were a thinly connected backwater tributary of the High John the Conquer theme. Scholars have largely viewed the John stories as a natural response to enslavement. In the character John, many have seen the trickster character familiar in the animal stories in which an underdog triumphs over a stronger, larger adversary. In these expanded, often bawdy, and humorous continuations of the High John the Conquer legacy, Niggah John always got the best of the white folks. Among African Americans, he was almost always called "Niggah John," rarely called just "John." When he was referred to as simply "John," it was often done with a twinkle in the eye so that informed listeners knew that the term *niggah* was implied in the omission. The effectiveness of the John stories lies in the juxtaposition of black and white under racial oppression. Though John is reduced to servitude, he still manages—through some quality of his personality or behavior—to debunk the myth of white racial superiority and get the best of the white man. Though he is ostensibly a mere "niggah," he is capable of outwitting members of the master race, thus challenging and undermining white superiority and challenging the white right to authority and control over black lives, thus restoring the significant principle of balance.[16]

Like the blues and the African American dances, the John tales developed and grew by incremental repetition.[17] As they grew, the very concept of John

CHAPTER 3

began to convey a certain generic anonymity and familiar distance; but it also galvanized a community and became part of the commonly understood mythology and folklore of African American culture. Once this happened, John was free to move in the common consciousness as a stock character representing multiple options. The very mention of John among some older blacks invoked a secret code of hope and resistance. High John the Conquer may have been the first deified ancestor of the Hoodoo religion who gradually became a secularized spiritual alternative.

The most effective teller of John stories I have ever encountered was a man called Mr. Jim, originally of Sarasota, Florida. Whenever he told one of these stories, his entire being would take on a new countenance. He would tell the story as if talking in a secret code that whites couldn't understand. His style of delivery to an all-black group of listeners implied the presence of powerful and controlling whites even when they weren't present. Mr. Jim would establish the white presence with his body language, stooping his shoulders, shuffling his feet, feigning the "stupid Negro" of white folks' expectations. As Mr. Jim wove the story and John eventually triumphed, Mr. Jim's countenance would transform into one of cunning and triumph, which spoke of real intellectual and practical superiority, defiance, and power. During the telling of the story, Mr. Jim would punctuate significant moments with a half smile and winking eye, which signaled that John knew something that the white folks did not.

MR. JIM'S BAWDY JOHN TALE

John was so defiant that he promised himself that he would never respond to a question from whites with the proper answer of "yes'm" or "yes, sir." And he never did. There was nothing that the white folks could do to make John say "yes, ma'am" or "yes, sir," he just wouldn't do it. Whenever John was asked a question by white folks that would normally solicit a "yes'm" or "yass'r" answer, John would answer affirmatively like this. If the white folks asked John, "John, did you chop the wood?" John would reply, "Stacked it, too." "John, did you water the horses?" "Groomed 'em, too." "John, did you weed the garden?" "Watered it, too." John always avoided the deferential answer that the white folks wanted to hear. Well, the white folks decided that they had had enough of John's impudence and they devised a plan to force John to answer appropriately. The twenty-year-old unmarried daughter, Lisa Belle, was to hide in the shower naked and surprise John with a question that would force him to reply "yes'm." So, Lisa Bell went upstairs and hid behind the shower curtain, naked in the shower. She called out to John as he cleaned the bathroom, "John, did you wash the dishes?" John replied, "Dried 'em, too." "John, did you cut the hay?" "Baled it, too." Finally in total frustration, Lisa Belle threw back the curtain, revealing her naked white body to John. As she stroked her breasts, she demanded that John look at her as she asked him the final question, "John, have you ever sucked a white woman's tittie?" John replied, "Pussy, too." And with that reply he left the bathroom.[18]

Through these and other stories, as well as in jokes, proverbs, and folktales in African Americans' daily conversations, John the generic Negro resisted, outsmarted, and exacted justice on whites. In his fullest manifestation, John was an actor in more than John tales and jokes. He could become an example of esteemed behavior in almost any context. The notion of John celebrated African American ingenuity under adverse circumstances and could be applied to the daily encounters of the average black man. John represented all African American men. When Mr. Jim was confronted with a challenge, he would often ask, with a smile, "Now, what would John do 'bout dat?"

The significance of High John the Conquer root in Hoodoo cannot be overstated. In the old conjure tradition, High John roots were often tied around either the waist or other body parts; it was embedded into walking canes and constructed into necklaces. Capable of being used in nearly every traditional Hoodoo ritual, High John has at least three namesakes, running John, cut from pieces of the High John vine and carried for good luck;[19] middle John, whose uses are most obscure of the three; and low John, the galanga root used in courtroom ritual. Galanga root, a relative of the ginger plant, is the famous chewing John. In his book *Fifty Years as a Low Country Witch Doctor*, J. E. McTeer describes Dr. Buzzard's root-chewing presence in a 1930s Beaufort, South Carolina, courtroom: "At a term of the general sessions court, the Doctor was very much in evidence, sitting among the spectators. He was busy 'chewing the root' on the judge, the solicitor, the jury and me, so that his clients would either be let loose or would receive a light sentence."[20] Another descriptively informative account of Dr. Buzzard's root chewin' states: "One of Robinson's best paying clients was the one who employed him to 'chew the root' on the judge, sheriff and solicitors during criminal court. Many times I've looked back into the courtroom and seen the purple sunglasses glaring at me as Stepheney 'chewed the root' on me. The basic goal of 'root chewing' was to render the evidence harmless and provide the best outcome for the accused. Dr. Buzzard couldn't lose, no matter what the verdict read."[21]

Root chewing, once quite common, has all but vanished or been replaced by something else. In 1980 in Robson County, North Carolina, professor Frank Schmalliger interviewed ten conjurers concerning their courtroom and legal casework. Though they mentioned rituals, powders, spells, roots, even track gathering, there is no mention of chewing the root to aid a courtroom defendant. Had root chewing disappeared in North Carolina by 1980?[22] Or was it nonexistent there for some other reason? It was known among conjurers and root workers that if a court case promised to be a difficult one, then root chewing was combined with other rituals such as dressing the courtroom with a spiritually potent substance such as lightening dust. According to conjure man Jim Vaugn of Menola, North Carolina: "Lightening dust is the red dust coming from insects boring into the exposed wood of a lightening struck pine tree. It becomes a powerful control agent when mixed with other things by a skilled conjure doctor."[23]

High John, as the *ipomoea jalapa* or *ipomoea purga* root is called by Hoodoo patrons and practitioners, could once be purchased from apothecaries as a type of laxative, from curio shops, candle shops, spiritual supply stores, and botanicas as well as from mail-order catalogs and Internet businesses. In the community of bondsmen, the root was obtained through the slave pharmacy assistants and doctors' assistants who had access to it where they worked. It was a medicinal root used to treat fevers and constipation and for its purgative qualities. If one can obtain it today, it can be rather expensive and is becoming more prized as *ipomoea* plant parts are illegal coming into the United States from any country except Canada.[24] Much to this author's surprise, when I tried to purchase jalap root I learned that most merchants advertising High John root would not sell the whole root, but would cut it into pieces and sell those instead or soak the root in oil and sell the oil for the same uses as the root.

This author's quest to purchase whole Mexican jalap root led to an Internet search of the area around Xalapa, Mexico, and this further led to yet another, and more astounding, discovery, the story of Afro-Mexican slave rebel Gaspar Yanga. As I read the story of Yanga, I could see immediately the startling parallels and detailed similarities between the story of Yanga and his kidnapping and the story of High John. How could this be? According to all available sources, Gaspar Yanga was a kidnapped member of one of the royal families of the African country of Gabon. Early on, he became the Spanish authorities' most feared and dreaded rebel and Maroon leader. He lived nearly four decades in the mountains between Xalapa and Puebla, where he eventually established a successful Maroon community in the hills of Veracruz, similar to the Quilombo del Palmaires in seventeenth- and eighteenth-century Brazil as well as numerous other Maroon communities.

In 1612, a mass public execution of thirty-three blacks, four of them women accused of plotting an uprising, quieted the spirit of rebellion for a while and forced the Maroon rebel spirit into silence only temporarily.

Gaspar Yanga. The enslaved Afro-Mexican Maroon rebel leader
Gaspar Yanga, possibly the model for High John the Conquer.

In the mountains of Veracruz, the only native habitat of jalap root, the
Yanganista Maroons continued to raid plantations and Indian settlements.
The best known of all Afro-Mexican Maroon settlements, Yanga's Maroon
community was founded after a bloody rebellion in the sugar fields in 1570;
Yanga was its leader. Hostile relations between the Spanish authorities and
slave rebels continued for the next sixty years, and finally the Maroons
were officially settled near the slopes of Mount Totutla in 1630. The town
was moved again to better farmland and survived, known as the city of San

Lorenzo de los Negros. At the time of Mexican independence in 1821, the small town had 719 people. Today it is a city of over twenty thousand.

Like High John, Yanga was a kidnapped African prince who could not be broken. He made trouble for slave masters and managed to get the better of them. Yet the Yanganistas' quest for freedom and the vision of hope they provided those still enslaved were tempered by public executions in the area where jalap root grows most abundantly. Could Gaspar Yanga or executed members of his rebel party be the original model for the African American High John the Conquer? Or could one of the many Maroon leaders in Spanish America be the model? There were certainly a significant number of them. And Spain could have traded slaves from other Spanish territories, as well as from Mexico, into the mainland of North America. Certainly there were other possible models, like Benkos Bioho in Cartegena, Columbia, in 1603. Maroon rebels were responsible for beginning the revolution in Haiti. The Maroons of Accompong, Jamaica, were regarded as fierce fighters. Maroon communities existed from Virginia to the southernmost slave societies of South America. And each of them had their rebel leader. In many instances, the leaders were captured, executed, or killed by bounty hunters. Since indigenous people were native to the habitat, they were often used to hunt down Maroons. But in some instances, native peoples joined with Maroons to fight off European settlers and enslavers, as in the case of Florida's famous Negro Fort.[25]

Pointing to a potential Afro-Mexican or Afro-Hispanic origin, the name Juan el Conquistador contains a reference to the Spanish conquerors. No such equivalent term for the British settlers was ever used by North American Indians or enslaved Africans; this further points to potential Afro-Mexican or Afro-Hispanic origins of the story. But if High John was Afro-Mexican originally, how could such a story achieve such a high degree of penetration into the black communities of North America? The answer may lie in several possibilities, not the least of which is the infamous slave pens of old New Orleans under the Spanish occupation.

> The formation of community in the slave trade—the creation of networks of support and sometimes resistance among individuals previously unknown to one another—began as something quite different: passing the time, engaging in conversation, offering isolated acts of friendship or succor. . . . [O]ut of these contingent interactions could be fashioned connections that could sustain slaves emotionally and help them circulate important knowledge about the trade. The revolts and runaways, of course, are the most obvious examples of the subversive connections that took root in the interstices of the slave trade. . . . [T]he community of slaves in the trade provided information and support that slaves could use to their advantage.[26]

Just as Spain traded slaves from Mexico into its new center of commerce, New Orleans, it easily traded slaves from other Spanish colonies where there were Maroons and stories of their triumphs. Slave traders had well-established slave-trading networks and followed the same routes that had proved successful year after year. Slaves who were traded also learned these routes and networks and had knowledge of the major southern slave trading centers like Lexington, Richmond, Charleston, Atlanta, Savannah, and New Orleans, among others. The stories, tales of hope and triumph, spread along these networks. Each slave state had its slave sales and brokers. Slavery as a stable institution with social networks was important to the forging of social identity, and white men's social selves were known and respected according to a code deeply dependent upon slavery for its existence. In the major slave-trading centers, particularly the slave pens of New Orleans, tales of triumph spread, slaves received and sent messages thousands of miles to distant relatives, to stolen and sold children, to other family members and friends. According to Walter Johnson: "Some of those whose friends or relatives were carried away by the traders had the comfort of information that came across the filaments of connection which spanned the enslaved South. Ann Garrison, who had been a slave in Maryland, told an interviewer in 1841 that her son, sold to a southbound trader, was able to send a farewell from Baltimore via a friend who lived there."[27] Some routes were so well traveled that slaves might encounter other slaves they had known elsewhere. These routes and their social connectedness supported a fragile underground slave communication network essential in sustaining hope. William Wells Brown leaves us such an account in his narrative. Brown encountered at least two slaves, one in New Orleans and one in Natchez, Mississippi, that he had known previously in St. Louis, Missouri.[28]

According to Walter Johnson, "More than anything, the community of slaves in the trade seems to have been forged out of conversation."[29] Conversations and other forms of communication were of supreme importance to slaves in the pens: "[T]he once anonymous slaves built a network of mutual recognition through a communal remembering and retelling of the past."[30] These slave communications networks reached out, obtained, and disseminated information and tales of hope from around the nation as well as internationally.[31] Noteworthy in this respect is the role of slave stewards, hired-out slaves, and errand boys working in the pens.

Slave stewards were responsible for escorting other slaves in the pens; they carried the slaves' baggage as well as clothing, and they were in and out of the slave pens regularly. They carried messages to and from slaves from different regions belonging to different traders. They performed favors for slaves such as obtaining food or tobacco. Hired-out slaves brought in news from the outside and disseminated it inside the pens and vice versa and so did the errand boys. These slaves who circulated in and out of the slave pens accelerated the movement of all types of information, including folktales of resistance, articles, letters, seeds, messages, conjure bags, medicinal roots, and reminders of a former life in Africa or elsewhere. Because these stewards and errand boys were sometimes owned by the owner of the slave pen, they were traded less frequently and represented a linkage, a site for continuity, limited stability, and consistency across time as well as region. This increased the reliability rate for sociocultural transfers of all types.

The story of Yanga as well as other Maroons or rebels could easily have moved into the slave pens of New Orleans when Louisiana was under Spanish control in the mid to latter eighteenth century. There was significant trading of slaves between Mexico and New Orleans during and after Spanish occupation. In her database, historian Gwendolyn Midlo Hall lists, mainly from records of slave sales, enough slaves in the area around New Orleans whose birthplaces were recorded as Mexico to indicate a trade in slaves between Mexico and New Orleans.[32] One such male slave, Jose, age eighteen, was sold by Sr. Jose Briones for 788 pesos in April 1783. He was probably born around 1765, and his birthplace was listed as Veracruz, Mexico. Another male slave, also age eighteen, named Pedro, trained as a ship caulker, was born in Mexico and was sold in Louisiana from the estate of Sr. Pedro Biraso in 1795. Still another male slave listed as a mulatto and "criole" of Mexico, age twenty-seven, sold for 400 pesos in 1801. The seller is listed as "Presbitero Capellan del 2nd. Batallon of the Infantry Regiment of Mexico." The buyer was "the Archbiship [sic] elect of the Holy Cathedral and Diocese of Guatemala." Still another slave, Aniceto, age thirteen, apparently was purchased by a slave dealer for 550 pesos on October 23, 1801, from Maria Josefa De Echagary y Lazaga in Mexico City. Another male slave, Bernard, a fifteen-year-old domestic servant, sold for 650 pesos on May 13, 1809, was listed as a native of Mexico. And finally, a female mulatto slave, Petra Catalina, purchased for 700 pesos on May 28, 1800, by Jose Carballo, is listed as born in Puguano, Mexico. Not only slaves but also buyers and sellers themselves came from Mexico or they authorized others to sell or purchase slaves for them in New Orleans, potentially to be sold into other places in Spanish America. In Hall's database, this author found at least one transaction listed as follows: "Slave is sold with power of attorney of Jose Goma of Campeche, Mexico."

Certainly the slave population was, because of its condition of forced servitude, predisposed to embracing a hope bringer. Though the resemblance of Yanga to High John is remarkable, the Afro-Mexican Yanga was not the only famous slave rebel, nor was his the only Maroon community; there were others who could have provided a model of resistance like that found in the tale of High John the Conquer.

Throughout the New World, particularly in Latin America, from Mexico to Peru and throughout the Caribbean, over a three century time frame, Maroon communities and encampments, with their rebel leaders, sprang up. They are too numerous to list here. Examples include a slave rebel settlement that was destroyed on Hispaniola in 1522.[33] In 1545, two hundred Maroons living in the swamps and marshes north of Lima, Peru, engaged in a bloody fight in which all the rebels were killed.[34] More than two hundred fifty years later in 1795, thousands of Venezuelan slaves rebelled and established a Maroon settlement retreat that was eventually destroyed by the Spanish.[35] In Columbia in 1603, Maroon rebel leader Benkos Bioho founded Palenque San Basilio in the area of Cartagena, Columbia.[36] In Mobile, Alabama, a Maroon stronghold was destroyed by local vigilante planters in 1827.[37] The Afro-Mexican Maroon community known as Palacios de Mandinga, one of six Maroon settlements established around 1735 after a series of costly revolts, persisted until 1827 with some Maroons remaining in hiding until the legal abolition of slavery in Mexico in 1829.[38] The most famous of all Maroon settlements is the Quilombo dos Palmares in Pernambuco, Brazil; it is estimated to have contained upward of ten thousand runaways.[39] The numerous Maroon communities in Spanish America would certainly strengthen the myth as it entered and passed through the Spanish-controlled slave pens of old New Orleans.

There are several possibilities that could be drawn from the widespread activities of Maroons and rebels within the present limits of the United States. One notable possible model for High John is the Louisiana Maroon rebel known as St. Malo. According to historian Gwendolyn Midlo Hall, runaway slaves in lower Louisiana adapted to the conditions of the cypress swamp and established Maroon camps throughout the region. "The maroon communities that developed during the last half of the eighteenth century consisted almost entirely of creole slaves, though large numbers of Africans were brought in under Spanish rule. . . . Runaway slaves hid out for weeks, months, and even years on or behind their masters' estates without being detected or apprehended."[40]

During the Spanish period in Louisiana, St. Malo and his party of runaways were the most troublesome of several Maroon rebel bands in the area south of New Orleans between the Mississippi River and Lake Borgne. "The syndic of the Cabildo of New Orleans described St. Malo as 'audacious, daring, and active' (atrevido, osado, y activo), which was fair enough, but he also portrayed him as ruthless and bloodthirsty."[41] Like most Maroons forced to live as fugitives, St. Malo's band both raided nearby plantations carrying off needed supplies, food, and munitions and fought fiercely to preserve their freedom from bondage. A number of the Maroon groups occupying the area below New Orleans established working relationships both with plantation slaves and, on occasion, with white slave masters.[42]

St. Malo and most of his band were finally captured, tried, and publicly executed on June 19, 1784. We know that before his death he made a final statement proclaiming the innocence of two of his fellow Maroons.[43] What else did he say before his life was publicly taken? How often was this or a similar scenario repeated under the various slave regimes of the New World? The story of St. Malo opens many speculative possibilities concerning the myth of High John the Conquer, particularly when one considers the high concentration of African slaves, especially Bambara, in the area of New Orleans.

The Bambara as well as other African ethnic groups believed that special amulets could be created that preserved the souls of individuals especially those who died in warfare or through the administration of justice.[44] Similar beliefs persisted among other groups including some native Europeans. The European belief in the power of the "glory hand," the left hand of a convicted murderer is similar in some respects. Among the Bambara, amulets were created to be carried into battle that were believed to contain the soul of the warrior ancestors. These amulets were created to support both physical and spiritual struggles. In speculating, this author suggests that if St. Malo's body were left hanging to rot publicly, as stated in the Creole slave song about his capture and execution, then it is not beyond the realm of possibility that amulets and protective charms could have been made from his body parts such as bones, hair, nails even clothing. Amulet making certainly was traditionally African. Perhaps clothing, hair, or other items were ritually confiscated from the bodies of publicly executed rebels by slaves who knew of or witnessed the executions. Certainly the stories of the numerous slave rebels circulated among the slave populations of the New World.

QUARRA ST. MALO,

Aie! Zeinzens, vinifeouarra
Pou' pov' St. Malodansl'embas!
Ye c'asse li avec ye chien,
Ye tire li ein coup d'fizi,
Ye hale li la cyprier,

So bras ye 'tasse par derrier,
Ye 'tasse so la main divant;
Ye 'marre li ape queue choual,
Ye trainein li zouqu'a la ville.
Divantmiches la dans Cabil'e
Ye quise li life complot
Pou'coupecou a tout ye blancs.
Ye 'mande li qui so comperes;
Pov' St. Malo pas di' a-rein!
Zize la li lir so la sentence,
Et pis li fedressepotence.
Ye hale choual—c'aretteparti—
Pov St. Malorestependi!
Eine her solieldeza levee
Quand ye pend li si la levee.
Ye laisse so corps balance
Pou'carancrogagneinmanze.

THE DIRGE OF ST. MALO

Alas! Young men, come, make lament
For poor St. Malo in distress!
They chased, they hunted him with dogs,
They fired at him with a gun,
They hauled him from the cypress swamp
His arms they tied behind his back,
they tied his hands in front of him;
They tied him to a horse's tail,
They dragged him up into the town.
Before those grand Cabildo men
They charged that he had made a plot
To cut the throats of all the whites.
They asked him who his comrades were;
Poor St. Malo said not a word!
The judge his sentence read to him,
And then they raised the gallows-tree.
They drew the horse—the cart moved off—
And left St. Malo hanging there.
The sun was up an hour high
When on the Levee he was hung;
They left his body swinging there,
For carrion crows to feed upon.[45]

Could St. Malo be the model for High John the Conquer? Could his spirit or a part of his soul have been placed in the root that could have grown in the area of Louisiana below New Orleans possibly imported there by the Spanish? Or could the life of St. Malo simply have acted to strengthen the already existing story of the kidnapped, unbreakable Maroon prince who was publicly executed, and whose soul flew back to Africa after leaving a bit of his warrior essence in the root of a certain plant?

The Maroon rebel story was acted out in many places in the New World; including the area now the United States of America. Maroons established communities and camps from Virginia to Florida, from South Carolina and eastern coastal areas to Louisiana.[46] The possibilities are numerous, but I am inclined to think that St. Malo's and other slave rebel and Maroon stories further strengthened the already existing archetype of the unbreakable warrior prince developed through centuries of rebellions and maroon-age. And that the traditional African belief in a plant or bush possessing a "spirit" was enlivened and infused within the framework of the "spirit plant" model common in African traditional religion. And that wherever Africans were enslaved in the New World in significantly concentrated numbers, the circumstances of enslavement predisposed and readied them for the appearance of a "hope bringer." Once again Hurston speaks to us:

> Maybe he was in Texas when the lash fell on a slave in Alabama, but before the blood was dried on the back he was there.[47] . . . There are many tales and variants of each, of how the Negro got his freedom through High John de Conquer. The best one deals with a plantation where the work was hard, and Old Massa mean. Even Old Miss used to pull her maids ears with hot firetongs when they got her riled. So naturally, Old John de Conquer was around that plantation a lot.[48]

The legacy of High John de Conquer, though transformed, is continued today in African American Hoodoo practice and by those that keep the remaining fragments of the Hoodoo faith.

> The thousands of humble people who still believe in him . . . do John reverence by getting the root of the plant in which he has taken up his secret dwelling, and "dress" it with perfume, and keeping it on their person or in their houses in a secret place. It is there to help them overcome things they feel that they could not beat otherwise . . . You will know then, that no matter how bad things look now, it will be worse for those who seek to oppress us.[49]

Standin' at the Crossroads, I tried to flag a ride
Standin' at the crossroads, I tried to flag a ride
Didn't nobody seem to know me, everybody pass me by
You can run you can run tell my friend—boy Willie Brown
Lord I'm standin' at the crossroad, babe, I believe I'm sinkin' down
—Robert Johnson, *Cross Road Blues*

CRISIS AT THE CROSSROADS

Sustaining and Transforming
Hoodoo's Black Belt Tradition
from Emancipation to World War II

The period following emancipation was transformative in every sense for African Americans. Both the physical and social boundaries of their cultural lives would be expanded and would develop a more prominent national profile. It was a period of fragmenting and recoalescing values and practices as the nation shifted gears between the Civil War and World War I. Black belt traditional Hoodoo would find itself approaching a critical crossroads in its identity and existence. Though emancipation would prefigure the forthcoming loss of certain traditions, freedom of movement would simultaneously provide the social backdrop from which regional cultural variations would cross-fertilize one another. The crisis that was approaching would challenge Hoodoo's adaptability and would confront black America's desire and ability to reinvest in a tradition that clung to the sociohistoric bones of an ever-evolving African American culture. The old tradition, the Hoodoo of the old black belt region plantation, would be modified and transformed under the influence of both internal and external factors as an interregional cross-fertilization process would disperse locally potent customs, traditions, and knowledge throughout the newly emancipated African American nation more rapidly than had been done previously. In some locales, the breakup of the old slave-quarter community manifests its impact immediately as destruction of the slave quarter meant that new and different cultural spaces would have to be located or created. Prior to emancipation, the larger plantation slave communities, as well as areas of high black concentration, had functioned as culturally potent repositories and cultural germination sites where, partially due to demographics, the culture-making process was intensified. The intensification process supported African cultural retention, especially in slave communities where recently imported African slaves were deposited.

The end of Reconstruction and withdrawal of federal troops from the South after 1877 left most African Americans at the mercy of local white citizens, many of whom were former slave owners. With a reign of racial terror raging around them in a violently antiblack atmosphere, freedmen had few defenses. The increased stress attending the movement from slavery to freedom, coupled with the terrorism and racist exclusion of the period, strained every role in the black community, exacerbated both psychological and physical malady, and made successful assimilation and individual societal adjustment difficult if not impossible for all but a minority of blacks. Legal marginalization and racial terrorism unraveled still-developing and stabilizing community traditions and propelled blacks into a mass exodus, first into southern cities then northward into large urban areas, many lured there by the promise of "good" employment made by labor recruiters.[1] The massive migration began as a trickle, hardly resembling the great deluge it would soon become. In this massive flow of humans from the rural countryside into more urban environments, certain aspects of African American cultural life, including Hoodoo, would become more visible to the wider society than they previously had been. In the postemancipation environment, blacks would continue to depend on Hoodoo's support and protection both to anchor and to provide them with a degree of certainty in an uncertain new world. With the black community confronting an unfamiliar and less certain future, Hoodoo workers experienced an increased demand for protective mojoes during this period. There was certainly an increase in the visibility and number of Hoodoo practitioners in at least one southern Hoodoo center, New Orleans.[2]

Hoodoo's new visibility and presence would immediately stimulate mainstream popular artistic and scholarly interest that would continue into the twenty-first century, as the July 9, 2007, issue of *Fortune Magazine* demonstrates when it asks on its cover, "Can Harvey Weinstein get his mojo back?" In the American mainstream, the rapid commercial secularization of Hoodoo's sacred dance, the Ring Shout, would give America the foundation for dances such as the Big Apple, a "called" counterclockwise circling dance with high arm gestures; the Eagle Rock, derived from the traditional African American dance play, known as the Buzzard Lope; and the Shout, a possession dance ritual[3] translated into a secular dance step. But more important, African American sacred dancing's postures, gestures, and movements would influence all American theatrical dance and would eventually dominate American urban popular dancing even more thoroughly than it had dominated some of the older plantation country dancing forms.[4]

Continuing for more than fourteen decades after the end of Reconstruction, Hoodoo's impact on American literature, though significant, was less intense than its influence on popular dance and music. The works of early writers such as Mark Twain, Charles W. Chesnutt, William Faulkner, DuBose Heyward, as well as more recent ones like John Berendt and Toni Morrison are noteworthy here. In *The Adventures of Huckleberry Finn*, Mark Twain's slave character, Jim, lives in a world inhabited by witches, haints, signs, herbal medicine, and magic. Through Jim we get a glimpse of the governing principles and scope of conjure. Jim turns to the conjure tradition to interpret signs, cure rattlesnake bite, keep off the witches, ward off loss, and deflect negative occurrences and bad luck. He lives by the conjure code, and it informs much of his behavior and impacts upon those he encounters. Young and impressionable, Huck Finn has absorbed many Hoodoo beliefs and practices from Jim in the same manner that many whites, through close association with African Americans, had learned certain Hoodoo practices. One such belief interpreted the presence of spiders as a good-luck sign and clearly states that harming or killing one is destined to bring the worse kind of bad luck to whomever committed the offense. Huck informs us:

> Pretty soon a spider went crawling up my shoulder, and I flipped it off and it lit in the candle; and before I could budge it was all shriveled up. I didn't need anybody to tell me that that was an awful bad sign and would fetch me some bad luck, so I was scared and most shook the clothes off of me. I got up and turned around in my tracks three times and crossed my breast every time; and then I tied up a little lock of my hair with a thread to keep witches away. But I hadn't no confidence. You do that when you've lost a horse-shoe that you've found, instead of nailing it up over the door, but I hadn't ever heard anybody say it was any way to keep off bad luck when you'd killed a spider.[5]

A thousand miles away and more than a century later, a very similar and culturally tenacious belief would be echoed in the daily lives of Sapelo Island, Georgia, residents, where sightings of "Aunt Nancy" the spider, were interpreted as an especially fortunate occurrence portending good things to come—but killing Aunt Nancy made you highly vulnerable to bad luck and could doom you to unfortunate, even deadly retribution. A Sapelo Island resident reveals: "For good luck, there was that black cat, of course, and we also had Aunt Nancy the spider. We called the spider An' Nancy. An' Nancy was quite wise. You could play with that spider all day long but they would not let you harm An' Nancy. We did not harm it, we did not kill it, we did not do anything to it. That spider brings you good luck."[6] A retention from the Ghanaian Ashanti of the Akan nation, stories of the trickster, Anansi, who comes in the form of a spider, was the subject of children's game plays in both the American black belt South and the Caribbean where Anansi tales and stories shaped the content of folk wisdom in the form of riddles, stories, and proverbs.

A focal point in much of Chesnutt's work, conjure, as Hoodoo is called there, acts as a bedrock principle in the lives of his black characters. Hoodoo, or conjure, is the great equalizer in the face of white supremacy's terrorizing power; when events take an uncontrollable turn for the worse and circumstances seem insurmountable, conjure is the next resort. Through Chesnutt's characters, we can see the post-Reconstruction world of blacks and the deep intertwining of conjure in their daily lives. Through conjure, Chesnutt's characters can become invisible to "patterollers" (slave patrollers), they can administer medical treatments, ward off beatings, and guarantee justice. Born before the Civil War to free Negro parents, Chesnutt was intimately exposed to the daily uses of conjure as an alternative spiritual reality. His conjure tales reflect a well-organized spiritual philosophy achieving centrality as a life-organizing, problem-solving, and meaning-attribution principle. Through conjure, lives are made whole, loved ones are kept in one place and not subjected to the master's will. In Chesnutt's work, conjure continually challenges the assumptions of the dominant white world while Chesnutt's portrayals of conjure give us additional information about its capricious nature. Functioning on the principles of balance, reciprocity, and compensation, conjure can backfire and have unintended consequences, as it does in Chesnutt's short story "Hot-Foot Hannibal."

In this conjure tale, which demonstrates a traditional Hoodoo principle, the root pack or goopher to make Hannibal a slave well ingratiated to his master, "light headed" and "hot-footed" is fashioned in the form of a doll with a cornstalk body, splinters for arms and legs, elderberry pith for a head, and two little red peppers for feet.[7] The goopher comes with strict instructions for use, and the conjure woman explicitly states that when the work is complete, the doll must be retrieved and returned to her: "Fer it's monst'us powerful goopher, en is liable ter make mo' trouble ef you leabe it layin' roun.'"[8] Through Chesnutt's conjure tales, we learn something of conjure's boundaries expressed as time constraints, location restrictions, constraints on duration, and periods of maximum and minimum efficiency and effectiveness.

In another respect, Chesnutt's Hoodoo themes are particularly interesting when compared with contemporary and traditional African religious belief. Noteworthy here is the theme of a spirit embodied in a tree or bush. In one of Chesnutt's stories entitled "Po Sandy," Sandy, a hardworking, obedient slave, is turned into a tree so that he can stay in one place and not continue to be hired out by his master. The hiring-out process took Sandy away from his wife so often that she tired of the situation and she and Sandy agreed to have the local conjure woman turn Sandy into a tree in the forest. Once he was turned into a tree, Sandy could stay in one place. Eventually, through great difficulty and effort, Sandy the tree is chopped down and sent to the sawmill where, because he is conjured, he breaks the saws used in the milling process as workers attempt to cut him into planks. The sound of the saw blade on Sandy's wood is said to sound like the wail of a human voice.[9]

According to author James H. Neal, he encountered a similar spirit bush while he was stationed in Ghana working on a building project. During the course of building, a large bush needed to be unearthed and removed. This feat would prove to be impossible. Try as they might with the latest equipment, the workers could not unearth and remove the bush. Finally a traditional priest was called and with alcohol and offerings persuaded the spirit of the bush to go elsewhere. The bush was then removed by hand using no heavy equipment.[10]

Faulkner's work references components from the old Hoodoo belief system. Statements about "blue-gummed" Negroes, for example, though viewed as pejorative, reflect old tradition Hoodoo belief in markings, particularly the belief in birthmarks. It was believed that if a pregnant woman looked a blue-gummed Negro in the eye during the full moon, her unborn child would be marked in some way, often by being born as a blue-gummed child.[11]

Best known for the 1925 novel *Porgy* and the 1935 Broadway folk opera *Porgy and Bess,* author DuBose Heyward makes compelling use of Hoodoo traditional belief to more completely and accurately portray southern African American life in his work. His short story "The Half Pint Flask" uses Hoodoo burial tradition as a core element in the unfolding of the story. In this tale, a visitor to the area removes a rare half-pint flask from a Negro grave. This action proves to be a regretful faux pas for the visitor.[12] Little did he know of the old Hoodoo method of decorating a grave with beautiful items or items of significance in the life of the deceased. Given to the dead, these items both honor them as ancestors and appease the spirit of the departed. In the initial internment, the sacred counterclockwise dance circle is convened as items are deposited on the grave; other items are added later. The ritual surrounding the continuing decoration of grave sites often resembles ancestor reverence practices in West and Central West Africa and proves to be an African American remnant form of the ancestor institution.

John Berendt, in his best-selling novel *Midnight in the Garden of Good and Evil*, introduces the reader to a character named Minerva, a Hoodoo woman, alleged in the novel to have been Dr. Buzzard's mistress. Minerva's Hoodoo work on behalf of the novel's protagonist brings him to meet her in Beaufort, South Carolina, over Dr. Buzzard's grave. Minerva's work results in a not guilty verdict in the protagonist's murder trial. Through Minerva, the protagonist can access Dr. Buzzard's legendary power in the courtroom. Her use in the novel is a pivotal point in this story filled with local color.[13] For these five authors—Chesnutt, Faulkner, Twain, Heyward, and Berendt—as well as numerous others such as Ismael Reed, Toni Morrison, and Alice Walker, Hoodoo as an important element in their portrayals deepens and enriches their characters, setting, and tone and reveals a deeply informative and essential cultural element rarely seen today by outsiders to working-class black life.

Hoodoo references would also be used in monologues by performing comics. Richard Pryor's monologue involving Miss Rudolph the conjure woman is one of his most widely known and most entertaining. Pryor reveals a number of interesting observations on old tradition Hoodoo's use of insects, spiders, and urine as well as the old practitioner's willingness to accept alternative forms of payment, other than money, such as food items. In this monologue, Miss Rudolph requests a "goose or a turkey" at Thanksgiving time as payment for her services. This was typically true of old tradition plantation Hoodoos. The significance and referencing of conjure would not end with an increasing number of literary references or an abundance of blues lyrics; they would extend themselves into the 1970s as black consciousness turned toward Africa. An example of Hoodoo's lingering influence is evidenced in the naming and construction of a university research publication entitled *Ju-Ju*. The title is taken from the following quote by black arts movement cofounder Larry Neal: "We cannot abdicate our culture to those who exist outside of us. We should guard and protect our culture viciously, and work critical ju-ju on those who screw up."[14] Portending statements like this raise new possibilities for old tradition Hoodoo's rejuvenation and fusion with the black consciousness movement. But the embracing of Hoodoo by black nationalists would not occur in that cycle of the politicocultural movement. Instead, Islam was seen by many as both a more viable spiritual alternative to "the white man's religion" of Christianity and a revolutionary alternative to the conservative hold of Negro preachers on the black spiritual community. Nevertheless, latter-day artists such as Renee Stout would continue using Hoodoo as a source of creative inspiration.[15]

Having been freed from constraints imposed by chattel slavery, conjure after emancipation would continue to figure significantly in black consciousness of self, family, and community under the new freedom. Just as newly enslaved Africans brought their historic memory of traditional African life with them into American bondage, the newly emancipated slave retained and carried part of the enslavement experience into the environment of freedom as well as into the next century. Since both the conjurer and the belief in conjure were often maligned, creating and sustaining Hoodoo involved a battle of spiritual and psychological energies for the ex-slaves as it had for their bondsmen predecessors. Following Hoodoo's birth under bondage, a new and constantly shifting battlefront for its existence would reinforce the belief that only through a highly adaptable profile could Hoodoo sustain itself. Initially, Hoodoo's dynamic and ever-evolving roles were partly a response to immediate as well as long-term needs among the bondsmen. Included among those roles were religiomedical practitioners such as treaters, midwives, healers, and slave "doctors." These individuals continued to appear in the slave population, and their overlapping roles as well as the role of conjurer would later broaden among freedmen and become both stabilized and institutionalized within Hoodoo practice.

Hoodoo's first phase of development occurred under enslavement and ended with the period surrounding emancipation. Hoodoo's second developmental stage began after Reconstruction and continued until World War II. This period marked the birth and development of marketeered Hoodoo, remodeled and controlled primarily by "middlemen minorities," in this case European Ashkenazi Jews who were outsiders to the Hoodoo tradition, even as old tradition black belt Hoodoo was fully functioning among African Americans. This second phase was roughly a seventy-year period that was distinguished by the full emergence of both the conjurer/ treater as an independent practitioner and the intensified homogenization of the three regional variations into one Hoodoo practice with a newly emerging national African American profile; this second phase of development occurred in two stages.

The second developmental period, particularly the last two-and-a-half decades preceding World War II, was marked by Hoodoo's full entry into the mainstream commercial marketplace, with full commoditization of many of its most publicly visible implements, tools, and supplies as well as a proliferation of exploiters of various types. Early on during this second developmental period, there is diversification and specialization by those offering various types of Hoodoo services both inside of and outside of the African American community; the conjurer often also functioned as a treater or folk doctor.

Often known as a root doctor, he or she, like their plantation counterparts, had the knowledge of herbal medicines and could use plants, animals, and other objects to cure or ward off illness or to attract good fortune. He or she was a master of spells and recipes—the term preferred by old tradition Hoodoo workers—potions and amulets, and could use plants and other objects not only to heal but also to cause harm. Supporting the root doctor's use of Hoodoo herbal remedies, patent medicines were both extensively used and advertised in early black newspapers in an attempt to reach black clientele. Already well established among blacks, the herb and root tradition would face competition from medical professionalization.

The role of conjurer doctor transferred directly and intact from slavery into the postemancipation environment. In some instances, the role of conjurer would split into two roles, and the two roles would not always diverge completely. In other instances, the dual function of root doctor and conjurer would continue to further diversify into completely separate roles, with the conjurer performing fewer and fewer of the healing functions and the root doctor performing fewer and fewer of the religiomagical tasks. By relinquishing more of the religiomagical functions, the root doctor could both function as an herbalist and divorce himself from the association of Hoodoo with "devil's work," a troublesome and pejorative label that would stubbornly persist in more than a few quarters.

Early in this second stage, immediately following Reconstruction, there appears to be a firm and visible stabilization of the old Hoodoo tradition resulting from the establishment of new internal norms and conventions as well as the strengthening of existing ones. Couched in a widely occurring transformative process, these modifications in the older plantation Hoodoo tradition were in part the result of the unprecedented movement of hundreds of thousands of newly freed slaves immediately following Emancipation. This massive migratory movement of people rapidly transported regional Hoodoo customs and traditions to new areas where they were quickly integrated into existing practice, contributing to a newly emerging national rather than regional profile. The national identity of Hoodoo parallels the redefinition of African American identity following Reconstruction. A new African American national profile sparked by migration and movement toward urbanization was influenced by forces similarly impacting upon Hoodoo. There was also further diversification in roles related to Hoodoo as well as in the division of labor within Hoodoo tradition, particularly between midwives-treaters and conjure men and the respective traditions they represented.

It is in the early years of this second stage that Hoodoo established a durable national profile as an African American spiritual-medicinal tradition while maintaining some regional uniqueness. In this stage Hoodoo rapidly transformed into a self-contained national African American institution complete with several divination systems, including the walking boy, the dancing dime, bones, playing cards, dice, dominoes, as well as animal signs such as low-flying birds and "frizzlie chickens" used as divination devises. Incantations in the form of Christian prayer, particularly the Psalms, would eventually totally replace the traditional West and Central West Africa chants and prayers. An example can be seen in slaves' traditional use of Psalm 10 when requiring protection during travel, especially when running away, Psalm 53 for God's divine protection, and Psalm 109 to curse and damn those who are wrongdoers.[16] Regional Hoodoo beliefs like the belief in witches, haints, and demon spirits like Plat-eye, Robination Horse, Jingo's Horse, or Hampshire's Horse spread. These spiritual entities were believed to be capable of changing form and luring away or chasing its victim into danger, confusing the mind and leaving the victim to die.[17]

There were sacred days in Hoodoo, particularly Friday, about which it was believed that no new project or piece of work should ever begin. Established procedures for recruitment and training of Hoodoo successors existed. They included training in the magical and medicinal uses of plants and other substances as well as training in reading signs in nature, such as in cloud formations and in the behavior of certain animals like barking dogs and low-flying birds. During this period, there were also socially strengthened Hoodoo myths and legends, some in the form of personal testimonials or syncretized African and perhaps Native American and European folk beliefs and tales. These were often delivered as stories like those of High John the Conquer, the fabled Dr. John of New Orleans, Marie Laveau, the Seven Sisters of Algiers, famous East Coast Hoodoo legends Dr. Bug and Black Herman,[18] and the most famous of them all, Dr. Buzzard of St. Helena Island, South Carolina.

Hoodoo truly had entered its golden age, and it had not yet fallen under the exploitative and controlling influences of occult marketeers; it was largely an African American dominated and controlled institution. Root doctors, midwives, conjurers, treaters, and those doing "the work" gained increased access to other occult traditions and supply paths, and all interfaced more freely than they had under slavery's inhuman confinement. Most locales with significant black populations had someone who provided the community with Hoodoo services. So a Hoodoo ritualist was available whenever the need arose. Some of them became very well known both inside and outside of their regions. Their clientele usually learned of them by word-of-mouth testimonials and referrals.

Early in this second stage, Hoodoo had its ritual practices and had achieved some degree of consistency with respect to philosophy and material culture. Though limited, ritual animal sacrifice, sometime performed at the crossroads, persisted. One observer leaves us this account from 1891:

> One terribly hot Sunday afternoon as I was sitting on the piazza, I happened to see at some distance through the pine grove Uncle Robert and his two little grandchildren, and at first could not determine what they were doing. I soon saw that the children were picking up leaves and small sticks and putting them on a pile under Uncle Robert's direction, and presently I noticed a little smoke rising from it. Wondering what it could mean, I walked out towards them and saw a pile of leaves and twigs around a small stake, the whole burning by that time quite briskly. "Isn't it hot enough to-day, Uncle Robert, without building a fire? What are you doing?" "I'se offering a sacrifice." "A sacrifice. What do you mean?"
> "Why, you see, Mister Gus, the distemper has got among my chickens, and they are dying off fast. Now when that happens, if you take a well one and burn it alive in the fork of a path it will cure the rest, and no more will die."
> I then noticed that he had built the fire in the fork of a footpath through the grove."[19]

Though some regional variation still existed, implements, materials, formulas, incantations, and initiation rites[20] all attained a degree of widespread consistency across regions during this phase. While some remaining African elements such as animal sacrifice were eventually lost or discarded, other practices such as amulet making and knot tying stabilized and remained part of the old black belt Hoodoo tradition. Black worship during this period was already highly African, and there was a continual movement of both African spiritual practices and approaches to worship into African American Christian worship. This simultaneously resulted in the formation of both a new Hoodooized Christianity and a nonchurch spiritual and controlling tradition.[21]

In the Hoodoo church, Hoodooized Christianity would become infused with African American Hoodoo sensibility and practices from the African Religion Complex (ARC), including water immersion, sacred dance, head shaving, spirit possession, faith or spiritual healing, amulet making, and rites of passage. But other Hoodoo practices were also dragged kicking and screaming into the black Christian experience, where they were frequently contested and denounced yet precariously balanced between toleration and condemnation. Hoodoo belief was so strong in some Afro-Christian churches that ministers resigned their posts in acquiescence to the strength of Hoodoo belief in their congregations. Consider the following passage from Newbell Niles Puckett written in 1922:

> In a rural Negro church near Columbus, Miss., there was a constant change of ministers because of the reliance of the congregation upon "jacks" (charms wrapped up in red flannel). A new minister was more quick-witted. He wrapped a large hunk of coal in red flannel, planked it on the pulpit one night and said: "Folks, dis yere de daddy-jack I'se got. Bring yo' baby-jacks on up." The members of the congregation were afraid not to do this. Thus the minister found out who had "jacks," destroyed their charms, and was able to hold his position without further trouble."[22]

One can speak of a Hoodoo-informed lifestyle developing and lasting in certain local and black communities. In some of these communities, such as that found on Sapelo Island, Georgia, everything was done under the canopy of luck and protection and laid upon a foundation of sign interpretation, including dreams as signs.[23] Though Hoodoo's early religious components could not coalesce into a recognizably sustainable religion, as traditional African religion did in the Caribbean and parts of Latin America, they heavily influenced the foundation beliefs and life approaches of a majority of African Americans. For most American blacks, the spiritual world in which they lived was one that included both Christian practice and Hoodoo belief in a noncontradictory coexistence. Hoodoo belief functioned as an epiphilosophical canopy and commonsense guide to life.

The early years of Hoodoo's second stage following emancipation was the period of classical Hoodoo practice and refinement when it fully flourished in the postemancipation era and achieved a national profile. It was this first phase of Hoodoo's second stage, the years from emancipation up to the few years surrounding World War I, that both Zora Neale Hurston and Harry Middleton Hyatt longed for but felt that they missed.[24] During this time, Hoodoo was freed from the legal bonds of plantation slavery and rural confinement as independent Hoodoo practitioners emerged and began to strengthen the tradition while developing Hoodoo as an African American community-owned commercial enterprise. The tradition blossomed in response to the black community's tremendous psychoreligious need during this postemancipation period of displacement, turmoil, upheaval, and change. Some locations experienced such phenomenal growth in the number of Hoodoo practitioners as to generate a concern for public safety. Speaking of the post-Reconstruction proliferation of spiritual practitioners in New Orleans, Louis Pendleton had this comment: "It has been stated that the number of Voodoo professionals among the negroes of New Orleans was found to be so great in 1886 as to compel the Board of Health to interfere, with a view to their suppression."[25]

Following Reconstruction, the descendants of African slaves in America had a new independence thrust into their lives as they became responsible for administering to their own needs. A reign of racial terrorism gripped the black communities of the South following emancipation and subjected the nation's newest citizens to the most brutal forms of murder, public beatings, torture, lynching, and starvation; nevertheless, this period was filled with both new fear and new hope. Harsh forms of repression touched all areas of black life, coupled with public pogroms in which racists openly dragged thousands of African American citizens from their homes and burned or otherwise destroyed their property and murdered them and their families. The wider American society felt little obligation toward its former chattel and outright denied people of African heritage refuge from terror as well as life-sustaining materials and services, frequently thrusting them back into the terror and to their own socially circumscribed, marginalized, and limited resources. There were new contingencies to their existence, and the conjurer/treater was one sure resource for dealing with instability, insecurity, poverty, and anxieties that invaded the lives of African Americans of the period. Intensified community anxieties and concerns centered on issues of securing a livelihood, family and marriage, health care, housing, police harassment, legal issues, vigilante terrorism, and the numerous dangers of the new freedom. All this was coupled with an onslaught of both public and private psychological intimidation and economic crippling that constantly circumscribed and limited black advancement while both state and federal governments turned a blind eye to the terror.

During this second stage of Hoodoo development, the divergence of roles between the conjurer and the former plantation preacher gained higher visibility. Again, W. E. B. DuBois leaves us this observation:

[T]he chief remaining institution was the Priest or Medicine-man. He early appeared on the plantation. . . . Thus, as bard physician, judge, and, priest, within the narrow limits allowed by the slave system, rose the Negro preacher, and under him the first Afro-American institution, the Negro church. The church was not at first by any means Christian nor definitely organized; rather it was an adaptation and mingling of heathen rites among the members of each plantation, and roughly designated as Voodooism. Association with the masters, missionary effort and motives of expediency gave these rites an early veneer of Christianity, and after the lapse of many generations the Negro church became Christian.[26]

Hoodoo's second phase was additionally marked by role diversification, specialization, and increasing Christianization. Though neither the plantation preacher's work nor the ordained reverend's calling was totally separate from many of the tasks and functions of the conjurer, the African American preacher, as a separate role, firmly emerged during this second phase of Hoodoo and presented itself as a full-blown alternative to the old-style plantation conjurer. Further diversification and specialization were evident in the widening split between medicinal herbalist, Hoodoo workers, lay midwives, and conjure women.

The diversification process, which early on marked this phase, temporarily expanded role definition and the structure within which the conjurer operated; but a quick-following period of specialization and disassociation limited conjure's purview and function.[27] The roles of preacher and conjurer diverged in a process, influenced initially by the same regional variations that influenced the character both of early Hoodoo and of early black Christian belief and worship. Significant numbers of early African American preachers allowed, even maintained, traditional African spiritual practices, and many of them had and today have a thorough knowledge of both Hoodoo and early African American Christian practice. Under the protective canopy of the church, Hoodoo could maintain a connection to a theological backdrop; in this context, one Hoodoo divinity, High John the Conquer, in some instances became associated with and partially merged with John the Prophet. While helping to define what Hoodoo was not, the early black folk preacher was essential in forging a new Christianity, an African-influenced Christianity, a Hoodooized Christianity that was socially flexible and fluid and would eventually find a future and permanent home in both the Spiritual churches and the Sanctified Church that would develop in numerous African American communities.[28]

Divergence in the roles of conjurer and preacher had begun during the enslavement period with efforts aimed at Christianizing bondsmen.

Christianization notwithstanding, both bondsmen and freedmen insisted on adhering to both traditional African religious patterns and their newly accepted Christian expression of faith; convening the sacred circle, one of numerous African religious practices, was just one means of doing this. Born in 1811, in Charleston, South Carolina, of free colored parents, Bishop Daniel Payne, sixth bishop of the African Methodist Episcopal church and founder and first president of Wilberforce University, leaves us this observation on African American response to Christianization: "This young man insisted that 'Sinners won't get converted unless there is a ring . . . at camp meeting there must be a ring here, a ring there, a ring over yonder, or sinners will not get converted.'"[29]

Shaving the head upon conversion, a practice known among traditional West and Central West Africans, was another African religious pattern observed among American bondsmen. Henry Brown, a fugitive slave, leaves this account of his sister's conversion experience: "[S]he shaved the hair from her head, as many of the slaves thought they could not be converted without doing this."[30] What did this head shaving mean? Were the converts reenacting what remained of a traditional African ceremonial rite of passage transformed into standard ARC practice and transferred into the early black Christian church, the Hoodoo church? Probably so; because head shaving marks a number of African rituals and rites, we can speculate with reasonable certainty about its African religious origins among bondsmen in the United States.

Hoodoo practice was broadened and enriched as a result of the regional migration taking place following the end of the Civil War. It took on a new profile as it repositioned itself to address new needs and confront new environments and new expectations. Traditions and practices that had been confined to isolated regions now became more available as freed slaves migrated intra- and interregionally. Hoodoo practices and standardized conventions, which prior to emancipation had been fairly isolated in Virginia or Mississippi were now—more rapidly than ever before—encountering one another with increasing frequency in cities such as Atlanta, Richmond, Montgomery, and Memphis and mixing with local Hoodoo practice there. It was indeed the coming of the golden age of Hoodoo practice.

Gradual and protracted, Hoodoo's transformation into its urban counterpart was, as with many institutions, uneven, so, too, with Hoodoo's move ment into postemancipation black cultural and religious arenas. Born of the rural environment, Hoodoo's existence and survival in the city verified its adaptability and functionality. Prior to World War I, Hoodoo's urban practice was barely distinguishable from the rural tradition that gave rise to it. The site for the most potent African American cultural creation was still in the rural South, with its high concentration of African Americans, but the mass migration process would create similarly functioning sites in the urban North.

Around the turn of the twentieth century, the increase in Hoodoo in the urban environment, particularly in the North, forced certain changes and adaptations in its practice. Changes such as the increasing use of both commercial advertising and commercial supply houses and curio shops became more widespread. The older rural Hoodoo men and women were skilled herbalists who supplied their own needs, rarely using commercially produced supplies. These traditionalists were the direct carriers of a slowly disintegrating, moribund African American herbal tradition sustained through a period of forced enslavement. The urban practitioner, on the other hand, was far more dependent on suppliers and was exposed to a higher rate of cross-fertilization from other spiritual traditions than the rural conjurers and the rural Hoodoo tradition. By the 1930s, the old-profile Hoodoo priest, also known as a swamper, would all but disappear. Zora Neale Hurston leaves us this account of one of the last of the swampers, Dr. Duke: "Dr. Duke is a member of a disappearing school of folk magic. He spends days and nights out in the woods and swamps and is therefore known as a 'swamper.' A swamper is a root-and-conjure doctor who goes to the swamps and gathers his or her own herbs and roots. Most of the doctors buy their materials from regular supply houses."[31] By the publication of this account in 1935, the latter phase in the second period of Hoodoo's development, marked by a proliferation of supply houses and urban clientele, conjure's older traditions were giving way to a more specialized practice, limited and heavily commercial. This would have indirect psychological impact. Participation in the mainstream marketplace, even if it were only at a Hoodoo curio drug store or supply house, allowed blacks who had been, and in most instances were still, marginalized economically and forced to the fringes of the American mainstream marketplace to minimally validate their economic location and way of life by buying from a store that targeted black specialty products. This dynamic was exacerbated by mainstream white merchants who refused to trade with blacks, making the reception in the Hoodoo shop all the more appealing.

By examining the visible practices of freedmen, their children, and their grandchildren, one can draw a partial picture of the scope of Hoodoo's domain and reveal something of the depth of Hoodoo's cultural penetration into black life as well as its level of social tenacity during the postemancipation period. Some Hoodoo practices have direct African antecedents, and depending on when they are first recorded, they allow us an extended view backward into the invisible world of African American folk religion and magic. Other practices were possibly derived from mingled European or Native American practices. Both groups certainly had folk magic traditions that likely strengthened the spiritual context in which Hoodoo could expand and flourish. Accounts from colonial records of European settlers give vivid evidence of widespread belief in the supernatural, particularly witchcraft. Witchcraft trials were well known and publicized throughout the colonies. Indeed the evidence indicates that belief in fairies, hobgoblins, bugbears, willis, enchantment, witches, and witchmasters was strong enough for there to be the official office of "witchfinder general."[32] Beliefs in phenomena such as shape-shifting and existence of spirits were found among the Native Americans. Speaking of the American aboriginal religious practice, Dr. John Brickell leaves us this account from circa 1737: "These people [the Indian conjurers] . . . are great Enchanters, and use many Charms of Witchcraft. . . . [I]t is reported by several Planters in those parts, that they raise great Storms of Wind, and that there are many frightful Apparitions that appear above the Fires during the time of their *Conjuration*."[33] Whatever the origin, many Hoodoo practices and beliefs with strong African antecedents would persist into the twenty-first century; others would be lost in the massive dislocation known as the great migration.

The African American mass migration from rural areas into the urban industrialized North would transform Hoodoo practice as it would all other aspects of African American life. Some practices transplanted easily to the new urban environment, others could not. Practices that in the rural environment addressed both the individual as well as his relationship with the community and the surrounding environment were often impossible in the city, which dislocated the individual from nature. One such practice was the act of erasing one's footprints or tracks.

Hoodoo adherents believed that a conjure fix, or spell, could be put on someone or, to use the language of Hoodoo, "someone could work you" by either gathering the dirt tracks where you had left your footprints or by dusting or pouring a mixture onto the footprint. This magic was potentially more potent if the victim walked barefoot, leaving invisible traces of perspiration and dead skin. This picking up tracks was easy to achieve in the rural environment of an African village or rural southern community of unpaved dirt roads and walkways. But in the urban areas, paved roads and walks as well as the more frequent wearing of shoes made track gathering nearly impossible. Track gathering was the origin of the commercially marketeered hot foot powder and would later be subtly and overtly reflected in African American blues songs long after many blacks had given up the practice.

Chester Arthur Burnett, known to the blues world as Howlin' Wolf, reminds us of the practice in one of his biggest hits, the Willie Dixon blues hit "Tail Dragger":

> I'm a tail dragger
> I wipe out my tracks
> I'm a tail dragger
> I wipe out my tracks
> When I get what I wont (want)
> Lord I don't come sneakin' back[34]

Adherence to the Hoodoo belief system represented more than operationalized faith; it provided an alternative reality paradigm. Throughout the black belt South, African Americans could be observed at sunset sweeping or raking the dust yards and walkways leading to their abodes; this activity was more than mere yard maintenance. Many sweepers were ritually removing any tracks or family members' footprints before they retired for the night, lest an evildoer pick them up while the family slept.

Track gathering was practiced throughout West and Central West Africa as an integrated part of many of the traditional religions of the area. It should therefore not be surprising to observe it in African American communities of the black belt South. The following account tells us:

> "Pickin' up tracks" is a common practice among the extremely superstitious, not only among negroes, but "po' white trash" as well, who have presumably adopted it from the former by intimate association.
>
> Not long ago great excitement prevailed in a country district in Mississippi, caused by a young negro woman who had "picked up tracks." It broke up families; everybody was afraid. Nobody knew whose track might be picked up next.
>
> It seems that the young woman had a grudge of some kind against a man and a woman. She had followed them and had "picked up their tracks." Then she had gone off and buried the tracks she had picked up. She had put dog's hair with the tracks of the man, and cat hair with the tracks of the woman. After that the man and the woman could not live together anymore than a cat and dog could. They separated and the whole community was in an uproar. The belligerents finally becoming awestruck at their own lawlessness, caused by fright, superinduced by superstition, agreed to send for an old negro preacher who lived in an adjoining county, and who was popularly supposed to "have power over evil spirits." He came at their request, remained several days and finally succeeded, by some method known only to himself in pouring oil on the troubled waters and in patching up affairs. The female originator of the trouble

was publicly rebuked as well as privately taken to task by the preacher; he visited among scattered members of families, and by exhortation, public open-air service, and private lectures, restored peace once more. The most important of his injunctions, and one that was strictly carried out under penalty of "a spell," of undefined character, was that the girl dig up the tracks and hair and burn the latter. The spell of "picked up tracks" can be destroyed only by fire.[35]

The incredible power of the gathered track was such that many African Americans deeply feared being conjured by someone using their footprints. Again, Tom Peete Cross writing about folk belief in North Carolina leaves us this account:

> The same principle explains the terror with which the negroes and poor whites in some sections of the South regard the action of "picking up tracks." Because of their accessibility and their close association with the person, especially in country districts where there is much traveling on foot and many people go barefooted, foot-prints are especially liable to be used by witches in working their will upon the maker.[36]

Knowing the power of the gathered track, it is not surprising to find the deepest Hoodoo believers among the elders, who sometimes carried old twig brooms with them to sweep away their tracks if they traveled any distance by foot. One such individual, Aunt Memory, was observed in Tallahassee, Florida. From the Florida State Archives we are left with this account:

> Aunt Memory was a negro slave in Tallahassee. . . . She walked with a drove of slaves from Virginia and was sold for $800 at the age of 4 in Tallahassee. . . . [S]he acquired the habit of always carrying a satchel, . . . broom and a watering pot wherever she went. The satchel was for gifts given her by the people for whom she did house work, but the broom and watering pot were used to efface witch tracks. Small boys frequently placed suspicious marks at street corners and watched her dispose of them. She had a well dug inside her house "so no niggers can witch my water." She was a Methodist and was allowed to sit in a special part of white church and take communion after others finished.[37]

Aunt Memory carried a broom with her to wipe out her tracks, thus assuring her immunity from footprint conjure. She may well have been a conjure woman herself. She was observed washing away and neutralizing suspicious marks at street corners, the site of the crossroads, a sacred location in Hoodoo.

What was it about track gathering that people feared? It was common knowledge among many older African Americans that the soul rested in the palms of the hands and soles of the feet. Rubbing the palms together could activate or stir up the soul's special power.[38] The belief in the palms of the hands and soles of the feet as conductors of the soul's unique power was further manifested in the variety of Hoodoo signs associated with those body parts.

One of the most dreaded uses of the gathered track other than causing death was the walkin' foot, a charm made in combination with ants, ant hill dust, or a red ants' nest. Another greatly feared use of the gathered track was in combination with running or flowing water, as in a stream or river. Both ritual charms were designed to compel the target to leave and go elsewhere. But certain manipulations of the footprint could cause a restlessness in which the victim was compelled to walk backward or in other strange patterns at unusual and dangerous times, such as out in a rainstorm at midnight. As late as the 1970s, according to some who knew him, one walkin' foot victim in the small East Texas town of Leesburg was seen walking the same route daily against his will, no matter what the weather. When the appointed time came, he appeared to be compelled by some unknown force to walk the same pattern during several months as he gradually slipped into insanity.[39] The local two-head, Mr. L. J., was known to have one of the most powerful walkin' foot charms available, but community members believed that someone other than Mr. L. J. "worked" this victim.[40]

His methodological shortcomings notwithstanding, Harry Middleton Hyatt interviewed Hoodoo adherents and practitioners from St. Petersburg, Florida, to Norfolk, Virginia, from Brunswick, Georgia, to Memphis, Tennessee, and he collected and recorded various uses and types of actions associated with the gathered track. Depending on the ritual and the intention, gathered tracks could be used in a variety of ways, including to attract a new lover, prevent a mate from straying, return a straying mate, drive off a rival, break up a romantic union, gain power or control over someone, force someone to leave or stay away from you, cause itching or unbearably hot feet, inhibit one's ability to walk, cause one to travel constantly and wander aimlessly from one destination to another, induce insanity, induce bodily weakness and wasting, and induce a general state of bad luck.[41]

Though track gathering has all but vanished or forcibly degenerated into the use of commercial hot foot powder, Hoodoo practices such as the safeguarding of discarded hair, menstrual flow, fingernails, and personal items such as underwear are still alive in the second decade of the twenty-first century in African American communities. In earlier times, hair trimmings that fell to the floor were gathered up and secured from conjure and root work through various disposal techniques. Burning the hair was the easiest and most often used method of secure disposal. Similar to the beliefs of their African ancestors, the belief that one's hair could be used to harm, control, and manipulate the owner is deep-seated and long standing even among many young African Americans. The practice is most visible today in institutional contexts in which people are forced into close proximity with one another, such as army barracks, prisons, or dormitories. In these contexts, African American believers are more vigilant about hair disposal and often burn their hair in discarded cans or in ashtrays. When questioned as to why they burn their hair, all revealed that if an enemy obtained your hair they could "work you" or "put roots on you." The hair was not flushed down the toilet because it was and still is believed that sewer rats will get it and use it to build a nest, resulting in the owner of the hair experiencing unexplained and sudden headaches, blindness, insanity, or death. The same logic is applied to discarding hair in the trash. It is believed that certain birds will use the hair in nest building, with similar tragic results for the hair's owner. These practices are both in evidence today and previously observed and recorded in various types of literature.

The increased mobility of freedmen after Reconstruction would certainly allow for increased exposure and contact with other religions and spiritual practices as well as occult traditions. One such source was certainly present in the many traveling tent shows, gillies, or carnivals. In addition to featuring magicians, these traveling shows sometimes featured occult artists such as Gypsies, palm readers, crystal ball gazers, fortune-tellers, Indian medicine men, or even African witch doctors. On special nights designated for "Colored," African American consciousness of supernatural possibilities would encounter commercial occultists at work who would expose blacks to new and often fabricated models of exotic and spiritual presentation. This exposure would awaken the new marketing possibilities for Hoodoo on the urban landscape. Internationally, the Western world's interest in the exotic as a theme in theater, dance, music, literature, and painting during the period surrounding World War I led to a proliferation of exotic stereotypes and images. The postemancipation African American community was not unaware of these commercial themes, stock images, and stereotypes, but they would run head on into them as the rapidly developing snake-oil Hoodoo industry's exploitation of old plantation Hoodoo accelerated. Hoodoo was still largely a black-controlled rural phenomenon during the first five decades following emancipation; significant numbers of root work practitioners collected fresh roots and dried them for storage. Frequently an older family member, often a female, had some knowledge of roots and herbs and administered various treatments. Swampers still collected their own roots, herbs, and other supplies themselves. A well-connected conjure doctor, root worker, or two-head had access to a black-controlled underground supply network that included, but was not limited to, midwives, apothecary workers, root diggers, gravediggers, and undertakers. The supply network was an economic asset among poor blacks, providing much needed economic resources in the highly charged racist atmosphere that outright denied and limited African American life chances. Each type of Hoodoo traditional specialist could and frequently did supply the conjurer with items that they had unique access to. Midwives supplied cauls, afterbirths, and umbilical cords. Consider the following quote:

> To "blin" a child, that is to ghosts, the caul should be kept; but were it lost, another caul might be secured, bought from "de docter shop." The doctor has a supply, because "dese midwife steal de chillun caul an' kyarry an' sell 'em to de doctor."[42]

Even this marginalized pipeline to economic hope and access was attacked and destroyed by marketeers who were well aware of the powerlessness of the recently emancipated community. Enslaved African Americans and later free blacks working in apothecaries had access to numerous supplies, including Hoodoo's most sacred root, the legendary High John, also known as jalap. High John root was kept on hand in most apothecaries for use in making laxatives. Gravediggers and morticians had access to graveyard dirt, human remains, and personal articles belonging to the dead, all of which were used in certain types of conjure work. Consider this article in an 1883 African American newspaper: "James King and George Gaddis, negroes, were arrested Tuesday, charged with robbing the grave of Mrs. Hattie Howell. They confessed the crime, informing the officers that they stole the body for the purpose of securing the bones of the arm, which they used in their profession of conjurers."[43]

In addition to an underground network of suppliers, a well-connected, reputable conjurer, Hoodoo, or two-head man or woman inherited the conjurer's "oral textbook" and practical experience through apprenticeship, oftentimes in families. The secrets of Hoodoo were guarded by the true old tradition practitioners, as access to spiritual power had been carefully protected in traditional West and Central West African societies. Hoodoo priests knew the guarded secrets and proper procedures for harvesting, processing, and working certain roots, and they also knew the scope and specifics of each plant's power, were knowledgeable of harvesting times and techniques, and knew which roots could be harvested by human hands and which ones should be harvested by animals only. They knew when to harvest for maximum effectiveness and knew the particulars accompanying each plant, animal, rock, and twig. Roots that required harvesting by animals often were extracted from the ground using an aged or ill dog or mule. A cord was tied to the animal and attached to the plant, then the animal pulled the plant from the ground. Plants that required this harvesting technique were believed to have the power to drain life force energy from any living creature attempting to unearth them. So an animal near death from ill health or old age, rather than a healthy one, was put at risk. Harvested thusly, these roots were used only in the most serious life-and-death matters. Other plants were believed to emit a scream or to cry tears when harvested. Still other plants like "wonder of the world root" required that it be spoken to and ceremonially addressed before it could be harvested successfully, lest it release forces that will harm whoever handles it.[44] Like their traditional African predecessors and their Native American counterparts, an African American conjurer, well trained in the old tradition, believed in the life force potentiality in each sacred plant, sacred animal, and sacred inanimate object.

Conjure and root work during the postemancipation pre–World War I period achieved and maintained some degree of public legitimacy and visibility among blacks, enough for some African Americans to feel no need either to conceal or to secret their belief in and use of conjuring. This is made clear even in urban areas like late-nineteenth-century Philadelphia. In W. E. B. DuBois's landmark study *The Philadelphia Negro,* at least two of his informants openly list their occupation as root doctor.[45] Though the rituals and practices of conjuring and root doctoring were largely secretive and invisible, their quasi-public legitimacy among blacks contributed to Hoodoo's vulnerability to middlemen minority exploitation and detrimental mainstream market influence. It was well known among whites that significant numbers of African Americans believed in supernatural phenomena such as spirits, root work, Hoodoo, and conjure. With a large pool of believers and no formalized power to regulate either Hoodoo development or its uses and practitioners, this struggling tradition was especially vulnerable to pitchmen and other types of appropriative exploitation. And no exploiters were more skilled than the immigrating middlemen minority European marketeers.

Prior to emancipation, the black community had very much been a part of the plantation and frontier health care tradition, heavily contributing its traditional healing principles and techniques while developing new ones. But the first two decades following emancipation witnessed the birth of two divergent and competing lines of Hoodoo development: one, the old tradition of African root doctor/conjurer from the plantation, the other, an exploitative quasi rendering of the tradition from primarily middlemen minority marketeers, the traveling medicine shows, and other similar related venues that reached a peak in popularity during this period.

Following emancipation, Hoodoo was essentially an internally contained "race product," and neither its magical practices nor its naturopathic medicine aspect was yet fully exploited by hucksters, dream merchants, snake-oil salesmen, spiritual merchants, or con artists, and the practice of healing was not yet regulated by a medical establishment. The result was that in the rural segregated community, one could find either a reputable two-head doctor or a local root worker through personal referral. The American medicine show, its imitators, and its spin-offs would, in some areas, challenge those traditional networks. But no challenge was as great as that posed by the middle minority manipulators and exploiters of Hoodoo.

To attract potential customers, the American medicine show took on elements of the Wild West show, the carnival, the circus, and the healing center. It was not beyond exploiting any and all cultural themes or traditions to make money. Indians, both Native American and Hindu, were frequently portrayed on advertising handbills distributed prior to the show's arrival in town. Often a medicine show featured someone dressed as and impersonating a Native American medicine man. Native Americans, like African Americans, certainly had acquired a widespread reputation and acceptance as adept healers, so their presence at medicine shows and their appearance on advertising handbills served to legitimate the snake-oil sales pitch.

Both African Americans and African witch doctors, like other exotics, Arabs, Hindus, and Native Americans, were often portrayed by white minstrels in blackface. White people in the United States had enjoyed blackface portrayals of African Americans since Lewis Hallam "performed a 'drunken darky' act on the American stage in 1769."[46] But it would not be until 1829, nearly sixty years later, before the blackface minstrel prototype known as "Jim Crow" would be portrayed by Thomas "Daddy" Rice, a white man. Instantly popular, Jim Crow was copied, imitated, and embellished. With his immense popularity, he was a fine fit in the medicine show or among other types of pitchmen and ballyhooers. According to medicine show historian Ann Anderson:

Minstrelsy was easily incorporated into medicine shows. Blackface comedy dominated most medicine shows even after minstrel companies per se were in decline. The bright, upbeat shows were the sort of simple, nontechnical fare that Main Street loved, and the producer could insert a medicine pitch at any point. . . . A typical medicine-minstrel show might have begun with the tried-and-true fake stabbing to draw the crowd. Then a banjo solo and a big musical number with the whole cast might follow. . . . After that, there were the specialty bits like magic, mind reading, or ventriloquism."[47]

Though the pitchmen, hucksters, and snake-oil industry had no access to Hoodoo's deep ceremonial nature, herbal treatments, myths, beliefs, procedures, and practices, their misportrayals and exploitation of aspects of the Hoodoo tradition ultimately exercised influence on public discourse, opinion, and expectations. By selling amulets, mojoes, and "luck bags," which they had neither authority, traditional training, community ground- ing, nor experience in making, they helped both to transform the Hoodoo tradition and to contribute to an atmosphere of distrust, denigration, and opposition to Hoodoo while fostering a misshapened portrayal of Hoodoo in the imagination of a significant percentage of their displaced and well- fleeced audience. Traditionally, only the conjurer, root doctor, or two-head could make effective mojoes because only the conjurer knew the incanta- tions, prayers, herbs, and rituals necessary to empower the charm. Only a called, trained, and anointed Hoodoo priest or priestess could prepare an authentic, traditional, and effective mojo bag and instruct the client in its care and uses. Blacks were especially vulnerable to marketeers who had both racial and economic power over them.

Before the takeover of Hoodoo by marketeers, there were different types of mojoes, tobies, jacks or luck bags, depending on the purpose for which it was constructed. One type, a luck ball, was carried for general protection. To empower the mojo, the owner was instructed in how to enliven, sustain, and strengthen the charm. A close, personal relationship was established between the charm and owner; the charm was protected, cared for, and fed in fashions similar to those performed in many parts of West and Cen- tral West Africa, the Caribbean, and Latin America. Originally encased in either leather, shells, seeds, or raffialike grass, African American mojoes eventually turned to cloth as the outer containment bag. Charms to attract, repel, or control another were often named for their target, while charms constructed for personal protection were often named for the owner or a revered protective ancestor. Mary Alicia Owens leaves us this account of old Aunt Mymee and her luck ball, which she named for herself and fed once a week:

> . . . of which was the loss of her most powerful fetich, the luck-ball she had talked to and called by her own name as if it were her double. . . . "What are you doing, Aunt Mymee?" "Gwine to gib Lil Mymeeer drink. . . ." "Shall I

bring you a gourd of water?" "No, honey. Lil Mymee, she don' sup watteh," said Aunt Mymee, lifting a dirty little yarn ball out of the dirty little linen bag. "She sup wut Big Angy name *eau-de-vie,* an' datsholy am de wattehob life foh huh, kaseef she don' git un she die." Aunt Mymee produced a black bottle of Little Mymee's elixir of life, better known to the general public as whiskey, and proceeded to moisten, first the ball, then herself there-with; after which ceremony she restored the ball to its proper receptacle, mended the broken string, . . . and made it an ornament to her person by slinging the string over her right armpit. She had, beforehand, be it understood, slipped out of her various waists of her raiment, so that the ball should lie against her naked body, with no intervening fold of calico or flannel to absorb its "strenk."[48]

After emancipation, African Americans had worked often in all-black medicine shows, tent shows, and gillies that played to segregated audiences. There was one outstanding exception, Jim Ferdon of Litchfield, Illinois, who impersonated a Quaker to sell his cures. Described as "the most blatant of the religious medicine show cons,"

Ferdon's show was much more lively than a real Quaker meeting, but audiences didn't seem to mind the discrepancy. After years of Indian shows, they were charmed by the novelty. He toured the midwest with an African American quartet dressed in the latest fashion: bulldog yellow shoes, three-inch collars, and wide-brimmed fedoras for the men, leg o' mutton sleeves, wasp waists, and peek-a-boo hats for the women. Ferdon was one of the few medicine showmen who had a mixed-race troupe. They were quite a spectacle in a region that didn't see many African Americans—or Quakers, for that matter. They carried their own stage, which consisted of a large platform surrounded by high canvas walls.[49]

Contact with pitchmen, hucksters, and the exotic themes they employed was one conduit through which the Hoodoo folk tradition would be turned into a field of exploitation, dream salesmanship, and in many instances outright thievery of tradition as well as money. J. C. Julian, an oil field worker near Seminole, Oklahoma, took the nickname "High-John-the-Conquer" and sold mojoes and toby charms as a sideline; he used the following snake-oil sales pitch:

Put up and built by the Seven Sisters at the Crackerjack Drug Store at New Orleans, Louisiana. My Toby will bring you Honor, Riches, and Happiness. It will help you Win in all Games. It will bring you Health and Wealth. It will Protect you against Evil Spirits and Witchcraft. Thieves nor Enemies cannot bother you. Now listen, everything you turn your hand to Prospers you and makes you Money. You succeed in your Trade, Job, or Business. You got Seven Wishes to make with each Lucky Bag. Hold the Bag in your Left hand, blow your hot breath on it Three times, and Make your Wish, and see if it don't come to Pass before the Seventh day is gone.

To hold your True Loved one. To get anyone you love. To Protect yourself against all Law. To Kill all Voodoo and Witchcraft. Buy a toby. Just One Dollar. And if you ain't satisfied with my Toby, I give you your Money Back. Don't be Foolhardy. Don't run no Risk. Keep a Toby on your person all the Time. Just One Dollar. But it's worth Fifty.[50]

While the true keepers and practitioners of Hoodoo's old tradition fought for its survival, they were overwhelmed in the deluge of oppositional and undermining forces, including attacks from certain Christian fronts, bastardization of its practices, and an association with trickery and con artistry. Prior to the appropriation of traditional Hoodoo charms by the con industry beginning in the latter half of the nineteenth century, Hoodoo had little, if any, identification with con artistry, with superstition perhaps, but not with outright deception and financial trickery, at least not yet.

As the racial terror of the black belt continued to escalate, the great migration intensified; urbanization and movement northward would displace some of the migrants from their traditional web of tried and trusted old tradition Hoodoo contacts, leaving them potentially vulnerable to con artists and market forces beyond their control. With at least a temporary loss of network, migrating blacks had to reconstruct a partial web of contacts in the new environment. How was this to be done? Hoodoo believers and practitioners had no formal advocates, no formal institutional structures, and no nationally organized hierarchy and regulatory body. Hoodoo's presence was visible to some and invisible to others. An example of its most visible public presence is described by Clyde Vernon Kiser in his landmark study of early-twentieth-century migrants from St. Helena Island, South Carolina, to Harlem, New York. Virtually indistinguishable from each other in some contexts, the old plantation Hoodoo tradition and the turn-of-the-century snake-oil Hoodoo competed for the potential market represented by both newly freed and migrating blacks. Both traditions brought their appeal directly to the potential consumer, as demonstrated by this statement:

It is almost impossible to go through Harlem, especially on Saturday afternoon when the streets are filled, without encountering several quack doctors surrounded by the curious and gullible. Some display well-worn charts of the human anatomy and by help of a pointer, indicate to the on-lookers the supposed nature of certain diseases and the reasons why potions, herbs, and salves can eradicate the ailments. Others seek to draw a crowd by exhibiting snakes wrapped around their necks, and by performing sleight of hand. Some venders are white, some black, but apparently the most successful are the light West Indians who pose as East Indians. Nor is quackery confined to medicine for the cure of physical ailments. At 162 West 129th Street, the following sign was displayed in an apartment window: "Prof. Ed. Barritt, School of Metaphysics, Spiritual Messenger, and Divine Healing Meetings." A few steps beyond and across the street was another placard in an apartment window, "Zandros Good Luck Incense Sold Here. 25c a can."[51]

In the urban North, the problem of locating an independent conjurer or root worker was partially solved as it had been in the rural South, by word-of-mouth reputation. But the urban environment offered the exploiters, imitators, and con artists a new entrée into the black community through print media advertising, especially magazines and newspapers. Competing with the old tradition, the snake-oil Hoodoo industry was the first to use commercial supply houses and would come to heavily exploit the increasingly present print media. Appealing primarily to both an illiterate and a semiliterate clientele, snake-oil Hoodoo and its peddlers would benefit from and take advantage of the push toward increasing literacy that occurred in the black community during this period. They did so by advertising in African American newspapers.

Not long after 1877, the year marking the end of Reconstruction, there was a noticeable increase in ads for spiritual services in African American newspapers. Like the beginnings of the great migration, the earliest ads were few and of limited use or influence. The old plantation Hoodoo tradition was still intact, self-contained, virtually self-supporting, and nearly independent of mainstream market forces. The earliest print media targeting black potential spiritual clientele that this author found was in the New York journal *The Rights of All* on Friday August 7, 1829 (vol. 1 no. 4). The advertisement for "Sarah Green Indian Doctress" informs her friends and clients of her new location. Undoubtedly a root doctor, she claims through her ad that she can cure a range of maladies, including piles, smallpox, and "Bite of mad dog." Perhaps she was a black Indian; nevertheless, her claim of Native American identity is intended to legitimate her claims at doctoring.

Prior to World War I, the African American population in the North was small compared to the numbers of blacks who were still in the South, but those less numerous, northern blacks were significant enough to support black newspapers in cities like New York, Baltimore, Detroit, Cleveland, and Pittsburgh. The number and types of ads would increase by leaps and bounds as the southern black population in the urban North increased. Newspapers and other print media would bring snake-oil Hoodoo's appeal and hook directly into previously inaccessible areas like black-owned businesses and households.

The pre–World War I ads were few and less elaborate than the later ads, but their snake-oil veneer clearly established a pattern that would influence future spiritual advertising aimed at blacks. The postemancipation pre–World War I ads would chart the course, set the style, and establish the conventions of future Hoodoo ads. The growing southern and northern black urban presence would find itself in a mutually reciprocal relationship with spiritual and occult traditions other than Hoodoo and Christianity. Unable to sustain autonomy from market influences, Hoodoo found itself mixing with and having an impact on other traditions as well as popular trends; astrology was one such influence.

Unknown in plantation Hoodoo, astrology or "planet reading" began soon after the end of Reconstruction to openly influence the newly developing urban variant of old tradition Hoodoo. As early as 1879, ads for a practitioner who combined psychic mediumship with root doctoring and astrology appeared in a Baltimore newspaper that served the black community, thus potentially expanding his clientele and establishing the framework to lay claims of increased power and effectiveness. Both the patent medicine ads and snake-oil handbills had established an easy path on which outside traditions and influences would enter Hoodoo and enable it to gradually replace aspects of the declining rural old tradition. A natural decline in the rural-based Hoodoo, resulting from increasing urbanization and transplantation northward would leave sociocultural crevices, holes that would be partially filled by the integration of external traditions and outsider influences and information. The opportunity for a commercial supply industry, supplying both traditional and snake-oil Hoodoo workers and their clients, would be seized and exploited. There were several books openly advertised in pre–World War I black newspapers that would become considerably influential among some urbanized Hoodoo practitioners. These texts would support the newly developing urban snake-oil Hoodoo to further disconnect from the old tradition while allowing certain practices to strengthen their relationship within the black church as a result of their alleged Old Testament legitimacy. Salesmen of *The Sixth and Seventh Books of Moses, Albertus Magnus,* and *Long Lost Friend* vigorously sought the African American market, and these texts were actively advertised in black newspapers and promoted. The following ad was in the local news section of a 1912, pre–World War I issue of the *Pittsburgh Courier:* "Sixth and Seventh

Books of Moses," "Albertus Magnus," "Long Lost Friend" At Mount's Old Book Shoppe, 626 Penn Avenue.[52]

As the more earth-based aspects of old tradition Hoodoo proved unsustainable in the northern urban environment, Hoodoo transplanted northward as well as to southern urban areas and would become more dependent on outsiders and outsider traditions and influences for procedures, incantations, prayers, paraphernalia, and supplies. The transition from the old tradition to the new marketeered urban Hoodoo was partly facilitated by the patent medicine industry that legitimized root doctoring and homemade medicine treatments. Like the ads for patent medicines, many of the ads for Hoodoo specialists emphasized their adeptness at treating both physical and spiritual concerns; these ads, their frequency, variations, and intensity would increase as the twentieth century dawned and unfolded. Influenced by its proximity to the rural community, southern urban Hoodoo, capable of stronger resistance to marketeering, faired better and sustained its connection to its rural parent longer and more intensely than the rapidly transforming northern urban form. But it also would eventually be altered by the forces of both the cultural marketplace and the great migration as urbanized Hoodoo, black Christian practice, snake oil, and the old tradition cross-fertilized and competed with one another for both "the souls of black folks" and their pocketbooks. The migration into both southern and northern urban areas provided a ready-made and potentially exploitable economic community. Coping with new pressures and driven by the desire to improve their lot in life, black migrants wrestled with whether to retain or discard Hoodoo as a relic of their former lives, lives filled with racial oppression in its most hopelessly barbaric form.

Some Hoodoo believers and practitioners viewed Hoodoo and Christian practices as complementary parts of a whole. Hoodoo's presence was justified then as it is today by the tenet that root work and spirit work are complements to God's power through the church but that the totality of God's power is disbursed and not totally located in church ritual, belief, and practice. Hoodoo philosophy, the oral text that sustained and justified its existence and that explained its motives and the spiritual foundation for all Hoodoo procedures, evolved as migration, urbanization, modernization, commercialization, and fragmentation all pulled to disconnect urban Hoodoo from the old plantation tradition. The post–World War I social environment would witness an intensification of all these trends. The confrontation between Hoodoo and its opponents, detractors, and undermining influences was nowhere more protracted than in the context of the black church. A previously cited account illustrates the depth of tension and contestation that Hoodoo believers experienced; they viewed their mojo bags, jacks, or tobies as spiritually essential to their role in black Christian worship and they carried them to church. I turn again to a previously quoted passage in which Newbell Niles Puckett reminds us:

> In a rural Negro church near Columbus, Miss., there was a constant change of ministers because of the reliance of the congregation upon "jacks" (charms wrapped up in red flannel). A new minister was more quick witted. He wrapped a large hunk of coal in red flannel, planked it on the pulpit one night and said: "Folks, dis yere de daddy-jack I'se got. Bring yo' baby-jacks on up." The members of the congregation were afraid not to do this.[53]

The dynamic tension of this passage fades into poignant irony upon closer examination. Only a technique that acknowledges and uses the power of the Hoodoo jack could rid this Christian congregation of their traditional African charms, known here as jacks.

In addition to jacks, other practices, characteristics, and aspects of African traditional religion would move from old tradition Hoodoo ritual and worship into the black church. The use of at least two types of sacred voice—a voice that was nasalized toward falsetto and a second gravelly voice—would move from the traditional African priest and other sacred workers into plantation Hoodoo and finally into the black Christian pulpit. But their movement would not settle there, like the Ring Shout, sacred voice would move into black secular song and eventually become a hallmark convention of stylized blues singing, while falsetto voice, observed in the Yoruba cult of Osayin, as an example, would reach a new widespread popularity nearly a century later in the doo-wop rhythm-and-blues songs of the 1950s and early to mid-1960s.

Certain modes of speaking and pronunciation would be imprinted on black Christian worship early on, with the plantation conjurer assuming a leadership role in accepting and converting to Christianity. In the religious dialogue between the leader and the participants/congregation, there was the use of elongated vowel emphasis to establish rhythm in their incantations, invocations, and prayers. These conventions would transfer from Hoodoo into the black church as part of the style and character of black worship, particularly black preaching. But as some African Americans slowly and painfully struggled to publicly legitimize their existence and to become more assimilated, some of them would relinquish these traditional conventions in their worship styles.

The division between the root doctor and the conjurer would become even more entrenched reflecting the pressure from the black church and

Hoodoo healing symbol. This symbol was traced in the sand by an enslaved woman whenever she experienced a pain in her side.

the movement toward specialization and professionalization that generally marked the period. Some root doctors would become known as expert herbal healers, like Dr. James Still. Specializing in natural treatments and naturopathic healing, "Dr. James of the Pine Barrens" empowered his treatments with a spiritual component, his strong belief in prayer, and the sacred healing power of nature as created by God.[54] Other two-heads made the conscious decision to relinquish the supernatural work and to pass on only the medicinal healing aspect of their folk religioscience.

Despite all that raged around them and tore at the fringes of an unraveling tradition, in some rural areas the older plantation Hoodoo traditions would continue. Some African Americans would still call their infant's name in the crossroads.[55] Others wore the African healing string tied with sacred healing knots.[56] Others engaged in sacred healing symbol manipulation. Ruby Andrews Moore leaves us this account of a rarely observed and recorded healing symbol used by bondsmen and their descendants. Entranced and using an unintelligible incantation, the afflicted woman knelt and drew a symbol in the sand.

One negro woman suffered a pain in her side, which she firmly believed to be the work of a witch. To exorcise the pain, when it grew severe, she went out into the yard, got on her knees in the sand, and making the following figure of as large dimensions as she could without moving, muttered words to herself that I could never find intelligible, indeed, barely audible, and she would never enlighten me when I asked what she said. Below is the figure she made, very slowly, with her eyes "set," and an intense expression on her face. When she had made a certain number of lines the pain ceased, she said. It appeared that the same number was not always requisite.[57]

Still others considered the water from the forging process sacred, as it had been regarded by their African ancestors, and they used that water in their church's indoor baptism pool when the practice of baptizing in the river significantly declined. Elsie Clews Parsons tells us: Just as they have "cut out" "baptizin in de riber." They now baptize in a pool in the church with water from the foundry.[58]

Though transformation bore down on it, the old tradition sought and found refuge in the rural community of practitioners who would extend, but would not be able to permanently sustain, its life in the face of accelerating urbanization and targeted commercialization occurring between the two world wars in the latter half of Hoodoo's second stage.

I said, "Hold it, Doc, a World War passed through my brain"
He said, "Nurse, get your pad, this boy's insane"
—Bob Dylan, "Talkin' World War III Blues"

THE DEMISE OF
DR. BUZZARD
Black Belt Hoodoo between
the Two World Wars

The period between World Wars I and II would play host to diversification in spiritual merchandising that contributed to an ever-strengthening subversion and undermining of Hoodoo's traditional old black belt practice. Aspects of the black belt Hoodoo tradition that the snake-oil industry could not exploit would begin a slow transformative decline into increasing invisibility while the spiritual merchants would marketeer Hoodoo merchandise into a lucrative and full-blown industry. The all but complete domination of the Hoodoo marketplace by spiritual merchants and marketeers produced a transformation in Negro supernatural folk knowledge. But the marketeers were merely one active and essential element in the transformation process. Another element was the medical community's attack on midwifery, Hoodoo's thriving and powerful link with the black folk medicine tradition. Marketeers could not penetrate and control this aspect of the old black belt Hoodoo complex. The medical establishment's attack contributed to the destruction of lay midwifery, an institution that controlled a wealth of sexually specific root and herbal knowledge as well as tradition. This destruction further disrupted the Hoodoo supply network and terminated the supply line in items such as cauls, placentas, and umbilical cords controlled by the midwife-conjure woman.

Old tradition Hoodoo was not an exception to the cultural change and further homogenization that was in process throughout the United States. American regional culture across the board would continue to become more homogenized and more national in its potential scope. As cultural access across regions became increasingly available, deep ethnic as well as regional uniqueness would become less encompassing while still retaining some core differences, but within an intensifying national identity. With the coming of railroads, radios, automobiles, movies, dance halls, company catalogs, print media, airplanes, standardized public education, and the birth of a free-floating, urban, popular culture consumer, Americans were becoming more similar; they could engage in similar experiences across regions. The two great wars that framed the period would further contribute to an intensification of national identity as they called forth national over regional loyalty, sentiment, and identification.

The three regional black belt Hoodoo clusters experienced a widening access to one another's unique Hoodoo expression in both the South and the North. This had a twofold effect. It enabled Hoodoo to resist and decelerate the limiting commercial standardization process by increasing regional diversity through exchange, but it also gave a unique visibility to those elements of Hoodoo that were not regionally specific and were widely known across regions. In some regions, Hoodoo recipes called for the use of local plants or other natural substances. These local supplies would not prove to be nationally recognizable and therefore were less marketable. In all three regions, certain aspects of Hoodoo would become even more visible in the era of Dr. Buzzard. Though it remained alive, Hoodoo's old tradition would be further weakened and would continue to slowly contract and transform as market forces as well as economic and social pressures mounted on the back of this highly vulnerable and exploitable tradition.

Advertisements in black print media for Hoodoo services, a trend started in the nineteenth century, increased dramatically during the period following World War I. Ads that targeted the primary areas addressed in Hoodoo ritual, including love, health, sexuality, finances, jobs, and legal trouble or court cases appeared in black print media, particularly newspapers and magazines. The marketeers addressed every area except that which was a central theme in plantation Hoodoo: protection from whites and their violent, controlling, and exploitative behavior. Most of the Hoodoo ads appropriated and emphasized several catchphrases and fictive kinship names frequently used in African American churches. Fictive kinship titles such as "Mother,"

"Brother," or "Sister" would serve not only to identify the ad's owner as a Hoodoo practitioner, but also to signify a connection with a church or sacred tradition, thus legitimizing the practitioner. Phrases such as "have you lost your nature?" "do you have bad luck?" or "are you in legal trouble?" served a similar purpose: getting the attention of a believer in need.

Hoping to exploit and benefit from the Hoodoo belief system, the practitioners behind the ads cast a wide net of appeal by advertising in the black print media of several cities simultaneously as well as carrying on a brisk mail-order trade. Targeting the dramatically increasing urban black population, ads appealing to Hoodoo believers appeared in all major black newspapers. Continuing, reflecting, and expanding the trend begun before World War I, ads appeared in *The Cleveland Gazette, The Chicago Defender, The Baltimore Afro-American, The Richmond Planet, The New York Age, The Amsterdam News, The Washington, D.C. Colored American,* and numerous other African American newspapers. Exemplifying this expanding trend in mail-order Hoodoo, *The Chicago Defender* in the 1930s carried an ad for "The Real and Original D. Alexander," whose address was listed as 200 West 135th Street in New York City, more than a thousand miles away. Another ad was for M. Williams, whose address was listed as 901 Bergen Ave. in Jersey City, New Jersey. In addition to the Hoodoo ads, there was an assault of ads for spiritual mediums, fortune-tellers, clairvoyants, "old Indian herb medicine men," and astrologers. In addition, ads for horoscopes, occult books, Hindu occult secrets, Egyptian talismans, Hindu magic mirrors, lucky hands, New Orleans luck powder, and root and herbal treatments and cures, all appeared in black newspapers between the world wars. The presence of these ads intensified and diversified the spiritual atmosphere in which both commercially marketeered Hoodoo and old tradition Hoodoo would compete to exist. Hoodoo's urban face would find itself submerged in an ever-changing sea and spiritual marketplace in which both access to supplies and competition with outsiders and nonbelievers for clients were challenging Hoodoo's once exclusive and self-sustaining supply market. Urbanized Hoodoo would experience a dynamic tension between its plantation origins and the contemporary urban marketeer-controlled marketplace. But the marketplace was limited in what it could offer and would eventually impact upon the direction of Hoodoo's urban development, severely circumscribing and transforming it. It was indeed a hostile takeover.

Spiritual merchandising by nonblacks would reach a plateau in the 1930s, 1940s, and early 1950s as the black urban population continued to increase.[1] Once they were carried to the cities, the old practices, legends, and beliefs did not die immediately. Instead they changed, metamorphosing into urban forms, as did other core aspects of African American culture such as music and dance. But unlike music and dance, old tradition Hoodoo could not hold its own against the negative undermining onslaught of outsider influences and marketeers. Negro dance and music had few successful imitators and external competitors during this time, but this was not true for Hoodoo, which faced both pressure and condemnation from some Christian quarters. Other competing philosophies as well as the spiritual merchants sought to control the trade in Hoodoo supplies. For many of the new migrants, the urbanized marketeered Hoodoo, with its almost total use of warehoused and commercially supplied roots and herbs, was insufficient when compared to the freshly harvested supplies and personal touch, cultural familiarity, and modes of community exchange of the old swampers. Though a number of these commercial establishments attempted to personalize their services by offering readings in a private area of the shop such as a back room, the down-home personal touch could not be duplicated in the commercial atmosphere of the white-owned Hoodoo drugstore or the curio shop with its comings and goings of customers. Even the fresh herbs of the urban root peddlers[2] could not keep pace with the demand and would eventually fade away. In addition, the newly acquired urban veneer of northern spiritual workers—particularly the snake-oil variety, who often combined forms of exoticism such as Islamic names, East Indian or Sikh turbans, contrived accents, Gypsy palm reading, and astrology as well as other spiritual and occult forms—often lacked appeal to the older southern-born Hoodoo believers. Many of the older migrants were unimpressed with the slick marketeering that had invaded northern urban Hoodoo. Consequently, many of them journeyed back to the black belt South where they believed they could find a purer and more powerful genuine carrier of the old tradition. Many East Coast residents found themselves journeying to St. Helena Island, South Carolina, seeking the Hoodoo services of Stepheney Robinson, America's most famous root and conjure doctor.

Known as Dr. Buzzard, Robinson built a reputation that spread far and wide up and down the eastern seaboard; he worked the old tradition as his enslaved African grandfather had taught him to. His conjure was free of exotic influences, he used only noncommercial products, he was a living link with the old plantation Hoodoo folk religion, and his life spanned Hoodoo development through several of its rapidly changing stages. Because both Robinson's father and his son-in-law and great-grandson were all known as Dr. Buzzard, there is sometimes confusion about the identity of the practitioner under discussion. The title as it applies to Robinson's progenitors had to have developed and remained well established in the plantation culture of African American bondsmen. The name Dr. Buzzard functions here as more of a title than a name. Probably derived from a commingling of African and Native American religious elements, the notion of the buzzard as spiritually significant can be found in both traditional West African culture and among southeastern Native American ethnic groups. Discussing Cherokee animal lore, Gayle Ross reflects: "Each animal had its place. Buzzard was known as a great doctor, while Turtle knew the secrets of conjuring. Frog was to marshal at the council house. Rabbit's job was to be the messenger."[3]

The exact date of Stepheney Robinson's birth is unclear. The *St. Helena Island Cemetery Survey* of 1999 gives his birth and death dates as 1860–1947.[4] But the best-known accounts of his presence are in two books by J. E. McTeer, *High Sheriff of the Low Country* and *Fifty Years as a Low Country Witch Doctor*.[5] In both volumes, McTeer underestimates that Dr. Buzzard is around fifty years old when McTeer becomes sheriff at age twenty-two in 1926. If this is correct, then Robinson would have been born circa 1876. This date contradicts other reports as well as St. Helena Island folklore, which states that Robinson was born a slave.[6] These two volumes by McTeer give some indication of how deeply entrenched Hoodoo practice was among the local residents, particularly the African American ones. Hoodoo was so important in controlling area residents that Sheriff McTeer found it necessary to imitate at least the appearance as well as minimal aspects of Hoodoo practice in order to more effectively administer justice in his jurisdiction.[7] Robinson was most famous for his work on legal matters, especially for clients charged with a crime. When a client contracted his services, he would don his famous blue-purple tinted glasses and sit in the courtroom chewing the galanga root and spitting whenever and wherever possible. Known as "chewing John," "low John" or "little John," the galanga, a member of the ginger family, was also used in other situations requiring neutralization and control. The practice of releasing the magical power in the root of sacred plants by mastication is common in West and Central West Africa and was passed on to African American Hoodoo practitioners by their parents. In the more difficult court cases, Robinson would have dressed the courtroom ahead of time, sometimes paying and sending in the unnoticeable Negro janitor to deposit the root. Robinson directly and fearlessly confronted the white man's world represented by the power of the courtroom. This was something that few African Americans could or would do.

Robinson's reputation is legendary in black communities, especially up and down the eastern seaboard, but it carries mythological weight on the

Gullah Coast, an area stretching from south of Savannah, Georgia, northward to Georgetown, South Carolina, and dotted with sea islands and Gullah communities. In an interview, lifelong Awendaw, South Carolina, resident sixty-four-year-old Frances Nesbitt stated, "I always thought 'Dr. Buzzard' was someting made up by de old folks. I always hear folks talk about going to see Dr. Buzzard 'bout some root work or to get a licky hand or some such ting ever since I a child I hear dem talk."[8]

Robinson's notoriety increased as the World War II draft trial of one of his fellow root doctors, Dr. Bug, came to public attention. Peter Murray, also known as Dr. Bug of Laurel Bay on the Broad River, was arrested in connection with his role in administering a root designed to produce a cardiac flutter in a man during his draft board medical examination. This root assured the exemption of his client from service in World War II. Murray's client was given a small amount of whiskey laced with minute amounts of lead arsenate, which Murray apparently ordered, purchased, and signed for through a Beaufort drugstore. He was taken into court, tried, and convicted of aiding a young white man from Georgia to "evade selective service." Murray was given a one-year suspended jail sentence and ordered to pay a $1,000 fine.[9]

The investigating authorities then turned their attention to other root workers in the area, particularly Dr. Buzzard. But neither the draft evasion charge nor the mail fraud charge against him could be made to stick, so federal authorities abandoned the pursuit of the eighty-three-year-old Dr. Buzzard to South Carolina authorities. The state of South Carolina arrested and charged Robinson with practicing medicine without a license. Contradicting his own practice, Robinson did not employ a member of the root brotherhood to chew the root[10] on his behalf at a possible costs of $250 or $300. Instead he hired a top-notch attorney, State Senator Brantley Harvey, to represent him.[11] He entered a guilty plea and paid a $300 fine in cash. It is believed that shortly after his conviction, Dr. Buzzard abandoned his root work practice, passing the mantle to his son-in-law, who continued working roots and being referred to as Dr. Buzzard. Robinson died about four years later in 1947, purportedly from stomach cancer.[12]

Robinson's burial site continues to be a carefully guarded secret known only to a select few. It is believed that his final resting place would be continually plundered by those wanting graveyard dirt, pieces of clothing, and even bones and hair if the burial site were well known. Robinson's status as a powerful old style conjurer and root worker makes articles and dirt retrieved from his grave more powerful in Hoodoo work than articles from the graves of lesser-known and less-powerful conjurers and root workers.[13] Both his reputation and his name are frequently appropriated by marketeers and used to sell their products.

With his life spanning from the end of U.S. chattel slavery to the end of World War II, Robinson witnessed stark transformations in American life and culture, particularly in Hoodoo practice and the targeting of Hoodoo by marketeers and the growth of the spiritual marketplace. Though Robinson rarely used them in his early years, commercially produced and mail-order Hoodoo supplies would be used by his descendants and, later, occasionally by him as these products became more accessible and natural harvest grounds became less available. Though most root workers during Robinson's earlier years maintained their own fresh root and herb supply when possible, certain products necessary in old tradition Hoodoo such as cauls, jalap root, sulfur, mercury, and bluestone were almost always obtained through purchase, exchange, or barter from African American midwives, morticians, or pharmacists. Robinson witnessed that change.

The era between the world wars was one of rapid transformation that cascaded and rippled throughout African American life as it was witnessing an increase in the number and quality of streets and highways. Each time a new highway or street was etched into the countryside, some essential Hoodoo harvest ground was potentially disturbed or destroyed. And in years to come, suburbanization with its concomitant malls and parking lots would ruin a significant number of harvest grounds. The destruction of harvest grounds, coupled with the ever-growing spiritual marketplace, would begin to squeeze old tradition Hoodoo practitioners out of their place as their own suppliers. In the years to come, some manufacturers and suppliers would attempt to corner at least their regional markets, locking out African American access to the traditional supplies and paraphernalia of Hoodoo practice. According to Lady Dale's Curio Shop, longtime employee Albert Hampton, he and shop owner Alex Silverberg would drive to Mexico and purchase all the jalap root available to them, usually enough to fill a large delivery truck, and drive it back to Philadelphia, thus monopolizing the High John the Conquer root trade in the Philadelphia area and shrinking the national mail-order supply for the competition.[14]

The major Hoodoo marketeers and commercial suppliers experienced significant growth and diversification during this period. Carolyn Morrow Long in her work *Spiritual Merchants, Religion, Magic and Commerce* outlines and describes the major manufacturers and suppliers of Hoodoo-inspired products. According to Long:

Many of the early manufacturers entered the spiritual products business through the publication of books on the occult; the production of toiletries, patent medicines, and household cleaning products; or the manufacture of candles and incense. Some got their start in neighborhood Hoodoo drugstores. Family connections have been another means of entry into the spiritual business. Most spiritual supply companies are family owned; spouses and in-laws are involved, and the current owners are often the children and grandchildren, nieces and nephews, of the "founding father" who established these companies in the 1920s-1940s.[15]

The growth of the spiritual marketeers is directly related to both the turn-of-the-twentieth-century eastern European Jewish immigration and the great migration of southern African Americans into northern urban communities. These migrants, their children, and their grandchildren, divorced from the African religious foundations and now further divorced from the southern Hoodoo folk religion, were especially vulnerable to these marketeers. How and why the community of Hoodoo believers could not make the adjustment to remain self-sustaining are questions for future research. The answer requires an understanding of American race relations and the convergence of several factors, including community dislocation, assimilationist pressures from significant numbers of black American churches, the level of poverty and lack of education among blacks, as well as the timely, shrewd, and exploitative business practices of the marketeers.

According to Long, the manufacturing of Hoodoo supplies was primarily controlled by whites from either Christian or Jewish backgrounds. A significant number of the Jewish spiritual merchants selling Hoodoo products were like Philadelphia-born Alex Silverberg, who was trained as a chemist but because of anti-Jewish sentiments found that getting the work he wanted was difficult in a white Christian environment. So he, like many of them, turned his business skills to exploiting the market in Hoodoo supplies and Negro cosmetics. The Christian merchants came from a variety of ethnic backgrounds. Whatever the religious background, none of the manufacturers or marketeers, according to Long, were practitioners of any African-based religion, nor were any of them participants in the Hoodoo belief system.[16] This situation of nonbelieving outsiders exploiting the African American market lends itself to a range of possible interpretations not explored here.

The Hoodoo of this period, as compared with both earlier and later Hoodoo, was at its most diverse, culturally widespread, most complex, best organized, and most interactive with other occult traditions. Though unstable and facing both continuing contestation and removal from its old tradition origins, Hoodoo during this period was at its fullest, richest, and most vibrant social placement. Here every aspect of Hoodoo overlaps into this period. In the earlier part of the era, black midwifery was still fully functioning. Undertakers, pharmacy workers, and swampers of the old tradition maintained the older Hoodoo networks and were fully functioning alongside the spiritual marketeers. Eventually the marketplace would prevail as the old tradition continued to decline. But during a brief social moment, the old tradition stared directly into the eyes of its Janus-faced nemesis and held its own against both the spiritual marketeers and the assimilationists from inside the African American community who viewed Hoodoo as a shameful relic of barbarism, ignorance, and forced subservience.

The oldest and longest-standing of the spiritual products manufacturers was the de Laurence Company of Chicago.[17] Chicago, like other northern manufacturing cities during this period, was a major urban industrial center receiving significant numbers of southern black migrants. Encouraging and facilitating this mass movement, Chicago industry sent labor recruiters into the South who offered one-way tickets to workers who would come to the North to work in the factories. Like the spiritual marketeers, Chicago industry placed ads in black newspapers inviting potential migrants with the promise of "good jobs" to journey "up north."[18] The flood of black migrants strategically, though inadvertently, placed a ready-made market at the disposal of spiritual merchants. When Laurens William de Laurence actually began his business in publishing occult books on hypnotism, magic, kabbalah, spiritualism, and Hindu mysticism is undetermined. But he soon expanded his offerings to include herbal medicines, candles, incense, perfumes, oils, seals, and other items that served a growing northern urban Hoodoo clientele.[19]

Founded in 1928 by chemist Morton G. Neumann, the Valmor Company targeted the so-called race market in Negro products such as hair straighteners, skin lighteners, soaps, tonics, and laxatives using four subsidiary names: Madam Jones and Sweet Georgia Brown for women's products and Lucky Brown and Slick Black for the men's. In addition to cosmetics, medicines, and Hoodoo spiritual supplies, Valmor produced "race records" and printed dream books.[20] The company achieved penetration into black communities through its sales agents, a technique it adopted in imitation of Madam C. J. Walker's successful business methods.[21] According to Long:

> Valmor covered all bases: the company sold wholesale to smaller stores, did a retail mail-order business, and recruited sales agents from all over the country through advertisements in its retail catalogs and dream books and in the *Chicago Defender*. Valmor's spiritual supplies were marketed through

subsidiary companies called King Novelty and Famous Products. The back cover of the *Valmor Dream Book* advertises Famous Products incense in seven fragrances—John the Conquer, Aunt Sally's Lucky Dream, Lodestone, Lucky Mo-Jo, Lucky Spirit and Frank-Incense.[22]

Established in Memphis, Tennessee, in 1925 by Morris Shapiro and chemist Joseph Menke, the Keystone Chemical Company was later known as Keystone Laboratories.[23] Through advertisements in black newspapers and the use of African American sales agents, techniques proven by Valmor and other companies, Keystone offered Negro cosmetics and Hoodoo spiritual supplies directly to the African American community. But Keystone went one step further by penetrating the black spiritual community directly through maintaining a sales booth at the Sanctified Church conventions.[24]

The Sanctified Church, the most African of black American Christian Protestant churches, according to Zora Neale Hurston, has two branches: the Church of God in Christ and the Saints of God.[25] In these churches, several components of the African Religion Complex were retained in the old rituals of sacred music and dancing the remnants of the Ring Shout; baptism by water immersion, preferably outdoors in a lake or river, spirit possession; speaking in tongues; and naturopathic and supernatural healing. There they had a stable institutional base for continued existence. There also, just as the label and title "midwife" could serve to protect the conjure root woman, the two-head man could modify his persona and find protection as a Sanctified or Spiritualist church official, and many did just that.[26] Certain Negro religious behaviors observed in Sanctified churches in the 1960s urban North had remained relatively unchanged since the early 1800s, St. Clair Drake and Horace Cayton tell us: "Urban life puts its stamp on this religion, and while the basic features of the old beliefs and rituals persist in Bronzeville they have been modified by contact with the complexities of a large northern city."[27]

Distinguished from the Spiritual churches in label only, the Sanctified churches and their yearly conventions were a fertile marketplace where spiritual marketeers could gain access to potential Hoodoo consumers and further tighten their unchallenged control of the Hoodoo supply market. Drake and Cayton further reveal the growth and existence of the Spiritual churches and independent tangential spiritualist in Chicago in a ten-year period. In 1928 there were seventeen Spiritualist storefronts in Bronzeville; by 1938 there were 51 Spiritualist churches including one congregation of over 2,000 members. In 1928 one church in twenty was Spiritualist; in 1938 one in ten.[28] As African American migrants became increasingly assimilated and removed from easy access to the old tradition, the truncated Hoodoo of the spiritual merchants narrowed and transformed the image of Hoodoo into a shadow of its former powerful and meaningful existence.

Keystone sales agents could purchase kits containing Hoodoo curios and peddle them in black communities.[29] Kits typically contained certain herbs such as life everlasting, a plant well known in Gullah folk medicine and native to South Carolina, as well as High John the Conquer root, lodestone, Adam and Eve root, Devil's shoestring, controlling powder, and lucky candles.[30] New products, new names, and new labels were continually introduced. These new marketing ideas were based partly on older Hoodoo images, beliefs, and charms, a knowledge of which was gleaned from African Americans themselves through customer requests and from the black sales agents.[31] The job of traveling salesman was short-lived and would soon disappear, and with it went the door-to-door marketing of these products. New sales venues would also appear during this period and Hoodoo product sales would continue in a new modified sales format via catalog and direct sales in curio shops and Hoodoo stores.

Venues such as the candle shop would emerge as successful Hoodoo enterprises. Candle shops specialized in selling spiritual work candles. The proliferation and success of these shops demonstrate one aspect of Hoodoo transformation, adaptation, and functional change. Cassandra Wimbs calls candle burning "Hoodoo's modern-day incarnation."[32] Closely tied to the spiritual merchants, the production of spiritual candles is controlled by some of the same companies that produce and market other Hoodoo supplies. The candle shop focuses Hoodoo ritual on candle burning as a means to affect the desired result. The process of burning replaces the intervention and old rituals of the plantation conjurer. Candle burning to affect change exists at the intersection of Hoodoo, New Orleans Voodoo, and Santeria/Lucumi. But in the precommercial days of candle burning, a flame was sustained with a wick in the appropriate oil for that divinity, saint, orisha, or *lwa*. For example, a flame for Oshun, Yoruba orisha of female sexuality, was simply a wick in sunflower oil. Oshun enjoys sunflowers; they and their oil are sacred to her. A flame for Obatala would use coconut oil, and a flame to Ogun, lord of iron, would include used motor oil. The flame consumes the oil as a sacrifice to the force that one is petitioning.

As significant as candle burning would become to post–World War I Hoodoo ritual, candle burning does not appear to have been a major part of the old plantation black belt Hoodoo tradition. Candles were costly and were rarely seen by slaves except in the "big house." Slaves used grease lamps in their cabins to supply them with light. Ex-slave Louis Hughes leaves us this description: "For light a grease lamp was used, which was made of iron, bowl shaped, by a blacksmith. The bowl was filled with grease and a rag or wick placed in it, one end resting on the edge for lighting. These lamps have a good light, and were in general used among the slaves. Tallow candles were a luxury, never seen except in the 'great houses' of the planters."[33] Candle burning could have achieved some inclusion in plantation Hoodoo, but only on a very limited basis. Southern Louisiana appears to be the exception to this with the influence of Catholicism, Haitian Vodun, and the emergence of New Orleans Voodoo, which all used candles.

Candle burning represents the reduction of Hoodoo ritual to one principle ritual artifact: the spiritual candle. According to Wimbs, "Candle wax is replacing roots as the most common ideal holding agent."[34] Candle burning became acceptable partly because candles avoid some of the stigma attached to Hoodoo holding agents such as mojo bags or other ritual amulets. Some candles can be displayed and are readily available in candle shops, in supermarkets, in drugstores and pharmacies, and in some churches.[35]

Candle burning addresses all the areas addressed in old tradition Hoodoo, including love and family, employment, legal matters, and mental and physical health concerns. Unlike the traditional Hoodoo amulet in which external color was far less important than the materials and rituals used to construct it, candle color is especially significant. Most of the candle shops surveyed by Wimbs also sold other items used in Hoodoo, including oils, baths and washes, powders, and incense. Many of the ritual items as well as the candles take their names from their intended outcome. In both modern Hoodoo candle burning and classical old tradition Hoodoo, intent is of supreme significance. Names such as "bend over" candle or oil, "jinx removing" oil, "steady work" oil, "chase away" powder, "love me" oil, "fast luck" candle, "money drawing" candle, "do as I say" oil, and "controlling" oil and powder all speak to intent.

Candle shops are primarily an urban phenomenon, and their increasing proliferation and visibility in urban areas are closely tied to black migration into large urban areas, particularly in the North. By the time World War II ended and blacks were continuing to move northward both to escape the rule of racial terrorism and to access postwar employment and prosperity, Hoodoo was being transformed into something observably different and severely limited as compared with the old tradition. The spiritual marketplace was limited in what it could deliver no matter how creative, exploitative, and well developed it became. Marketeered Hoodoo could not deliver the fresh herbs and roots, nor could it tailor a ritual or a mojo to the client's specific needs. It could not know the old incantations, it could not tie the sacred knots or use the walking boy for individual diagnosis of malady. It could not know the proportions in which High John was mixed with "rattlesnake master" to empower and strengthen a client. As the old tradition slowly died, marketeers continued to make inroads in supplying those root workers, conjurers, and independents who claimed to still practice what was left of the old plantation black belt tradition.

During this period, there developed a deeply intertwined relationship between Hoodoo dream interpretation, the illegal lotteries known as "the numbers," and Hoodoo sign interpretation. An important component in Hoodoo belief has always been the sign. A sign is an unusual occurrence that portends or warns of a coming event. A sign may be great or small, subtle or bodacious. It may be something simple that occurs out of place or it may be something abrupt and commanding your immediate attention. It may appear to be perfectly explainable and suddenly become complex and mysterious. Every human interaction is pregnant with possibilities and has potential to be a sign. Signs may come in dreams or during waking hours. The stories that illustrate the function of the sign are numerous and are told frequently in African American culture. Here are two such tales. A neighbor of mine, Mrs. Austin, an elderly African American woman then in her seventies, told the story of her brother's passing. She explained that a clock, which was believed to be broken and incapable of chiming, chimed at one o'clock. This unusual occurrence was viewed as a sign, a harbinger that something out of the ordinary and unexpected had either happened unbeknownst to her or was about to happen; that something was her brother's demise. The chiming of the clock was the related sign forewarning or informing the family of the impending death.[36]

Another informant in his early nineties told the story of his sister leaving her wristwatch on his kitchen table and how this was a sign. Upon discovering the timepiece on his kitchen table, he insisted, against his family's wishes, upon personally taking the watch to her rather than mailing it from his home in Cleveland, Ohio, to her home in Montgomery, Alabama. He packed the watch in his luggage and boarded a bus for Montgomery. Upon arriving in Montgomery, he went to his sister's house, they ate dinner, enjoyed an evening together, and retired late. Upon awaking in the morning, he entered his sister's room to awaken her; instead he found her dead.[37]

A list of common contemporary signs includes itching palms, usually interpreted as having to do with either losing or acquiring money. It is most often interpreted as a sign that you will soon receive some money. Some believers distinguish between the itching occurring in the left or the right palm. Muscle spasms in the eyelid called "twitching eye" are seen as a sign, usually a sign that trouble is coming. If your feet are swept by someone using a broom to sweep a floor, that is seen as a very serious sign that either bad luck is coming or you may be bound for jail. Dogs barking or howling excessively at night means death is coming.

Some signs such as sweeping of feet must be neutralized by some immediate gesture in order to deflect the coming negative consequences and to restore the balance disrupted by the sign event. Most bad luck signs could be immediately neutralized by gestures that became standardized, like spitting on the broom after one's feet were swept or biting and stepping on one's index finger if you had pointed at a cemetery or a recently covered grave. These latter-day standardized gestures were likely derived from early Hoodoo belief. Other gestures were displayed at the Hoodoo shout that neutralized negative spiritual energies for the plantation slave community.

The faith in signs heavily informed African American spiritual belief and could extend into all areas of black life. As they functioned, signs provided the believer with a rudimentary form of divination that was accessible to everyone, even youngsters. Signs were always regarded as spiritual in nature even when they signaled a secular event. The consciousness of signs extended itself into unexpected areas of African American life, including participation in the illegal lotteries, known in black communities as the numbers.

Though the relationship between sign interpretation, dream interpretation, and the numbers would often prove to be exploitative in nature, that triangular relationship formed a supporting component in the vibrant, alternative, underground economy of many black communities. The daily and sometime weekly income from the numbers was lucrative enough so that African American men often were able to support their families with their weekly take; others supplemented marginal or seasonal employment. Still others prospered and some amassed small fortunes. Numbers was an equal opportunity employer. Though men primarily were numbers runners who carried bets to the numbers station, anyone, regardless of gender, could make a book—as collecting and writing numbers was known—and women often did. The money derived from such an endeavor supplemented scarce household income.

Buttressed initially by post–World War I prosperity, then again during the Great Depression, playing the numbers[38] experienced tremendous growth and expansion in urban black communities. Although the numbers began before World War I, they grew exponentially as black urban population density increased from northward migration. Hoping to hit[39] on a bet as small as one cent, gamblers often saw numbers as a hoped-for possibility for financial gain in the face of limited employment access and the "last hired, first fired" policy. As the growing black urban population began playing numbers, Hoodoo would influence black participation in numbers betting as it had done for other forms of gambling.

It was during this period that dream books and their association with the numbers became familiar to a great many African Americans. A dream book is a book of dream interpretation that assigns corresponding numbers to the subject of the dream. If one dreams of a black cat, then the dreamer looks up "black cat" in the dream book index and finds its corresponding number. Dream books and written numerological interpretations of dreams are much older than one would imagine. According to Gustav Carlson: "The dream book is a very old item of culture since there is evidence of its existence as far back as the time of the ancient Egyptians. . . . We read of dream books being used as long ago as the 16th century in connection with the Italian lottery."[40]

Ancient Greek priestesses of Zeus and Apollo interpreted dreams. Hippocrates, the Greek father of medicine (460–370 BC), believed that dreams could predict upcoming struggle and could reveal information about health, including which organ was affected. Artemidorus, a second-century physician from Roman Asia, wrote what is believed by some to be the first book of dream interpretation. Entitled *Oneirocritica* and written in five small volumes, this book is regarded as the parent of all dream books.[41] Subsequent books on dream interpretation were printed in Greek and translated into Italian and English. Achmed ibn Sirin (born AD 653 in Basra, Iraq) wrote a work of dream interpretations that was printed in Frankfurt, Germany, in 1577 and in Paris in 1603. *The Universal Dream Dictionary* was published in Philadelphia and in Baltimore in 1797 and in Wilmington, Delaware, in 1817. In 1835, U. P. James published the *Complete Fortune Teller and Dream Book* in Cincinnati, Ohio, and in 1848 he published *Sibylline Oracles; or Dreams and Their Interpretations.*[42]

The earliest known dream book thought to have been written by an African American was entitled *The Complete Fortune Teller and Dream Book,* by Chloe Russel, a woman of color; it was written in 1824 and published in 1827. It contained no numbers and gave an alphabetized list of dreams and their interpretations, from "adversity" to "weight." The text also included a discussion of palmistry and the reading of moles on the body.[43]

In 1862 and 1863, publisher Dick and Fitzgerald departed from the previously published dream books and released *The Golden Wheel Dream Book, and Fortune-Teller* and *Le Marchand's Fortune Teller and Dreamers' Dictionary.* Different from all heretofore printed dream books, these two included "luck" numbers following each dream interpretation. From 1862 onward, nearly all dream books published lucky numbers.[44] Today dream books sold in African American communities rarely if ever interpret dreams, they merely give numbers.

Many dream book publishers were like Ed Kay, owner of Dorene Publishing, and Alex Silverberg. Both published dream books, and Silverberg manufactured Hoodoo products as well as supplies and sold them in his store located on South Street in Philadelphia. These spiritual merchants targeted blacks and exercised a very profitable control over the Hoodoo marketplace and Hoodoo ritual artifacts. Silverberg, although he was neither a Hoodoo believer nor a two-head, would make mojo bags for unsuspecting, and oftentimes unknowledgeable, clients. For those same unknowledgeable and culturally displaced clients, his wife invented and manufactured "power pouches."[45] None of these products was properly prepared according to old tradition Hoodoo protocol, the divination was not performed, the problem was not diagnosed, the proper rituals were not enacted, the appropriate incantation or prayer was not said by the appropriate number of "prayer warriors," and the proper forces were not harnessed. Divorced from their own cultural traditions by migration and the desire to discard the past, African American clients were at a loss and could easily be sold the marketeered, snake-oil version of Hoodoo. The marketeers controlled dream book distribution, they profited from the sale of gambling and lucky mojoes, they profited from the sale of incense and candles that revealed numbers when burned, and they controlled the transformation of urbanized Hoodoo artifacts.

Dream books and dream interpretation seem to be a natural outgrowth of the numbers. Like dream books, lottery-style numbers games are far from new. The numbers was based on the old Italian lottery, which, according to sources, began circa 1550 when Benedetto Gentile organized a lottery based on election results. By 1634, the first Genoese Republic instituted a lottery tax, and by 1644 the state had control of the game. By 1860, the Reggio Lotto existed in every Italian state except Sardinia[46] and has continued as the model for American lotteries. Numbers lotteries were probably introduced in America from several independent sources, but by 1720 lotteries actively existed in the colonies and along the East Coast.[47] Believed to have derived from earlier French and Spanish sources, the famous Louisiana lottery began in 1868. But the modern-day lottery in the United States probably appeared somewhere around the end of the nineteenth century with the influx of southern Italian immigrants who controlled the numbers games in several cities.

Other sources state that the numbers game that dominated cities like Tampa and Jacksonville, Florida, in the late 1920s and early 1930s was imported from Havana, Cuba, around the turn of the century. The game

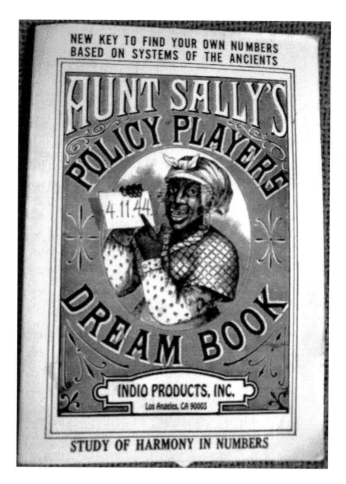

NEW KEY TO FIND YOUR OWN NUMBERS
BASED ON SYSTEMS OF THE ANCIENTS

AUNT SALLY'S
POLICY PLAYERS

4.11.44

DREAM BOOK

INDIO PRODUCTS, INC.
Los Angeles, CA 90003

STUDY OF HARMONY IN NUMBERS

Dream books were an important element in Hoodoo's
relationship with the numbers racket.

spread northward and westward to Baltimore, Pittsburgh, Cleveland, New
York, Atlanta, Kansas City, Toledo, and Detroit.[48] Some sources cite Chinese
numbers games Gee Fah and Pak Kop Piu, which are based upon symbols
rather than numbers, as the source for some lotteries. The Chinese lottery
paid two to one odds and mostly remained confined to the Chinese American and Chinatown communities. Along with these three types of lotteries,
numbers games of numerous types sprang up around the country.

Another widely played type of numbers was based on bets placed on horse
races. Known as both clearinghouse and mutuel race horse policy or simply
mutuel policy, this system used an independent source, rather than an in-

house numbers wheel, or bolita bag to determine the day's winning numbers.[49] Still another type of policy gambling was based on numbers published by the various stock exchanges, including some smaller local exchanges in Cincinnati and Indianapolis. In areas such as Minneapolis and St. Paul, where milling was significant, the number was obtained from the totals of the grain exchange. On the West Coast, the total poundage of the salmon catch was used to determine the number. And in some southern mining regions, the total number of tons of ore mined was used to determine the daily number. Even the figures from the Chicago Butter and Egg Market were used in certain cities. And at one time, the figures of the Weather Bureau Report were used in Washington, DC.[50] But by far the universal favorite was numbers published by the New York Stock Exchange; the number was based on the total stock and bond sales and could be obtained by simply consulting the market close edition of local metropolitan newspapers. Popular all over the country, the stock exchange number was the most widely bet upon, and Hoodoo was used to forecast a winning possibility.

More often than not, Hoodoo patrons placed bets on a winning number or lucky number that they played frequently and even became identified with as "their number." But when the lucky number did not hit quickly enough, some anxious policy players wrote letters to the New York Stock Exchange asking for the upcoming winning number and sometimes proposing types of schemes to win and share the winnings if the stock exchange would comply. Between 1932 and 1935, the New York Stock Exchange received hundreds of letters from the numbers playing public from cities large and small around the country, including Baltimore; Columbus, Ohio; Sharon, Pennsylvania; Sarasota, Florida; Mount Vernon, Ohio; Pittsburgh; Atlanta; Youngstown, Ohio; Detroit; and Buffalo, New York, to mention only a few. Here is an example of one such letter written on November 15, 1935:

New York Stock Exchange,   November 15th, 1935
New York City.

Gentlemen, -
   For many, many weeks I have been trying to "catch" the New York bond on No. 375 – and in looking back upon my records for over a year I note this number has never come out on the Bond – the final three figures of the dollars on the daily transactions of the Exchange as published in the daily papers.
   Is there a reason why 375 has never come out or has it just happened so? Also I note "ooo" has never dropped – there must be a stock exchange superstition against throwing this particular number.

If by any chance 375 could come out once it would save my home and something else besides. Please let me know if I should continue playing 375 or had I better change. And thanking you kindly for your consideration in reading this, my letter, I am,

Very truly yours

———————————

P. O. Box 1334
Tampa, Fla.

Both numbers gambling and the spiritual marketplace experienced tremendous growth during this period. The spiritual marketeers expanded their product lines to include not only more dream books, but an entire line of products aimed at numbers gamblers. Cashing in on the black community's cultural and economic vulnerability, the spiritual marketeers added products such as lucky candles and lucky incense, which revealed a lucky number when burned. They retooled existing products to include luck at the numbers along with other types of luck at gambling. Lucky oil and incense packets, when not prepared to reveal a number when burned, simply included a list of lucky numbers in the package, but at a price. Concerning financial and cultural exploitation of the African American community and the policy player, one researcher had this comment:

> Lucky products command fabulous prices. For example an inch-long piece of Adam and Eve Root is sold for $3.00, the cost of an ounce bottle of holy oil ranges in price from $2 to $20, a snuff of graveyard dust is worth 50 cents, while a good luck ring will bring anywhere from $20 to $100. It is interesting to note that the cost of the ingredients for an ounce of holy oil selling for $20 is a fraction of a cent. Lucky products constitute an important place in the stock of every negro drug-store. They are sold also by salesmen who go from house to house as representatives of such organizations as Oracle Product's Co., Sovereign Products Co. Valmor Products Co., and Alexander's Psychic Aid, Inc.[51]

The older African Americans who knew the old tradition and journeyed back down South to access it were disgusted by, yet powerless against, the urban middlemen minority spiritual marketeers who were actively exploiting, redefining, and helping to transform a long-standing black folk tradition. The demise of the old tradition, symbolized in the death of Dr. Buzzard, signaled the transformation that was taking place in Hoodoo between the two world wars. African American health care, another area of Hoodoo tradition, would also undergo transformation. We will now turn our attention to it.

HEALIN' DA SICK, RAISIN' DA DAID

Hoodoo as Health Care, Root Doctors, Midwives, Treaters

The full dimensions of Hoodoo have been overlooked. Even recent scholarship on Hoodoo has not included a discussion of the medicinal aspect of the tradition. In addition, that scholarship has totally overlooked a discussion of traditional Hoodoo healers: treaters, midwives, and root doctors. Even African Americans who know anything of contemporary Hoodoo will usually not immediately associate it with medicinal herbalism. Hoodoo marketeers were neither interested in nor had access to this aspect of Hoodoo. While much of the magical aspect of Hoodoo would be discarded under the strict dictates of Christianity, science, and commercialism, much of Hoodoo's medicinal herbalism would be kept alive under another label. Home remedies were passed down in extended families from an earlier time, thus assuring that the postemancipation African American community would inherit a well-developed and long-standing folk medicine tradition rich in regional variation. That community, like African communities elsewhere, would also inherit the deep belief that physical illness could have a supernatural cause. This belief would persist among African Americans into the twenty-first century. Hoodoo was believed to be able to cause all types of illness as well as unusual physical and mental symptoms. Even in the late twentieth and early twenty-first centuries, Hoodoo is believed to be capable of causing the following:

1. Paralysis
2. Weight loss
3. Hair loss
4. Loss of willpower
5. Miscarriage
6. Falling obsessively in love
7. Breathing problems
8. Bodily infestations of lizards, snakes, salamanders, worms, spiders
9. Hating one's own family
10. Prolonged constipation/locked bowels
11. Acting like a dog or cat
12. Eliminating feces through nose or mouth
13. Unexplained bodily pain
14. Fits
15. Insanity
16. Impotence/loss of nature
17. Financial trouble
18. Ugliness
19. Swelling of limbs
20. Blindness
21. Arthritis
22. Death
23. Disfiguration
24. Insomnia
25. Paranoia/intense fear[1]

In a majority of poor and working-class black neighborhoods, there was someone at least minimally skilled in administering herbal-based treatments, some of which are used today in African American communities as well as throughout the African diaspora.[2]

The slave "doctor" was a common feature on most plantations of substantial size, and on smaller plantations there was someone at least minimally skilled in naturopathic treatments for physical, mental, and spiritual malady. Herbal healing recipes were but one chapter in Hoodoo's oral textbook. Herbal healers and practitioners such as midwives, treaters, and root doctors mastered treatments and developed their regional pharmacopoeia. In addition, there was an existing body of common knowledge and information grounded in well-known treatment traditions that some individuals applied to themselves. We see an example of this in the slave who wore a buckeye on a string around his neck as a protective medicine.[3] In addition to bringing healing traditions from Africa with them and acquiring medicinal skill on their own, some slaves were owned by white physicians and were trained by them.[4] One such slave named Primus assisted his master, a white doctor, at surgery and began his own practice when his master died.[5] Another slave doctor, who practiced in New Orleans, bought his own freedom after having assisted and apprenticed under three doctors, all of whom owned him at one time or another.[6] Other slaves were owned by pharmacists and assisted in the filling of prescriptions and the making of medicines.[7] And at least one bondsman, Willie Elfe, published his own prescription book.[8] Still others acted as nurses both accompanying their owners and practicing independently applying their knowledge of herbal healing.[9] Midwives were among those who also had herbal medicinal knowledge.

Like their plantation predecessors, most post-Reconstruction midwives harvested their own herbs rather than purchase them. A well-stocked midwife's cabinet would contain "digitalis, golden seal, belladonna, lobelia, sage, henna, rhubarb, May apple, blood root, wild cherry, and numerous others," many that she cultivated herself.[10] Like the old conjurers known as swampers, most midwives were skilled herbalists, knowledgeable in both the identification of and use of plants and other natural substances such as natural clay dirt and insect nests. In addition to midwifery, she often used the herbs in other types of "doctorin.'" Sometimes known as a medicine woman, and skilled in herbal treatment, the doctor-midwife specialized in roots related to matters of romance and of the heart. She knew which roots, herbs, substances, prayers, and rituals would "get a husband," restore "nature,"[11] and help the childless to conceive.

The midwife tradition among enslaved plantation women emerged out of necessity and fulfilled a need in both the slave quarter and in the freedmen communities. These women would also be called on to deliver white babies. This aspect of the Hoodoo tradition would be handed down to the next generation through community apprenticeships by practicing midwives. Researcher Holly F. Mathews reveals:

> Most midwives learned their trade through long apprenticeships to older, established midwives, usually their kinswomen. The apprenticed girl would accompany her mentor on visits to pregnant women, sew and clean for them, and stay with them after their babies were born. After years of attending births and after having their own first child, the apprentice could begin to assist at deliveries and eventually answer night calls for the senior

midwife. When the senior midwife decided to retire, she would officially hand over her practice and patients to her chosen successor. In this way, the traditions of midwifery were passed from generation to generation and continuity in belief and practice were maintained.[12]

African women who were transported to the New World as captives would have been aware of traditional African birthing practices, and many probably had given birth. Some undoubtedly were traditional birth attendants in their homeland. The African American midwife in some instances was also a competent treater of ailments and possessed skill in aspects of conjure related to love, marriage, and family. As an essential part of a cooperative Hoodoo network that included conjurers, root doctors, apothecary workers, hospital workers, gravediggers, morticians, and other midwives, she frequently had contact with conjurers and other types of root doctors.

In her close contact with conjurers, the midwife was the only direct supply line through which conjurers could obtain umbilical cords, cauls, or other supplies associated with birth. Even midwives who worked with white physicians would secretly steal cauls and sell them to conjure doctors.[13] Frequently the midwife was also a conjurer, and she could use any cauls, umbilical cords, or placentas that she could obtain. Describing one such midwife-conjurer, author F. Roy Johnson describes Aunt Joe: "Aunt Jo (Sephine) Minton (1873–1927) of the Diamond Bridge area on the Nottoway River a short distance in Virginia from Como began to collaborate with her first cousin Jim Jordan. . . . She was recognized as a good mid-wife, herb doctor and conjure woman."[14]

Believed by some to have been a midwife, New Orleans Voodoo legend Marie Laveau appears to have accompanied midwives who attended births. Claiming to have known Laveau, ex-slave N. H. Hobley had this comment:

> Now that it's all over, here are some practices of Marie Laveau. She stood in with midwives and—as there was no law then requiring birth records—she obtained the bodies of babies soon after they were born. They were then dried out by being treated in some way, left to hang up a chimney and smoked until they was so black you couldn't tell whether they were born white or colored, and so shriveled as to be unrecognizable. You would not know they were human. These, she used in her ceremonies. She had a cabinetmaker make neat little boxes out of cedar, and in each one she put one of these mummies or skeletons. They were then bought by rich men who put them in their safes to ward off evil spirits.[15]

Whether the idea that Marie Laveau was a midwife was mythical or not, the association of midwifery with conjure was firm. Claiming to be a midwife and using the title imparted a level of legitimacy to women root workers and female Hoodoos. Numerous conjure women used the title and probably attended births, but their primary function was not in the area of delivering babies. In forty-six counties in Alabama in 1925, most of the women claiming to be midwives attended no more than one delivery in six months and 28 percent of the known midwives reported attending no births in that year. By comparison, 26 percent of the known midwives in the forty-six counties attended seventy percent of the births.[16] Why did so many women claim to be midwives when in fact they were not attending births or delivering babies? The title "midwife" imparted not only legitimacy but also community status as well as a degree of legal protection under which a conjure woman could safely operate.

Also known as granny midwives, these women were significant facilitators in both the spiritual and physical aspects of birth. Through prayer, incantation, potions, amulets, sacred objects, procedures, and rituals, they treated and safeguarded the birthing woman's heightened spiritual vulnerability. The midwife's bag contained materials from the old tradition that she clandestinely used even after state regulation of midwife practices forbade it. Some midwives even created two bags, one for state inspection and one for traditional ritual use.[17] Where the midwife's conjure skill and spiritual belief were well developed, she could engage in minimum ritual, something as simple as driving three brand-new nails into the threshold of the house to distract malevolent spirits that might interfere with the birth process.[18] These nails served also to warn bad spirits of the midwife's spiritual strength and power. In cases of premature infant death or death shortly after birth, the bereaved mother was given ritual instructions by the midwife to protect against death claiming another of her infants. This is reminiscent of certain practices among traditional West and Central West Africans. The Yoruba provide us with the example of *abiku,* a child who is born to die. If the cycle of stillbirth or sudden death is not broken, then the *abiku* will return and die innumerable times. In his book *Way of the Orisha,* American author Philip John Neimark tells of his ordeal with *abiku* and how, after losing two children at birth, he enlisted a Babalawo, high priest of the Yoruba religion, who fastened his newborn's soul to the earth using a traditional implement, an Ogun chain, in order to prevent his newborn infant's death.[19] African American midwifery was a place where Hoodoo ritual related to birth and sometimes death was fully functioning, inadvertently preserving and safeguarding what would otherwise soon become a moribund tradition.

The midwife, even more so than the conjurer, root doctor, or treater, stood in the doorway separating life and death, natural and supernatural, spiritual and physical worlds. Her methods were frequently part conjure ritual, part herbal tradition, and part folk medicine. Like the conjurer, root doctor, treater, and preacher, the midwife was often called into service through supernatural occurrence, such as a recurring dream or a vision. Describing the two-part vision that called her to her work as a midwife, Aunt Quintilla, an African American Virginia midwife recalls:

> Den I had annuder call, . . . I was washin' de clo'es on de back po'ch, and de suds pile up lak de clouds in de sky. All in a minnit I seen a bright light an' a han' come right up outen de suds hol'in a fiery sword an' a voice says, "Quintilla, why aint you obeyed de call?"[20]

As with the many Hoodoo practitioners and believers, the midwife was usually well connected and often prominent in several roles in the widespread network of her church community, which frequently provided her with client referrals. Often she was a church official such as a deaconess or church mother. And it was there that she was important in the movement of Hoodoo into black American church ritual that used aspects of the Bible, especially the Psalms, in replacing lost African prayers and incantations. An example of the Psalms used for healing and restoring ill health can be found in Psalms 42 and 43. A major player in the Hoodoo community, she was both a carrier of tradition and a significant elder with the power to label and sanction behaviors. Within her community, she was sought as a counselor, advisor, mediator, assistant, and visionary. Her counsel was considered expert in advising women on cultural knowledge of men. She was keeper of ritual and procedures that would allow a woman some degree of control over her husband's fidelity, loyalty, and devoted love. She knew the awesome legacy of the power of menstrual blood, perspiration, and urine, and she knew how to direct and use them with maximum efficacy. With a good supply of cauls, umbilical cords, and placentas available to her, she primarily controlled love charms and rituals related to conception and female sexual potency. She advised, soothed, counseled, and supported women, particularly in their role as mothers and wives. And she controlled the tying of the dreaded nature sack.

This old tradition Hoodoo charm has been confused and mislabeled "nation sack" by those who misunderstood certain African American pronunciation patterns and who believed that blacks were mispronouncing the word *nation* instead of *nature,* which was pronounced "naitcha."[21] Others confuse this mojo with the donation sacks carried by both tent revival preachers as well as some prostitutes around Memphis, Tennessee, in the late 1800s and described as existing only in Memphis. As referred to by seminal bluesman

Robert Johnson in his song "Come on in My Kitchen," it is a purse or sack smaller than but resembling tent show preachers' donation sacks:

> Oh-ah, she's gone
> I know she won't come back
> I've taken the last nickel
> out of her nation sack
> You better come on
> in my kitchen
> babe, it's goin' to be rainin' outdoors

This could possibly have been a true nature sack he was referring to, and the record company translated and corrected his pronunciation and wrote "nation" instead of "nature." Prostitutes who carried purses for their earnings began calling them donation sacks as a barb at the donation-collecting practices of the self-righteous traveling preachers who in their sermons often targeted prostitutes as examples of sin. On the other hand, the true Hoodoo nature sack, a female-controlled mojo, was wrapped from Virginia to Texas, not in only one city. Marketeers are responsible for asserting the misleading and ridiculous information.

Original Hoodoo nature sacks were tied by midwife conjure women all over the black belt South, not simply in Memphis. The confusion of the donation sack with the Hoodoo nature sack probably originated with misinterpretations of Harry Middleton Hyatt's work *Hoodoo-Conjuration-Witchcraft-Rootwork* and a misreading of southern black pronunciation patterns. The misinterpretation has been perpetrated by Hoodoo exploiters and marketeers. Various readings of Hyatt's work probably further confused the issue.[22] Like High John and midwifery, this and other types of mojoes have not been sufficiently discussed in either the scholarly or popular literature on Hoodoo; nevertheless, the midwife-conjure woman was the guardian of the dreaded nature sack. This type of amulet-mojo was believed to be extremely powerful when tied properly, tailoring and integrating all the necessary elements of time, location, direction, and ingredients.

The purpose of the nature sack was to enable a woman to control her man's ability to become sexually aroused and achieve an erection with another woman. To be most effective, the nature sack had to be tied during coitus, with the final knot tied during the man's ejaculation. The woman desiring such a mojo was given strict details, instructions, prohibitions, and warnings. This type of mojo was known to cause trembling in men who were Hoodoo believers and was feared by women and approached cautiously. If a woman was caught in the act of tying a nature sack on a man, her life could be in peril. Even the mere mention of the nature sack could incite extreme reactions in some men, even those claiming to be nonbelievers. Women as well as men sometimes sought out conjurer-midwives to restore a man's nature. These lay fertility and sexuality specialists prescribed herbs, potions, and certain foods to increase male sexual potency and increase a woman's chances of conceiving.

In addition to "catchin' babies," midwives were consulted for advice on marital problems. They acted as lay psychologists and community counselors. In African American neighborhoods, there was frequently at least one well-respected church community elder who was sought out for her advice, counseling, and support. These granny midwives performed any number of birth-related duties, including staying on with the new mother and infant for an extended time during the postpartum period. Like the contemporary doula, the midwife would help with housework, cooking, and child care. She would also instruct the new mother on diet, postpartum bodily care, infant care, household safety, and spiritual protection. A North Carolina midwife reveals:

> You teach them how to take care of themselves, to keep the house clean and proper for a baby, 'bout good food to eat so they'll have good milk and how to make the baby's clothes. Then you get ready for the birthin' so they won't be scared and you be there with them any time of day or night. Lord, I've been called at some strange times. But when that baby's comin' there ain't nothin' for it but to do it. And stay—stayin' after, that's the thing. That's when they really need you more than in the catchin' 'cause after is when the tiredness sets in and they're weak and that's when the baby prone to sickness. So I'se always been one to stay as long as they needed me; to help clean, cook, and sometimes show 'em what to do with that little baby. And I never lost but one baby in all my days of work.[23]

Revered for their knowledge, ability, skill, and power, midwives were women held in high social esteem in the rural African American communities of the black belt South.[24] This high esteem could possibly be another reason that so many black women claimed that title. Because she encountered medical personnel such as physicians and nurses and because she also attended birthing white women, the black midwife sometimes stood between two racial worlds, one black, one white, and forged a link by forcing open a door in mainstream society unknown to many African Americans of the period. Describing one such midwife-conjure woman, Aunt Molly Kirby, who attended white women and was allowed into areas off-limits to most African Americans, an informant tells us:

We didn't have a big time herbist. People got their own herbs from the field or the store. There was Aunt Molly Kirby, they called her, a great big black woman. She made herb medicines and hoodoos. Lots of men went to her when they had social diseases. She was also a midwife, delivered a world of babies. She's go out on the mountain and deliver babies. They didn't allow colored people out there much, but they allow her.[25]

Usually called in months before the delivery, the midwife supported the overall needs of the pregnant woman. Using parallel practices found in traditional West African cultures, including abdominal massage, belief in birthmarks, burial of the placenta, use of sharp metal objects to ward off a malevolent spirits, and geophagy, if the midwife suspected the possibility of miscarriage, she took a particular course of action. In an interview, Granny Ya, an eighty-six-year-old treater and former midwife, explains: "I put a red rag around them if I think they gon miscarry, and it hold the baby there. When child got asthma, or got attaché (overgrown liver), I put the cloth back on. (She used red strips of cloth for women of childbearing age)."[26] In her role as midwife and healer, the granny was the guardian of one aspect of the Hoodoo tradition. Her ceremonies, rituals, and practices involved a holistic approach to treatment and support. In the absence of twilight sleep and pain-deadening epidurals, the granny depended on the power of self-hypnosis and suggestion framed by ritual practice as she placed a sharpened axe under the laboring woman's bed in the belief that the axe would cut the pain.[27] To time the birth, she used her own natural timing devise, a dried fern with tightly curled fronds, known in contemporary botanicas as either rose of Jericho or resurrection plant. An informant tells us:

When she arrived at the bedside of a labor patient she put the dried plant into a bowl of water, lighted her pipe, sat down, and watched the fronds unfold. They gave her full information about the child's progress on its journey into this world. If the leaves caught on one another or opened unevenly she feared trouble and resorted to action. The value of this charm was far-famed, and because of it she had a large and respectful clientele.[28]

The Hoodoo-informed birthing ritual was both simple and elaborate and included the donning of ritual clothing, usually by the birthing mother. The items included ceremonial necklaces from either herbs, bones, animal teeth, or other items and ritual clothing, usually one of the husband's scent-laden, well-worn, and unwashed shirts or a hat. The midwife controlled the "sacred birthing flame" built in the hearth. This flame was used to convert and mark the fireplace as a temporary sacred altar with ritual care procedures. These procedures dictated how long the flame should burn as well as when and how the ashes were used and disposed of.

African American midwives developed and maintained a body of evolving spiritual knowledge and information about the use of plants and other substances as they responded to the changing needs of their clientele. They collected and tested numerous folk remedies and rituals; among them, remedies for diminishing childbirth pain, for avoiding birthmarks, and for treating abnormal conditions in both the infant and mother. Their knowledge and experience enabled them to establish and control the psychosocial atmosphere in the birthing chamber. The midwife engaged in behaviors and practices expected by the birthing mother. She also was the essential link between the birthing mother and the wider community. In the cultural context of birthing, she helped reinforce expectations and fulfilled them by moving the mother through the ritualized stages of birth.

While performing the necessary tasks such as cutting the umbilical cord, the midwife would also obtain the placenta; this she used as a divination instrument. The midwife would "read the knots" in the placenta to predict the number of children a woman would bear. Describing the procedure as performed by Miss Katie, a local midwife, Cornelia Bailey tells us:

> Now if Elise had been Ada's first child, Miss Katie would have read the knots in the afterbirth, as the midwife always did after the first child was born. By that, I mean she would have counted the knots when the first child came and predicted how many more kids you would have. Miss Katie would read those knots, and lots of time she'd say, "Oh Lord, plenty of knots in this one. You gonna have plenty chirren."[29]

The midwife was also directly responsible for ensuring a proper and secure burial for the placenta.

As with the conjurers, demeanor was an essential component in the midwife's success. She needed to move with the quiet authority of supernatural power, conveying confidence and spiritual support to the birthing mother. Most midwives were regarded as spiritually well developed as they used prayers and incantations to pull down supernatural power in supporting the birthing process and the midwife's work.

The midwife was also the essential person involved in postpartum care. As with the birth, certain postpartum ritual procedures were followed and brought into play. One researcher tells us:

> The midwife was responsible for instructing the mother in the performance of prescribed precautionary measures during the particularly vulnerable

postpartum period and overseeing rites to celebrate and protect the newborn. Since the acceptance of a range of living spirits, good and evil, is not unusual, the community valued the midwives' role in providing instruction on how to mitigate such forces during the postpartum period.[30]

She was directly involved in the related Hoodoo rituals of "taking up the mother" and "calling the baby's spirit." Frequently, on the ninth day after birth, the mother was both helped to her feet by the midwife and slowly walked counterclockwise, the circling direction of the sacred Ring Shout, around the house. Then she was given a thimble of water to drink when she returned indoors. The midwife also took up the newborn and walked the sacred counterclockwise circle around the house, speaking to the infant and calling its name.[31] In some places like central Alabama, the mother took up the infant and circled the house either three, seven, or nine days after the birth, and she consumed the thimble of water. A Eutaw, Alabama, resident informs us: "My baby was, I believe, it was two weeks old when they made me go around the house with the thimble of water. Mama brought me the thimble of water, and I had to carry it all the way around the house. Mama made me drink it when I got back. It was just a swallow. It was a little small thimble."[32]

During the period between the two world wars, the lay midwife profession among blacks declined; North Carolina appears typical. In 1917 there were nine thousand midwives in North Carolina; eight years later, in 1925, North Carolina led the nation with sixty-five hundred practicing midwives who delivered one-third of all babies born that year.[33] By 1931 there were 2,234 fewer practicing midwives delivering 31 percent of all babies born. By 1940 the percentage of midwife-assisted births declined to 24.6 percent, and by 1950 only 10.9 percent of all births in North Carolina were midwife-assisted. The number of practicing registered midwives declined concomitantly to only 915 by 1950.[34] Similar patterns of decline can be observed in all the black belt areas, especially Mississippi, Alabama, South Carolina, Virginia, and Georgia.

The rapid decline in black midwifery resulted in part from protracted attacks by the medical profession and its promotion of the new medical specialty of obstetrics and gynecology. Describing the process in North Carolina, Holly F. Mathews states: "War was declared on the granny midwife by the General Assembly of the state in 1912 with the passage of a law granting any county board of health the power to license and control midwives."[35] But it was not until 1917 that Rocky Mount, North Carolina, began to enforce a local law that required that midwives pass an examination.[36] The attack further included berating the midwife and distorting the contrast between midwives and doctors. A massive propaganda campaign was waged that used racist stereotypes and images to support its arguments.

Midwives were by no means the only type of Hoodoo health care provider available to the black community. Other types of Hoodoo health care personnel included treaters. Treaters were a type of healer, either male or female, who used herbs, roots, prayers, rituals, amulets, and incantations to effect a positive change in a personal malady. Contemporary treaters are the direct descendants of the old plantation conjurer doctors, though all of them, when confronted with the label "Hoodoo," "conjure," or even "root work," denied any relationship whatsoever.[37] Treaters were a diversified group, and the midwife was often also one type of treater.

Another type of treater was simply known as "doctor." Like the conjurer and the midwife, the doctor stood astride the physical and spiritual worlds in his or her approaches and techniques as well as in the supplies used. The doctor's work overlapped with both the midwife's and the conjurer's work. In the slave community, the doctor was often the same individual but frequently had specialized knowledge, ability, or gifts, such as the ability to "blow out fire" or ease the pain from burns.[38] Slave healers, like their African predecessors, used insects in addition to plants and other substances to treat malady. Enslaved African Americans were known to use maggots to treat external infections. The maggots ate away the dead and infected tissue, leaving clean, healthy tissue in its place, and the larvae produced a secretion that had additional antiseptic and medical value in healing and restoring the tissue. A popular novel of the 1960s leaves us this description of Mere Angelique, a slave conjure doctor, and her use of maggots, incantations, and prayer to heal and treat infected tissue. After applying a poultice of medicinal herbs and other healing substances to Drum's badly infected leg, she:

> . . . reached for the red cock, and she laid it on its back on the floor. Taking a long knife from her basket, she held it over the bird while she mumbled another series of unintelligible words. . . . With one slash of the knife, she laid the fowl open, neatly cleaving it from neck to tail. Spreading open its severed body, she laid it over the steaming poultice, . . . and bandaged the whole agglomeration tightly to Drum's leg.
>
> "Six days"—she counted them off on her fingers—"six days no touch. Bile this." She handed a tied bundle of herbs to Rachele. "Make him drink it. Keep him shittin' all-a time. Make him drink lots water. Keep him pissin' all-a time." She pointed to the bulging bandage on Drum's leg. "Pretty

soon big stink. Phew! But no take off. One day God de father, one day, Holy Virgin, one day Jesus Christ, three days conjur' spirits, much betta goddam strong." . . . Mere Angelique arrived again, took a long satisfied look at her patient, and then, with the same knife that had split the cock, she proceeded to cut off the putrid poultice attached to Drum's leg. It came off in a mass of crawling maggots, but after Mere Angelique had washed the leg with warm water, there was nothing but a clean, nearly healed wound in the midst of an expanse of pale lavender-colored flesh.[39]

One technique used by all three types of Hoodoo health care providers was the method of using string to tie sacred healing knots. Abayomi Sofowora speaks of this practice in West Africa, where both healing and preventative medicine used the string tied around the waist or worn as a necklace.[40] Once widespread throughout West Africa, the technique of healing and rebalancing by using string and sacred knots was carried to the Americas by captive Africans. The healing string would outlive American slavery and survive in isolated pockets of African American culture at least until the early twenty-first century.

The string as a healing device was recorded by Newbell Niles Puckett in South Carolina in the 1920s and 1930s. String or yarn soaked in turpentine and worn around the waist for nine days was used to cause abortion.[41] Tied around the head with a knot in front, the string was used to treat headaches.[42] Tied around the neck or, like the Yoruba/Lucumi "first hand of Ifa" (*primer mano de Ifa*), tied around the left wrist using sixteen knots and traditional prayer, the string was seen as a powerful protective device.[43] One of Puckett's informants, Ms. Hattie Harris of Columbus, Mississippi, prescribed the knotted string for treating chills.[44] The healing string was photographed in active use on St. Helena Island, South Carolina, in 1934, and its most recent use was recorded in Opaloosas, Louisiana, in 1994 by Wanda Fontenot. Though Puckett's and Fontenot's works were in different states and were separated by more than seven decades, the similarities that they documented in the use, approach, and techniques of string healing are undeniable. Tied by various peoples from Senegal down to the Kongo, the string in West Africa was used for rebalancing as well as for healing and protection.

Fontenot's work on African American ethnomedicine documented nine types of healing amulets, five of which use string and knots. The nine types are the single-knot string amulet, the multiknot amulet, the root necklace, the prayer bead necklace, the prayer cloth, the biblical scroll, the walking cane, religious lithography, and the silver coin,[45] but the most widely used is the single knot string amulet. According to Fontenot:

NUTMEG, RED FLANNEL, AND SILVER

Whole nutmeg strung around the neck, red flannel wrap,
and a silver dime strung around the ankle as medicine.
(Photo courtesy of Newbell Niles Puckett, *Folk Beliefs of the
Southern Negro*, Montclair, N.J.: Patterson Smith, 1968).

Of the nine amulets, the *single-knot string* amulet is considered the dominant ritual artifact. It usually is made with cord string and has nine knots
tied on it. In most cases it is a part of the healing rituals of the treaters and
is commonly prescribed for children and adults. The single string amulet
can be made to be worn around the waist, across the chest (the string fits
over one shoulder and under the opposite arm), the wrist, the ankle, or

Child in foreground wearing two medicine packets attached to the African
healing string. Photo taken in Colombia, South America, in 2000.
(Dr. Thomas. B. Morton © 2000)

the neck, depending on what area of the body is afflicted. The common
colors are white, red, and black.[46]

The various colors of string further specify its function. Fontenot continues:

> The red is used for women of childbearing age who suffer with a history
> of miscarriages, difficult pregnancies, excessive bleeding after giving birth,
> and irregular menses. The red string amulet is a specialty of midwives. The
> white is used for any sex, any age, and any disease. The black is used for
> young children suffering with worms.[47]

The multiknot amulet, considered very powerful and worn only around
the waist, is often prescribed for adults suffering from multiple problems.
Composed of the single-string amulet with a macramé-type knot in the
center, the multiknot amulet is used less often than the single-knot type.
More difficult to tie and considered very powerful, "the multiple center
knots," according to one practitioner, "represent every organ and bone in
an individual's body."[48]

The silver dime amulet was undoubtedly the most widely used by African Americans. Sometimes selected for its "man" or "woman" qualities, dimes were either male or female because the portrait on the coin was either male or female. If the required male dime was not available, then the charm was reversed so that a female dime could be used for male work if necessary, but that required additional knowledge and steps in the ritual. Observed in northern black communities in the early 1950s by this author, the silver dime amulet was nearly universally known by American blacks until the silver dime was modified with a copper filling by the United States Mint. The coin's modification coincided with, but probably had little effect on, the declining status of Hoodoo as an independent alternative approach and perspective on the world. Sometimes silver dimes and High John roots were sewn alternately on a narrow cloth belt that was tied around the waist to heal, strengthen, and protect the wearer.

The string, sometimes constructed either as a belt, an anklet, a bracelet, or a necklace, served to focus the individual's psychic energies on that part of the body that required medical attention. It provided the conduit for a uniting of the spiritual and physical energies, which were constantly being refocused and rebalanced by the string. It turned the self-healing receptors inward and opened up the individual so that healing could occur. It also prepared the individual for the healing process. It raised confidence and psychic strength and tapped into the individual's ability to heal himself through positive thinking. It focused the psychic healing resources on that part of the individual that required treatment. Medical personnel, including doctors and nurses, are now recognizing the healing benefits of spiritual beliefs and supports, and some doctors are even using their patients' belief systems to support their own treatment of patients.

Though more widely known today for his magical and spiritual manipulations, the conjurer was also sought as a health care provider. The conjurer, root doctor, health care tradition extended from West and Central West Africa to the North American plantation, where conjurers were often the sole health care provider treating both black and white patients. The tradition that united the magical with the medicinal in a balanced spiritual framework was the African medicinal legacy inherited by the plantation conjurer. According to historian Eugene Genovese, "The most important positive application of charms came in slave medical practice."[49] The slave conjurers, root doctors, and midwives passed on a vast body of knowledge of naturopathic healing techniques. The old tradition accumulated a storehouse of knowledge, such as pennyroyal tea used for female complaints, sassafras tea used for measles, mint tea used for abdominal problems, and Spanish moss used to treat asthma.[50]

Not only were herbs and roots, with incantations, ritual procedures, and prayers used, the earth itself was used as a healing device to restore use of limbs. In seaside communities such as Sapelo Island, Georgia, and Mobile, Alabama, the power of the earth itself was harnessed to treat both humans and animals stricken with impaired use of lower limbs. At the shore, a deep hole was dug in the sand and the afflicted individual was buried in a standing position up to the chest. A shelter was constructed over exposed body parts to protect them from the elements, insects, and inclement weather. Water would be continually fed to the patient to prevent dehydration; this treatment was continued for three days while pressure from the sand combined with the sand's mineral content and the raw power of the spinning earth straightened out and strengthened the afflicted limbs. Cornelia Walker Bailey informs us of the procedure described by her Uncle Nero:

> He believed in the power of the earth to heal—just sand, doing its work . . . said the Creator created us from sand from the earth, so the earth was special, it had special healing properties. . . . Uncle Nero said he would dig a hole straight down and he would put Ophelia in there and he's straighten out Ophelias legs and he's pack sand around them, and that sand would keep her legs straight. He would keep packing sand around her, just up to a certain point that was high enough, but not up to her head, so there wasn't gonna be any danger to Ophelia, she wasn't gonna suffocate or anything. Ophelia would just be in a hole in a standing position for three days and three nights.[51]

Another example tells us of thirty-five-year-old John Isaac of Montgomery, Alabama, who was suddenly stricken with an unknown affliction that made him unable to walk without the use of crutches. In an attempt to find a cure, he was sent to his older sister's house in Mobile, Alabama, where he was taken to the beach and buried in a standing position in sand up to his chest. He returned to Montgomery about two weeks later fully restored, walking without the use of crutches.[52]

Professor James Turner of the Cornell University Africana Studies and Research Center shared the following story of his personal encounter with the Hoodoo medical legacy. His aunt had a serious malady in her arm. Doctors were unable to cure the condition, and as it worsened, amputation was presented to the family as the only lifesaving solution. According to Turner, his aunt—as with many African Americans—had little trust of white doctors, and when the physician suggested amputation of the arm she refused. She instead turned to Hoodoo medicine, boarded a bus, and headed for upcountry South Carolina, where she had been born and had grown up. She embraced and had faith in the power of old tradition Hoodoo healing procedures. She was taken to community "doctors," who treated her from the rituals and herbal medicine of the old tradition and who saved both her arm and her life. After several weeks of treatment, she returned to New York with her arm fully healed and restored.

The attempt to eliminate slave medical practice, which began in earnest in 1748 and probably was made more so from fear of slave poisonings than of concern for competence, was never wholly successful among either blacks or whites in the antebellum environment. Though the late nineteenth century saw an increase in the attacks on the black herbal medicine tradition, that attack, like earlier efforts, was less than successful. Blacks and some whites continued to seek treatment, advice, and support from African American root doctors as well as other black health care providers.

Born in 1812 and probably America's most famous nineteenth-century root doctor, Dr. James Still of southern New Jersey was known to locals as "Dr. James of the Pine Barrens." The brother of abolitionist William Still, Dr. James Still was widely sought and consulted by both blacks and whites with medical concerns. Though he never claimed to be either a medical doctor or a Hoodoo practitioner, he did invest his herbal potions and remedies with spiritual potency through prayer. As the child of slaves, he was exposed to and adhered to disconnected elements of the Hoodoo belief system, such as the belief in luck, as the following passage indicates:

> Leaving Samuels, I started for Philadelphia. I went by by-roads and through woods. After traveling about two hundred yards in a woods, I spied a large black-snake lying a little to my left. I seized a stick close at hand, and killing the snake, threw away the stick and was about to gather up my pack and go on, when on the other side of the way, I beheld another as large as the first. I picked up the stick again and killed it, also. Now, thought I, good luck will attend me, as I had heard say "Kill the first snake you see in the new year and you shall kill your enemies."[53]

Like his contemporaries the swampers, Dr. James Still dug and harvested his own roots and distilled a wide range of oils, essences, and potions that he sold to Philadelphia druggists Charles and William Ellis.[54] He distilled sassafras roots and peppermint and used his own healing herbal recipes made from a range of plants and roots, including saffron, ipecac, pleurisy root, Virginia snakeroot, lobelia, bloodroot, cloves, comfrey, horehound, elecampane, skunk cabbage, spikenard root, Alexandria senna, mayapple, cream of tartar, catnip, boneset, and High John root.

Nicknamed "Mr. Buzzard" by other young men he encountered one day while chopping wood for a living, Dr. Still's nickname may have been an appellation applied to any man who was skilled in either medicinal or magico-spiritual root work. In African American culture, the buzzard has appeared in dance, song, folktale, joke, and riddle, attesting to its now lost significance as part of the Hoodoo worldview and applied not only to Dr. James Still but also to America's most famous conjurer, Dr. Buzzard, Stepheney Robinson of St. Helena Island, South Carolina. The reference to the bird may have been handed down either from African cultural tradition or from a Native American appellation easily adopted by Africans and their descendants.

By whatever name they were designated, all the late-nineteenth- and early-twentieth-century African American folk health care providers had one common concern relating to the wider society: being arrested and charged with practicing medicine without a license. It seems that this charge particularly was used to suppress anyone functioning as a folk healer, and it was used to suppress and legally threaten the root brotherhood. The control, containment, and suppression of patent medicines during this period had a further undermining influence on Hoodoo. The establishment of regulatory efforts at the turn of the twentieth century modified the public atmosphere in which folk medicine would be regarded and practiced. Two important regulatory acts overlapped and framed the period: the 1906 Federal Food and Drugs Act and the 1938 Food, Drug, and Cosmetic Act. These two acts addressed issues of truthful labeling and allowed government officials to assert some degree of control and regulation over products and substances that might threaten public safety. Those included nearly everything from drugs such as opium and cocaine to food additives and adulterants of all types.

Fueled by muckraking journalism, a new public discourse emerged that would favor government oversight and regulation of foods, drugs, and medicines. African Americans would be late to follow this trend. But their distrust of white doctors, the medical profession generally,[55] and the oppositional cultural attitudes toward the white mainstream reinforced the fact that blacks had profound faith in their own medicinal legacy and healing practices. This all predisposed them to supporting and seeking out a tradition passed down to them by their elders. The African American belief in the "night doctor" and the "needle doctor"[56] reminded and warned blacks that they should not trust the medical profession and that instead they should seek out midwives, root doctors, conjurers, treaters, and healers of the old Hoodoo tradition. Of the cultural attitudes contributing to the maintenance of Hoodoo medicine, the long-standing belief that the medical profession continues to experiment on blacks is the most potent and influential.

A 2002 questionnaire on Hoodoo belief revealed interesting results. Of the thirty-six African American women who returned the survey from a field of one hundred distributed, twenty-seven, or 75 percent, revealed that they have known someone who believes that doctors may be experimenting on blacks. Twenty-six, or 72 percent of respondents revealed that they personally believed that doctors may be experimenting on blacks.[57]

In the hands of either the uninitiated or the exploitative marketeer, Hoodoo medicine could prove to be anything from less than helpful to fatal, particularly when an ailing individual encountered a charlatan or when he or she simply asked a friend how to treat an ailment. In the case of a potentially fatal ailment or public health threat like venereal disease, the home remedies circulating in public discourse could prove fatal. By the time a young man asked someone to suggest a home treatment, that particular treatment may have been modified in the public discourse and assigned to an inapplicable malady, as in the following case:

> I drew them into a conversation, finally asking what I should do for gonorrhea. One of them said that he had had the "clap" several times and while he knew of others who spent large sums of money to get rid of it, he never spent more than ten or fifteen cents. . . . He told me to get ten cents worth of turpentine and take nine drops at a time on a spoonful of brown sugar.[58]

Public health studies document what some young men suggest as a treatment for either syphilis or gonorrhea. A 1931 New Orleans public health survey indicates that black men in the survey were only about one-third as likely as white men to seek out a physician or clinic when ill. Seventy percent of black men surveyed said that they would use some form of home remedy, while only forty-six, less than half, white men said they would use a home remedy.[59] Studies conducted in Chicago and Washington, DC, reveal similar trends.[60]

Many of the supplies used in self-medication and self-treatment could be purchased at the local drugstore, sometimes a Hoodoo drugstore. Hoodoo drugstores were commercial sites where the magical and medicinal aspects of Hoodoo were reunited; those establishments were common throughout the black belt South. Very different than today's drugstores, these establishments were sometimes owned by a doctor who filled prescriptions as well as created treatments for various symptoms. Hoodoo drugstores were a significant component in urban folk medicine and home remedies in the late nineteenth and early twentieth centuries. According to researcher Carolyn Morrow Long:

> [W]hite people were also entering the spiritual business, often through ownership of a neighborhood drugstore with a predominantly black clientele. The pharmacy was a common source for the "materiamedica" of hoodoo. In the nineteenth and early twentieth centuries, all pharmacies stocked botanicals, oils, essences, and flavorings for the formulation of healing preparations, and they sold common household preservatives and cleaners such as alum, saltpeter, ammonia, laundry bluing, lye, and sulfur. . . . Certain white druggist were willing to make up hoodoo "prescriptions" for customers.[61]

The most famous of all the Hoodoo drugstores was the Cracker Jack Drug Store, located at 435 South Rampart Street in New Orleans. Founded as an ordinary drugstore in 1897 by a white pharmacist physician, George A. Thomas, the Thomas Drugstore eventually became a spiritual market and in 1932 was renamed the Cracker Jack Drug Store, a name it retained until it closed in 1974.[62]

As a commercial folk health care site, the Hoodoo drugstore was a station at which numerous spiritual trains stopped. These establishments would eventually bring together a range of spiritual and occult practitioners and traditions that had previously little if any access to one another. These were sites for cross-fertilization and change, a place where the high practitioners and potential patrons met and exchanged information, knowledge, and tradition. It was also a place where new approaches to Hoodoo would be created and sold by outsider merchants and always with marketeering and profit as their primary intent.

7

BLACK BELT HOODOO IN THE POST–WORLD WAR II CULTURAL ENVIRONMENT

The aftermath of World War II, particularly its benefits in the form of educational supports, jobs, pensions, and housing benefits from the GI bill to returning African American servicemen, would provide the black community with both incentives and opportunities for continuing migration northward. Increased income, though racially circumscribed in northern black communities, intensified the movement away from old black belt traditions. In some cases, the old Hoodoo continuum would experience internally generated redefinition, particularly through church-connected Hoodoo workers. But in the northern urban environment, marketeered Hoodoo would dominate in many black communities.

Hoodoo's first urban face, which appeared in the smaller cities and towns of the postemancipation black belt South, was unlike its latter-day counterpart in large northern metropolises and even some large southern cities. The style of early, urban, black-controlled Hoodoo was very much like its rural counterpart, sharing similar characteristics, and was intertwined in the same supply networks. Commercial exploitation was less developed there. This would change as marketeers moved to take over, control, and profit from the sale of Hoodoo. Post–World War II urbanized Hoodoo would present itself publicly as a conglomeration of disconnected products, gestures, and procedures like candle burning and mojo bag making. Participation in old black belt traditions would eventually come to be viewed by some African Americans as incompatible with notions of "racial uplift." This view was informed largely by several factors, including the aggressive diversification and proliferation of the spiritual marketplace, increasing African American cultural disengagement from old southern black belt spiritual traditions and culture, migration to and employment in the urban North, and the thrust toward "race betterment" marked by assimilation to the mainstream. Confronting these factors, post–World War II urbanized Hoodoo would become nearly unrecognizable as it presented itself publicly as a conglomeration of disconnected products, gestures, and procedures.

Workers of old tradition Hoodoo would be outnumbered by and achieve lower levels of visibility than the marketeering outsiders interested in the commercial exploitation of Hoodoo. This would have potentially dangerous consequences for those seeking help with medical conditions or those preoccupied with a serious personal concern. Some of the spiritual merchants, who had so effectively financially exploited the African American Hoodoo belief system, would pass their businesses to their heirs and establish a continuing legacy of intergenerational exploitation and profiting from Hoodoo. They would further modify urban Hoodoo's face.

As old tradition black belt Hoodoo's influence and reach were weakening, it was both outflanked by commercial exploiters and becoming more difficult to locate inside the African American community. Concurrently, the old sites for locating the vast array of authentic old tradition Hoodoo ingredients and materials were becoming increasingly scarce.[1] For example, the supply line through the often elderly black man, who either assisted or became the local pharmacist, and the old-style drugstore with its compounding pharmacy selling patent medicines and ingredients used both in Hoodoo and for other purposes would, like the old swampers, become relics of the past. Both the conjurer-root workers and the clients they served would, increasingly, be forced to turn to the curio shop, the mail-order marketplace, and Hoodoo mail-order catalogs for supplies. Though the new sources could deliver only a limited and often insufficient inventory, the exploiting marketeers aggressively pushed their products in an increasingly receptive atmosphere contributed to by black belt tradition invisibility and racism. Loudell F. Snow, in her study of "mail-order magic," clearly documents the commercial exploitation of the old Hoodoo folk belief system by marketeers using mail-order catalogs.[2]

Several other factors would contribute to black belt Hoodoo's susceptibility to outsider control and further marginalization as well as loss of black control in the marketplace. The disappearance of the street-crying root and herb peddlers, the African American community's own door-to-door Hoodoo supply salesman, would disappear. The continuing shrinkage of old root and herb harvest grounds and the disappearance of natural sites such as forested lands for obtaining other old tradition Hoodoo ingredients further contributed. The disappearance of the African American lay midwife disrupted the traditional supply line needed for most sexually specific Hoodoo work. All left the black belt Hoodoo believer open to intense financial and spiritual exploitation by those who were nonbelieving outsiders looking to make a profit. Mail-order catalog Hoodoo would thrive in this cultural atmosphere, but it would not go uncontested.

In addition to an increase in the number and diversity of mail-order catalogs offering Hoodoo supplies, Hoodoo advertising would move from primarily newspapers to the new "confessions" magazines that were penetrating African American and white communities alike. Like the race records of the era, the confessions magazine initially targeted their racially segregated potential readership based considerably on race and gender. *True Confessions Magazine,* the best-known example on the market, though it would later expand its readership to include African Americans, initially targeted primarily, though not exclusively, working-class white females between ages sixteen and forty years old. African American consumers could partake of similar material in at least three comparable publications: *Tan, Sepia,* and *Bronze Thrills,* all published by the same company as *True Confessions,* McFadden Publishers. Targeted to working-class women, the confessions publications of the 1940s, '50s, and '60s offered stories that centered on themes of love, cheating, sexuality, secrecy, and betrayal. Confessions publications gave the reader a look from behind the "chastity curtain." Their stories involved home wreckers, premarital sex, out-of-wedlock pregnancies, infidelity, and young women who violated the moral code of the day and suffered the consequences. Titles such as "I Had to Put Out or Lose My Job," "He Only Wanted One Thing," "My Man Left Me for My Neighbor," and "My Parole Officer Stole My Woman" attest to the often melodramatic, soap opera quality of the magazines' contents. It is no coincidence that the characters in the confessions stories confronted the very same problems that plagued Hoodoo help seekers, thus reinforcing an instant identification between the readers and the characters while the Hoodoo ads promised help for such problems. These magazines acted as templates both by illustrating familiar thematic problems and by providing the numerous ads that directed readers to supernatural solutions.

Hoodoo confessions ads like these flood black confessions magazines.

The late 1960s and early 1970s, the era of heightened black activism and economic transformation would witness decline in confession market sales. But beginning in the late 1970s and early 1980s and by the 1990s, the confessions market would experience a rebound as well as an expansion from three to six separate magazines aimed at blacks. *Bronze Thrills* and *Jive* are the oldest at more than forty years old; the other four magazines, *Black Confessions, Black Secrets, True Black Experience,* and *Black Romance,* are all less than thirty years old and demonstrate the increase in demand for this material. Since their first publication, these magazines have become a major vehicle carrying advertisements for alleged Hoodoo practitioners. The ads are spread throughout the magazine, with the largest concentration of ads in the last few pages.

The Hoodoo ads in the confessions magazines were not and today are not unlike those in African American newspapers of an earlier era. Many of the same approaches and techniques of appeal, such as the use of fictive kinship titles like "Mother," "Brother," and "Sister," were and are still part of the sales pitch. Because these titles are also used in the African American church, they carry and impart a certain level of legitimacy in the world of African American spiritual work. As in the earlier advertisements, the use of these titles by Hoodoo workers signifies a connection with a church and thus an implied level of both spiritual stability and legitimacy as well as an assurance that the worker was doing only good work and not evil. But for the marketeer, the use of the fictive title was merely a marketing device.

According to psychiatrist E. Fuller Torrey, fictive kinship titles such as these serve another important function: They raise the potential client's expectations and they mobilize hope and confidence in the worker's ability and experience.[3] In the context of the black church, these titles are earned by individuals and bestowed by the congregation using the principle of working community consensus. An important church mother never assumes the title on her own; she cannot designate herself as "Mother Johnson" or "Mother Catherine." In core culture African American communities, these high-status indicators are bestowed by the church, sometimes formally in recognition ceremonies, but only after an extended period of time and only through community acknowledgment and consensus. The marketeers who serve an African American clientele often bestow these titles on themselves because they are not and will never be black church "mothers" or "brothers." Since the introduction of Hoodoo to the Internet, there is a new twist on the theme of "title taking" by those claiming to be Hoodoos. One can now see the use of academic titles such as Doctor or PhD in Internet Hoodoo Web sites. The false use of academic titles is not altogether new, as an examination of nineteenth- and early-twentieth-century black newspapers revealed. Web sites now make tailored, misleading Hoodoo advertising possible and available. As this investigator began searching for old tradition black belt Hoodoo workers and root workers for this study, I turned to the ads in the black confessions magazines to help me locate them. Wondering where the search would lead, I assumed that the ads were for legitimate African American Hoodoos. I would soon find out that my expectations were far from correct. Certainly, clients in the readership who need Hoodoo work performed turn to these magazines as sources for locating a worker. I collected a set of thirty-eight names and telephone numbers that frequently appeared in the magazines over a five-year period from 1997 to 2002. I designated these names as "frequent advertisers" and included those who advertised at least monthly for several years. Some of them regularly advertised in more than one of the black confessions magazines. I was searching for a traditional African American root worker who appeared to be connected with the old tradition and who had been trained by an older family member, church member, or a community elder, as was done in old tradition Hoodoo. I composed a list of thirty-eight names, all but a few used either a fictive title with a black church legacy or terms such as "gifted," as in "gifted root worker" or "gifted psychic." Nineteen of the thirty-eight, or half, were unreachable by telephone because the listed numbers had been disconnected since the ad was placed. Of the remaining nineteen that I was able to reach, none of them were African American Hoodoo or root workers. Most of them were middle age or beyond and were white women with a few palm readers from Romanian backgrounds seeking to expand their market and clientele in fortune-telling. Only one of the thirty-eight spoke to me with sincerity about her work and her qualifications and admitted not knowing the fictitious "Papa Juma" incantations, a name that I invented to test the knowledge and integrity of the worker. Several self-designated psychics that I spoke with assured me that they could recite these nonexistent verses but only alone and in secrecy. Several of them quickly told me that they could solve my problems, even before I told them what the problems were, and quickly added that I must immediately send them sums that varied between $1,200 and $1,500.

After no success in locating a black belt tradition Hoodoo worker through these magazines, I finally concluded that these ads allowed a legion of spiritual exploiters direct access to a wide-ranging readership of primarily young, poor, and lower-middle-class working African American women who have, at best, a slippery grasp on what appears to them as a fragmented and moribund tradition. Lured to Hoodoo by their own cultural legacy and social predisposition via folk stories and conversations among African Americans that still tell of Hoodoo's efficacy, the potential believers still seek spiritual help from a tradition now forced to the margins of black culture and heavily infiltrated by middlemen minority marketeers.

Black belt Hoodoo in the post–World War II period would find itself confronted with yet another repositioning. As old tradition Hoodoo became more invisible and marginalized, adaptations such as the candle shop would become a more prominent feature than they had been prior to World War II. Southern African Americans who migrated from the rural South into northern urban black communities after the war, would give the northern, urban adaptation of old black belt Hoodoo its last infusion of the remaining elements of the old tradition. Other modifications involved simply importing a black belt tradition, as did the old root doctors in Philadelphia when they began directly peddling fresh roots, herbs, and medicinal plants in the city's northern black neighborhoods.

Other adaptations were stimulated by both the new postwar sociocultural environment and expansion of marketeering sites that combined the sale of spiritual products, including roots, herbs, candles, incense, and books from diverse traditions such as Santeria, Wicca, kabbalah, Judaism, astrology, Christianity, Hinduism, Islam, New Orleans Voodoo, and Hoodoo. Eventually, the influence of the new age spiritual movements of the late 1960s and 1970s would be felt and demonstrated in the old shops through the addition of products such as crystals, crystal balls, astrology charts, tarot cards, and even spiritual wands. Some shops would hire readers, some of whom were charlatans, but who would perform readings and spiritual consultations right in the store. The old curio shops and Hoodoo drugstores would be forced to diversify or close; most closed.

In those shops that survived economically through the close of the twentieth century, diversification would become a standard; in the 1990s, Internet access would give a new avenue to both marketeers and legitimate old tradition black belt Hoodoos as well as potential clients. By the end of the twentieth century, a diversifying and widening range of marketeered Hoodoo products could be easily located by anyone with a computer and access to online Web sites. Many of the sites offer a catalog of products for sale and will ship them by mail order. Some of the sites will even offer to make up a mojo bag for a price. Fabricated, marketeered items such as "war water" or "peace water," nonexistent in old tradition black belt Hoodoo, as well as questionably constructed imitation Hoodoo/mojo bags, money-drawing oil, jinx-removing oils, powders, incense, air fresheners, soaps, and floor washes are all for sale. Some sites give information that contradicts historical evidence as well as common sense, such as the use of a chicken wing bone to indicate travel. Slaves were not likely to be traveling unless they were attempting an escape. None of the nineteenth-century conjurers' caches that this author examined had chicken wing bones; there were what appeared to be rib bones, but no chicken bones.

Old tradition black belt Hoodoo ingredients have always been all natural, recently harvested, or ritually preserved by traditional Hoodoo root doctor herbalists, using old techniques, incantations, and prayers. These would have been obtainable in the plantation environment before the emergence of marketeered Hoodoo. Many imitated and marketeered Hoodoo products would depart considerably, in both content and construction technique, from their original old tradition Hoodoo predecessors. Much of the material culture and nonmaterial aspect of old tradition Hoodoo work would be lost to those who exploited and commercially marketed these products. Two examples of this exploitation can be clearly seen in the marketeering of something known in the Hoodoo marketplace as hot foot powder and war water. No such products existed in plantation-based Hoodoo. Hot foot powder is an insufficient attempt to fabricate the old black belt Hoodoo charm known to well-trained and knowledgeable old tradition Hoodoo practitioners simply as "the walking foot." War water attempts to duplicate the old tradition use of a liquid substance to harm or protect. But unlike marketeered liquids, the individually prepared Hoodoo liquids usually contained some of the client's bodily fluid as well as the "blood" or sap from certain plants, roots, or herbs, depending on the intensity, speed, and results intended. According to both African tradition and old tradition Hoodoo, it was mandatory that the recipe be mixed from fresh or ritually preserved supplies. Unlike old tradition ingredients, some of the marketeered supplies have sat on the shelf so long that the plastic bags containing the herb or root became cloudy and brittle and the plant or root became stale and ineffective.

When an authentic black belt Hoodoo recipe required that it be diluted, only sacred water was used. Only water such as rainwater caught on either the full or the dark of the moon, water from the blacksmith's forge or foundry, or water from the baptismal pool or "baptizin' place" in the local river or lake was used. In the small town of Glen Allen, Mississippi, water from the local "baptizin' place" was used in 1971 and perhaps more recently. Local Hoodoo mythology often developed around the "safety" of the local "baptizin' place." It was believed that the spiritual power left in the water after a sacred ritual such as baptism rendered the water sacred and thus a "safe zone" where one could not be bitten by venomous snakes or attacked by alligators that normally inhabit the local waters. The spot was also used for recreational activities such as swimming because it was believed to be safe.

If a client needed to harness the swift power of the rattlesnake, then the plant known only as rattlesnake master was added to the mixture to speed the work along. Certain prayers, incantations, and words of power were spoken as the mixture was created; the words were changed to complement and call out the spiritual power of the herbs, roots, and substances that were used. Particular plants, with either short or extended growing periods, were used to time the release of the power in the mixture. With some mixtures, a counteractive substance was used to either slow, mute, or limit the time span of the action. The counteractive substance, particularly if it were a plant, was usually found within about an arm's radius of the root used. This rule was also applied to poisonous plants and their natural antidotes. The root worker simply stood astride the plant, spread his or her arms out to the side, and within an arm's length somewhere an antidote was to be found.

The Internet has allowed a flowering of Hoodoo merchandising and cyberspace exploitation. In the saturation of cyberspace, one can purchase spells, including a death spell, a spell to bring back a lover, get a husband, get money, get out of jail, harm an enemy or rival, and a host of other actions. One can also purchase a marketeered course on Hoodoo, find instructions on YouTube.com on how to make mojoes, create spells, make Florida water, make Hoodoo candles, and make Hoodoo oils. One can listen to radio blogs on such sites as BlogTalkRadio.com that feature shows on Hoodoo, which take calls while on the air. One can also learn to read cards and divine with shells, sticks, and rocks. Most of the Hoodoo products carry the label "sold only as a curio," with no refund. On at least one Hoodoo Internet site, the reader accepts the money and the client has no way of verifying that the spell was actually performed. In the case of an Internet mojo bag, the client is sent the mojo in the mail.

As old tradition black belt Hoodoo became nearly publicly invisible, some marketeers have been able to present themselves as self-styled experts on Hoodoo, even offering classes and certification. Lifting their information from others' scholarly research and printed materials, marketeers present what is by comparison a Hoodoo that is truncated, marked by disclaimers, superficial, without spiritual substance or healing content, and often fabricated by earlier marketeers. The sites that feature commercially exploitable versions of Hoodoo are flooded with the sale of their own products, many of which are poor imitations or limited versions of old tradition self-obtained supplies. In this vein, the marketeers have attempted to impose standardization from the outside, thereby further enabling themselves to both control and tap into the limited flow of African American dollars.

Marketeered standardization and control would eventually contribute to an open, oozing fissure of flowing black dollars into outsiders' pockets. In addition, the middlemen minority marketeers would also publicly present a badly misshapen image of an oppressed people's long-standing spiritual tradition. The problems that the marketeers claim to address are often presented with cavalier, self-serving, questionable images that substantiate and support old racist stereotypes. Some of the images depict "Negroes" as foolish with money and lazy and who would rather gamble than work, so much so that they seek supernatural assistance to achieve a positive end. Gambling, sex, police trouble, vice, broken families, and lack of work are all marketeered as the stereotyped, narrow image of African American concern and Hoodoo focus. Here Hoodoo is redefined in the language and imagery of the marketeers. And the problems that blacks have are the result of individual weakness and shortcomings and not systemic racism.

In the post–World War II environment, the division between old tradition black belt Hoodoo and the snake-oil Hoodoo of the commercial marketeers would be wider than ever before in most aspects except one. As the old harvest grounds continue to disappear, some old tradition workers have succumbed to pressure to use at least some commercial supplies. Though some African American conjurers have turned to marketeered supplies, most old tradition workers still use freshly harvested plants, roots, herbs, and other supplies, though they may not dig them themselves. Some still use diggers, professional harvesters, who dig roots and herbs for them and who are continually on the lookout for fresh wild-growing plants. On one of my visits to Sheffield, Alabama, to interview an old tradition root worker who now uses some marketeered products, Miss Mary, as she is known, had one of her diggers harvest a giant poke root and present it to me as a gift. Dried and pulverized, this legendary root has numerous uses in old tradition Hoodoo. And on a trip to visit Brother Gregory of St. Helena Island, South Carolina, I was given two freshly harvested rattlesnake master plants as a gift. In both instances, the diggers had spotted and dug up the fresh roots for their old tradition root workers. Even those old tradition specialists like Ms. Mary and Brother Gregory, who resist and limit their dependence on marketeered products, have been recently forced to concede and purchase some commercial supplies.

Wider sea changes in the sociocultural environment, particularly end-of-the-century deindustrialization and its impact on the overall economic health of African American communities heavily dependent on industry, have impacted old tradition Hoodoo workers. Significant numbers of them, like their clients, are forced to commit more time to their regular jobs, so they restrict their Hoodoo practice to a preferred specialty. Though most of them have been trained as generalists, they now specialize in a particular type of work, such as court case work or love and family work, and they carefully screen their cases when a request is made. The continuing loss of black-owned farmland has also impacted old tradition Hoodoo specialists because many of them had been independent small farmers feeding themselves from the land and practicing their craft. The loss of land has been a double curse upon Hoodoo that includes the loss of traditional Hoodoo harvest grounds as well as the loss of farming land for economic support and independence from wage labor.

In spite of everything that has contributed to old tradition Hoodoo's demise, influential vestiges persist that connect contemporary black belt Hoodoo practice directly back to the plantation community as well as to its golden age before the takeover by marketeers and ultimately back to areas of West and Central West Africa, particularly Nigeria, Benin, Ghana, Senegambia, Kongo, and Sierra Leone. Today black belt tradition conjurers and root workers still perform some of the functions performed by both plantation conjurers and African traditional priests. In an interview with a contemporary black belt old tradition root worker on St. Helena Island, South Carolina, the informant, Brother A. B. Gregory, the great-grandson of Dr. Buzzard, revealed that recently he had experienced an increase in requests for two types of work. One type was in court cases involving younger clients accused of murder, particularly shootings of young African American men related to gang violence or quasi-gang drug violence. The other type was in the "community sanction" function, indicated by the number of people who brought their children and grandchildren to him to be verbally lectured and reprimanded. He further stated, "More and more people are bringing their kids here for me to fuss at them and tell them to obey and listen to their parents, stay out of trouble."[4] Of significance to West and Central West African tradition society and important to the slave community, conjurers performed the community sanction function and passed it on to freedmen as a component of the conjurer's role in community life. This role and aspect of Hoodoo would not be replicated or even addressed by marketeers.

In the rapidly changing post–World War II sociocultural environment, contemporary root workers would interface with those students of and practitioners of various traditions, including African traditional religion, particularly Vodun, Santeria/Lucumi, Yoruba, Akan, and Kongo traditions. Drawn together in stores that serve as botanicas, Hoodoo curio stores, and candle shops, all under one roof, spiritual believers from a range of traditions would encounter one another. Each overheard conversation represents an opportunity for cross-fertilization as clients will sometime inform contemporary root workers of their own dabbling in other traditions. In the post–World War II cultural environment, there would be new venues in which old tradition black belt Hoodoo would encounter and interact with other African-derived spiritual traditions. Additionally, some children and grandchildren of old tradition workers have become educated in the fields of psychology and medicine and are raising important questions about Hoodoo belief and its role in African American community health. One such person is Dr. Wilbert Jordan of Los Angeles who was reared in a household that practiced and passed on the old plantation black belt Hoodoo traditions. He is now a medical doctor sensitive in his medical practice to his patients' folk healing and Hoodoo medical traditions.[5]

To subsequent generations of African Americans born in the North, three factors would further diminish the influence and exposure of old tradition Hoodoo as a first choice problem-solving spiritual alternative: the continuing black migration out of the rural southern black belt northward into urban areas, increasing income and identification with a northern urban lifestyle, and increasing access to mainstream medical care and more money to afford it. Though many African Americans did not trust white doctors or the health care system, and justifiably so,[6] greater access to health care would further challenge belief in old tradition Hoodoo's medical legacy and would completely and finally drive it either underground or into prayer-based faith healing rituals. Nevertheless, beliefs from the old plantation Hoodoo tradition would still inform behaviors of millions of younger African Americans. There is ample evidence that in spite of black-owned supply networks dying at least some Hoodoo belief is thriving.

Though Hoodoo would experience a diminished centrality causing subsequent generations of African Americans to know and experience less of Hoodoo than their parents and grandparents, many of them still turn to Hoodoo as either their system of last resort or to support actions initiated independently by them. This appears to be particularly true of young African American women in their late twenties and thirties who are looking for husbands. According to old tradition practitioner informants, work to "get a man, preferably a husband" dominates a major part of their practice.[7] And here we can note central concerns among blacks as believers. In post–World War II African American communities, the legacy and practice of old tradition Hoodoo would continue in the more fundamentalist African American churches. And today one can still find an old tradition black belt root worker using certain African American church networks. A significant number of those urbanized practitioners would increasingly be forced into at least minimally using commercially packaged curios or marketeered supplies such as powders, candles, roots, and soaps.

As black consciousness and political struggles of the postwar 1950s and 1960s intensified in the atmosphere of the Cold War, the influence of New World Pan-Africanism and popular black nationalism would inadvertently provide a new undergirding for old tradition Hoodoo. During the 1960s, a period of heightened black consciousness, African Americans in some quarters would view older elements of national Negro culture, including Hoodoo, tap dance, jook activity, and the blues, as antithetical to the new militant black man of the period. In some quarters, this view would find compatibility with notions of racial uplift, but for different reasons. The trajectories of Black Nationalism and assimilationist uplift would intersect in the 1960s to further stimulate the negative perceptions of Hoodoo as a relic of Negro superstition and backwardness. Tap dance in particular suffered a near-death experience.[8]

Though it would arrive at Hoodoo's doorstep in the late twentieth century and after an ideological struggle, the influence of both modern Pan-Africanism and African American nationalism would provide old tradition Hoodoo with new exchange sites free from the dictates and direct influence of exploiting marketeers and outsiders. These new sites have been allowing old tradition workers direct contact with both continental African and New World African traditionalists, priests, shamans, and spiritual specialists in African traditional religion.

African-founded and controlled licensing organizations such as the National African Religion Congress (NARC) are providing safe space for new types of exchanges free from the fear that marketeers will appropriate the tradition and continue the legacy of falsification, misrepresentation, and monetary exploitation. Founded in Philadelphia in 1999, NARC has established a governing body of African religion practitioners that includes Akan priests; Nigerian, Cuban, and Puerto Rican Babalawos; Olorishas; Iyalorishas; Kongo priests; Santeros; and Shango Baptist priests. The governing body is a certification and licensing body of African traditionalists. The safe spaces provided by organizations such as NARC allow old tradition workers to examine possible origins and to re-Africanize Hoodoo traditions modified, polluted, and exploited by marketeers' standardization and false fabrication of Hoodoo products. At NARC's yearly conference, Hoodoos and other priests can learn the subtly detailed tradition of making African traditional bagged amulets or mojoes and gain exposure to the traditional African parents of Hoodoo.

Exposure to other New World manifestations of African religious traditions allows practitioners to observe the evolutionary history and variety of demographic circumstances and their possible influences in producing other New World African religious traditions such as Lucumi and Shango Baptist. These conferences are rich in the exchange of old tradition information and ritual materials such as authentically made African traditional soaps, oils, powders, roots, herbs, and plants. Some items must undergo long ritual curing periods in secret, sacred locations before they can be exchanged; these sacred places are only known to the priests and priestesses initiated in the sacred tradition. The sites also serve as places for exchange of herbal traditions.

Snake-oil and marketeered Hoodoo networks thrived partly on African American disconnection from their own traditions, cultural ignorance, and denial of self, resulting partly from racial oppression from both past enslavement and contemporary social dislocation.[9] Economic marginalization and exclusion, cultural denigration, deceptive marketeering practices, and outright racist targeting of African Americans further contributed to this process. Gunnar Myrdal made clear the racist dynamic inherent in some exchanges between whites and African Americans in his landmark study *An American Dilemma: The Negro Problem and Modern Democracy,* in which he quotes interviewed whites as saying, "The only way a man can make money from farming is by stealing it from the Negroes. Some people get ahead by living close . . . and then there are lots that steal from the Negroes. Some of them will take everything a Negro has, down to his last chicken and hog."[10]

In addition to serving marketeered Hoodoo, new sites in cyberspace are challenging it through an African American reclamation of old tradition black belt Hoodoo. Although the Internet has become a favored medium of Hoodoo marketeers and in some instances con artists, younger African American conjurers, root doctors, and Hoodoos who work in the old tradition all around the United States are circumventing the marketeers and are in close contact with one another and are exchanging traditional folk recipes, old formulas, and rituals handed down in their families for healing, harming, and controlling. And few if any of these recipes, formulas, or rituals resemble anything peddled by catalog and Internet marketeers who set themselves up as experts but who have limited and often incorrect and corrupted information that could eventually even prove to be harmful. In the post–World War II environment, the Hoodoo ads that once proliferated in African American newspapers would dwindle and in most instances disappear. Only in the confessions market would the Hoodoo ads continue.

Hoodoo radio advertising has been limited to shows with religious content, such as Gospel hours that featured African American Gospel music and that attract fundamentalist believers. Certain black churches still sponsor these shows, and their listening audiences of potential clients can readily identify a local "prophet's" ads. Unlike radio, early television attempted no race-based marketing of Hoodoo practitioners or products. Only occasionally would an African American church have a local television show; Reverend Ike is the noteworthy exception here.

Born on June 1, 1935, in Ridgeland, South Carolina, Reverend Ike carried one element of old tradition black belt Hoodoo into the television age: the modified mojo bag and devotional amulet known as the prayer cloth. Unlike other amulets, prayer cloths were never prepared with the client present. And like the variety of preparation techniques used with the healing string, preparation of the prayer cloth involved different techniques. This updated version of the old tradition mojo bag functions similarly, and thousands of African Americans have sent for and received Reverend Ike's prayer cloths. These modernized amulet prayer cloths are internally conceived modifications and true adaptations from within church-based Hoodoo rather than from outsider middlemen minority marketeers. Similar cloths would be used and distributed by Louisiana treaters as curative amulets.[11] Both Reverend Ike and the treaters used only red cloth in the amulet's preparation.

The 1990s would bring to the public access to an updated, complex spiritual marketplace. Psychic hotlines, some endorsed by celebrities, would flood the airways with televised ads. Individual readers and advisors such as the now infamous Miss Cleo offered the viewing public telephone hotlines through which they could contact a psychic, astrologer, advisor, or reader. Though the TV psychics appealed to a wide-ranging and ethnically diverse viewing audience, Miss Cleo targeted black potential clients by using a well-established question in Hoodoo discourse: "Has someone put roots on you?" This language, designed to get the black viewer's attention, targeted not only African Americans but also other blacks familiar with similar traditions such as Jamaican Obeah.

Today in numerous communities, people still seek the help, support, counsel, and assistance of community laypeople. Some of these skilled lay community helpers have developed local, regional, and in some instances national reputations as knowledgeable and adept helpers, readers, and advisors. There are perhaps thousands of these lay community health practitioners in African American communities across the country, and it appears that the most effective are still associated with a traditional African American black belt style Sanctified church. These practitioners still address concerns that range from love problems and the general category of protection, to the general condition of good or bad luck, as well as legal problems and court cases, medical problems and concerns, and personal, behavioral, and discipline problems within families, such as disobedient youth. They also address a major concern for economically marginalized African Americans: the acquisition of money. Many of these lay practitioners have a considerable degree of traditional knowledge on the uses of medicinal herbs for healing teas and baths as well as for traditional spiritual treatments. They are consulted not so much for their medical knowledge as for their spiritual support and help in making important medical decisions and exploring what questions to ask a doctor. The most widely sought after lay helpers are still connected with a Baptist, African Methodist Episcopal (AME), or Holiness church that retains fundamentalist elements from the African Religion Complex in the style of worship. In most of these churches, there is an old style African-based exuberance in music, dance, and physical movement as well as a strong interactive, participatory style between preacher and congregation. Where these churches are the most numerous, visible, and dominant sites of sacred worship, old tradition black belt Hoodoo beliefs appear to be the strongest.

Though old tradition black belt Hoodoo was both originated and developed by African American captives on plantations in the southern slave states of America, today's workers in the tradition serve a more ethnically and demographically diverse population than ever before. Some clients are immigrants who have lost touch with their own folk magical and medicinal systems and now look for something familiar and spiritually compatible to turn to. For all of my informants, their clients are Chinese immigrants as well as first- and second-generation Southeast Asians, African Americans; West Indians of African, Chinese, and East Indian ancestry; Mexican and other Latinos; and southern as well as northern white Americans. Most of the clients were raised in a Christian environment, and most of them live in urban areas. The problems the workers are consulted for are in those areas of life addressed by both old tradition black belt Hoodoo and its marketeered, snake-oil equivalent: love and family relationships, work or job-related problems, financial problems, bad luck, protection from negative forces and energies including those that cause stress, as well as emotional and psychological difficulties, criminal court cases, and other legal problems. Problems of love, particularly those of finding a good mate, and finding a good job are the most requested.

As the national stability and social conditions of the African American family continue in rapid decline, marriage rates are decreasing and out-of-wedlock births and single-parent households are increasing. As the marriage picture in the African American community grows more dismal each year, there has been a noticeable increase in requests for work that would get a husband. As one informant stated, "Because it's so hard for a black woman to find a husband, you know with the white women and all going after our men, I'm getting a lot of calls." Most of these requests come from African American women in their late twenties and early thirties who want to get married immediately and feel a sense of desperation. Sometimes the marriage request is for a specific person, such as a professional athlete, or someone who is already married. In the case of the latter, a request to break up the existing marriage is frequently included, but most workers will not do work to break up a legal union with children.

Though few and far between, old tradition black belt Hoodoo workers still exist; four women and four men were interviewed for this study. They are Ms. Mary, Brother Gregory, Papa Ce, Djenra Windwalker, Arthur Flowers, Hougan Dafusky Jones, Dancingtree Moonwater, and Phoenix Savage. Each one is different and represents a responding variation on a tradition that has evolved underground and partly resisted commercialization. Ms. Mary was born in 1945 in Sheffield, Alabama, a few miles from Florence, Alabama, the birthplace of W. C. Handy, father of the blues. She was submerged in the lifestyle and culture of the old tradition black belt Hoodoo faith and the blues, the national music of the old black belt South. As a child, she was, as were many African Americans, reared in an extended family that included close contact with her maternal grandmother whom Ms. Mary remembers as an adept community healer, advisor, and root and herb specialist. According to Ms. Mary, her grandmother, a church mother known as Miss Mattie, who had "the calling," could treat any ailment and "could cure just about any type of sickness," including that with a supernatural cause; her grandmother knew just which plants and substances to utilize to successfully treat a range of maladies. While still a young child, Ms. Mary spent more time in intensely close contact with her grandmother than with her own parents. And as a result, she began to participate in her grandmother's root and herb operation by being sent to obtain certain items, such as plants, herbs, roots, or other objects such as rusty nails, whenever grandma requested them. Ms. Mary's mother lacked interest "in learning about all this stuff, so as my grandmother continued to use me in her errands, I learned more and more."

Eventually, through the informal apprenticeship provided by her grandmother, Ms. Mary acquired a storehouse of traditional black belt Hoodoo and root worker knowledge that she would not make active use of outside her own family and close friends until years later.[12] After doing the work for a number of years, Ms. Mary stopped "for about fifteen or so years. Then I was called back about fifteen or so years ago, and I've been doing it ever since."[13] Today she is both an active deaconess of her church and a traditional root working Hoodoo. She occasionally uses elements from the Lucumi tradition to enhance her work.

At the 2002 NARC meetings in Philadelphia, Ms. Mary became the first African American old tradition root worker to receive a membership certification acknowledging and verifying her status. That same year, Ms. Mary and I drove from Philadelphia to St. Helena Island, South Carolina, for several meetings and discussions with Brother Gregory, great-grandson of Dr. Buzzard.

Brother A. B. Gregory was born in 1954 on St. Helena Island, South Carolina, where he grew up; he resides there today. The great-grandson of the famous Stepheney Robinson, known as Dr. Buzzard of St. Helena Island, Brother Gregory, like Ms. Mary, encountered and began learning the work from an elder, his grandfather, Dr. Buzzard's son-in-law, in an extended-family setting, saturated with spiritual belief. Dr. Buzzard himself began training his son-in-law after his only biological son perished in a tragic automobile accident. As a child, young Gregory was very attached to and spent significant time with his grandfather, who began involving him in his work by sending him to obtain certain wild plants as well as giving him certain tasks to complete in the ritual preparation of mojoes. All the while, Gregory was learning the old black belt Hoodoo tradition and being exposed to a significant number of Gullah Coast root workers with whom his grandfather consulted. Gregory thus acquired the cooperative network he would later need to inherit his grandfather's practice. Both Gregory's grandfather and father were active practitioners of old tradition black belt root work.[14] Like Ms. Mary, Brother Gregory is an active member of his church, though he is sometimes questioned about his work and mildly admonished by his reverend to relinquish it.

Papa Ce is an example of a socially conscious and socially active Hoodoo working in the old black belt tradition. He uses no marketeered supplies and he tailors his work to his clients' needs. He sells no generic mojo bags or other untailored amulets that could be harmful. What makes Papa Ce's work unique is that he combines the techniques, materials, and methodologies of the old tradition black belt South Hoodoo worker with those of the traditional work of the Igbo of Nigeria, West Africa. His work includes all aspects of black belt tradition Hoodoo, including precision dream interpretation within the context of the client's sociocultural and historical experience.

Born in the southern black belt town of Caddo Parrish, Louisiana, on September 5, 1936, Papa Ce is like many old tradition root workers whose birth is announced by an unusual or significant occurrence, such as being born with a veil or an unusual birthmark. In Papa Ce's case, his birth was announced by seven peals of thunder. His family watched and waited as he grew, then when he was about age three he was recognized and designated as being two-headed. He had a gift picking winning horses at races and did so for several months for his uncle's friends. During his teen years, he ignored and ran from his gift; friends, neighbors, and community members called him names such as "spooky," and for twenty years he shied away from the work and refused to use the gift. All this would drastically change upon receiving a reading from an Igbo traditional priest who told him of his family history, recounting a kidnapped ancestor and telling Papa Ce of one of his dreams as well as of secret personal matters that only Papa Ce could know. He was told that he had the gift of traditional priesthood and that he must resume that work among his people here in the United States. His traditional name became Chukwunyere Eze Ndubuisi, a complex delineation of traits and status positions including "King, Chief Who Is Servant of the People" and "Life Is Paramount." Fifty years ago, Papa Ce began gathering together all that he had learned and began learning even more from grandparents, community elders, and traditional Igbo priests. He is thoroughly acquainted with the medicinal and magicospiritual properties of herbs and plants, and he uses only fresh supplies and environmentally compatible and available materials. He is a husband and father of ten.[15]

Diviner, priestess, philosopher, mother, grandmother, and wife, Djenra Ta-Rotah Ir-n Wa, also known by her Internet screen name Djenra Wind-walker, represents another contemporary variant on old tradition black belt Hoodoo. According to Djenra, "The Hoodoo lexicon and pharmacology (roots) was where I started—my cultural base, it is to my work what an individual's upbringing is to the formation of their personality—a big part but not all. . . . My working style has been modified & expanded as I developed. That is why I often refer to work done in the Systopia as a 'remix.'"[16]

Djenra was born to parents who migrated out of the North Carolina black belt to Mount Vernon, New York. Like Papa Ce's, Djenra's childhood was upset by her spiritual gifts. But like many traditionally called and gifted black belt tradition workers, Djenra "was fortunate to have people around who helped me to survive until puberty, when my personal questioning against all that a Baptist upbringing deemed 'holy' really kicked in." She began studying tarot on her own at age twelve before tarot and alternative spirituality became a popular fad and she began doing readings for friends and family.

In her early twenties, after graduating from Fordham University with honors, she began spending evenings at the famous Tree of Life on 125th

Street in Harlem, sitting in on some classes taught by John More, the late Hoodoo doctor. She went on to study with a series of famous African American sages, including Ethiopian Jewish scholar Yusef Ben-Jochannon, visiting professor at Cornell, the widely revered Dr. John Henrik Clarke, also visiting at Cornell, Dr. Ivan Van Sertima of Rutgers University, and psychiatrist Dr. Richard King. She also discovered the teachings of Ki-Kongo culture as espoused by Dr. FuKia Benseki of Kinshasa, Zaire, then at the Caribbean Cultural Center in New York.

Djenra traveled to Egypt, the Sudan, Ghana, Senegal, then to Havana, Cuba, where she was crowned Orisha Oya, thus the online name "Windwalker." She then took several trips to Haiti to complete her Vodun initiation. Earlier she had been initiated into both Palo Mayombe and Palo Kimbisa. Finally in the summer of 2002, she was initiated as a second rank (Reiki 2) practitioner. According to Djenra, "I use the Reiki and crystal grids for healing as an expansion of the 'laying on of hands' techniques used by traditional Hoodoo culture."

Today Djenra's work includes dream interpretation, candle work, bath preparation, making talismans or amulets, house fumigation, and spiritual cleansing, any of which may include the folkloric materials of old tradition black belt Hoodoo or other methods and ingredients from other systems such as Palo, Ocha, or Vodun, all of which she is initiated to. Like other workers in this updating of old tradition Hoodoo, Djenra avoids marketeered supplies as much as possible, preferring to mix and tailor the work to the client's needs.[17]

Professor Arthur Flowers is another root worker moving in the ways of the old black belt tradition. His primary focus is working with High John root while learning the older recipes, formulas, and uses. He is unusual in several respects; he is both a novelist and an assistant professor of fiction at Syracuse University. By his own admission, he came to working Hoodoo in the late 1970s, inspired by the work of author and satirist Ismael Reed. Flowers was familiar with Hoodoo from his mother's side of the family, "My momma came from Hoodoo folks in North Carolina," of whom he says, "half of my family gives consultations, the other half won't do anything without one." He became so invigorated by Reed's use and literary rendering of Hoodoo that he began to study, inquire, and reconnect what he had been exposed to as a child with what he was then reading. "In the process of inquiry, I came across Hyatt's work and began to sort out what was familiar to me, what I had seen or heard of growing up."[18]

For Flowers, Hoodoo is both a spiritual science and an inspiration for his work. He is a generalist but focuses most of his work in the realm of working with High John and creating protective and soothing mojoes crafted from High John the Conquer root in the old plantation tradition. He is the founder of The Hoodoo Way, a discussion group of mainly old tradition black belt African American Hoodoos.[19] Group members exchange information on old tradition recipes, harvest sites for fresh ingredients, and rituals for certain problems. A number of members are in touch with grandparents and elders who worked the old black belt Hoodoo tradition. In addition, a number of participants are Hoodoos, priests, initiates, and practitioners of other African religious systems, such as Lucumi, Palo, or Vodun. They do not recommend using the services of anyone who is outside of the Hoodoo faith or who does not have an African-derived tradition as their primary religion; this includes the Sanctified and spiritualist churches.

Like Flowers, Phoenix Savage is an artist with a scholarly as well as a practical interest in the spiritual practices of her African American ancestors. Her recent master's thesis from the University of Mississippi on contemporary health care and Hoodoo in Mississippi explores the concurrent belief and practical treatment parameters of Hoodoo as health care. Her findings indicate that in African American communities, health care providers must understand and in some instances integrate Hoodoo belief into the treatment model and approach.

Born in Philadelphia, Pennsylvania, into a family that on her father's side had its ancestry in the Virginia black belt region, Phoenix Savage came to Hoodoo early under the influence of an aunt and the aunt's mother who both read tarot cards and engaged in root work for their own purposes. She later discovered that the aunt was working to assist others. Early on Savage noticed certain gifts, such as the ability to will certain happenings, and she began using it to empower herself. Later in life, she would learn the details of her great-great-grandfather, an itinerant Hoodoo known in her family as Prophet Jones, not to be confused with the famous Prophet Jones from Detroit.

Savage began reading books on alternative spirituality but, as she states, "None of it connected with my soul until I discovered Haitian Vodun." This quest began when she asked herself the question, "What did black folk have before they got Jesus? I came to an intellectual reckoning with old tradition Hoodoo." For a period of time, she embraced the New World Yoruba tradition while living in Nashville, Tennessee, but Hoodoo was still at the foundation of her spirituality. Her art work is inspired by old tradition black belt Hoodoo as well as both the Kongo and Haitian religions. Her work implores the viewer to question his own senses through the use of energy-bound tactile and textual strands. Savage only does spiritual work for people who contact her. She does not advertise her spiritual work, and her reputation has been spread by word of mouth. Although she is a generalist, she concentrates most of her efforts in her specialty, assisting in the breaking and restoring of love ties. The ritual to accomplish such varies with each case. She uses no marketeered products, only those ingredients that are obtained fresh as needed. She currently resides in Louisiana.[20]

Dancingtree Moonwater is both an Olorisha of Ogun with the first hand of Ifa in the Lucumi/Yoruba tradition and an old tradition Hoodoo trained by a number of family members, most notably Louise Johnson, her great-grandfather's sister from Waughs, Montgomery County, Alabama. Born in 1875 of freedmen parents, Aint New, as she was called by family members, passed away at the age of 102 in 1977 when Moonwater was twenty-nine years old. On her yearly visits to family in Cleveland, Ohio, and Detroit, Michigan, Aint New would set up shop in one of her nieces' or nephews' small back rooms or kitchens and begin receiving clients, some she knew before the migration north. After church, family members would often inform potential or past clients that Aint New was coming north and would be doing work for just a few. Moonwater began doing small errands for her great-great aunt, such as helping to mix recipes and being called to recite prayers when an unbroken prayer circle was required. It was in these prayer circles that she was introduced to the use of Psalms as well as the tradition of creating and tailoring a Hoodoo prayer to the needs of the client.

Having witnessed the invasion into and transformation of preemancipation black belt Hoodoo's public face by marketeers, Aint New never used marketeered ingredients and steered all of her clients clear of outsider-owned Hoodoo drugstores and curio shops. In addition to spiritual work, Aint New was an old-style treater who used old tradition Hoodoo medicine combined with originally created prayers to treat ailments, swellings, coughs, headaches, and other maladies. Once while living in the Gulf Coast region of Mobile, Alabama, she conducted a ritual that restored her younger brother John's ability to walk.[21] Though Dancingtree Moonwater is a generalist who uses a traditional Lucumi divination device to help with diagnosis of all types of cases, her strength is with court or jail trouble primarily and love issues and concerns secondarily. She does not advertise and is contacted by word of mouth. Like other Hoodoos discussed here, Dancingtree Moonwater is formally educated, she has a doctorate from a prestigious university, and is currently a tenured professor.

The founder of In the Old Tradition, a collective of African American old tradition Hoodoo workers, Moonwater, along with the Hoodoos profiled here, are working to restore some and maintain other aspects of the old plantation black belt tradition in Hoodoo and to use it to support problem solving in the African American community where the need for a supportive alternative spirituality is more pressing than ever.

Hougan Dafusky Jones, the youngest Hoodoo interviewed, was born in Lynchburg, Virginia, in 1975. He was trained from an early age by old tradition Hoodoos. In addition to being an initiated Voodoo Hougan, he learned Hoodoo from the people in his home community. It was all around him in his daily life. As a child, he would hear older women particularly, quietly speaking of work to control their men. Although it was all around him and everyone did it and believed in it, no one spoke openly about it. The elders maintained the traditional code of silence found in African and black Atlantic communities. Jones collects his own Virginia snakeroot, devil's shoestring, and numerous other traditional medicinal and magical herbs used by his Hoodoo ancestors. He has a large stock of both fresh and ritually dried herbs that he collects according to African spiritual tradition. With no botanicas within reasonable distance of their communities, in the past all root workers dug their own roots and harvested their own herbs. Today Jones and his family gather the medicine at the right time of the year, right time of day, and right season. His specialty is a type of mojo bag known as the four corners of the earth. This is an old traditional mojo unknown to and inaccessible to marketeers.[22]

In discussions with several primary care physicians in the University of Pennsylvania system, it was confirmed for me that significant numbers of African Americans, particularly those over age fifty, believe in root work as a possible cause of illness.[23] Some of them have had their beliefs left unaddressed, especially in their health care. The medical profession is just beginning to acknowledge that patients' mental states and spiritual beliefs as well as prayer and ritual can affect the response both to illness and to treatment as well as influence recovery time. It is my hope that this culture-sensitive trend will continue to strengthen so that community practitioners can work with medical doctors and community clinics when needed by clients with beliefs from the old black belt Hoodoo tradition. Though the location and sites for old tradition Hoodoo are severely limited and more difficult than ever to locate, all black belt Hoodoo has not totally vanished. Its old approach, though requiring much more effort, is still preferred by African Americans knowledgeable of the old tradition and who have faith in its ability to serve those in need.

I shall be telling this with a sigh
Somewhere ages and ages hence:
Two roads diverged in a wood, and I—
I took the one less traveled by,
And that has made all the difference.
—Robert Frost, "The Road Not Taken"

POSTSCRIPT

With the previous discussion considered, it appears that the future of old tradition Hoodoo is uncertain. The only era in which Hoodoo was universally used by African Americans, as a vehicle for liberation, was the era of enslavement. Hoodoo initially focused on the needs of the enslaved African American community. There it was universally used both to protect one against slave owners, patrollers, and punishment and to discover and redirect evil. It was also used as a means to address both physical and spiritual malady. Initially, Hoodoo was a spiritual system that, at its core, assumed a posture of spiritual resistance to both enslavement and racist domination. Socialized by the enslaved African American women who reared, cared for, and breast-fed them, numerous whites in the black belt South encountered and believed in the tradition.

After emancipation, the rule of racial terrorism, mass migration, family disruption, economic deprivation, and racial circumscription rendered the newly emerging "free" African American community vulnerable. Traditional spiritual solutions were an arena in which blacks had a degree of independent agency in unhampered sociocultural space. That independent spiritual tradition would be seized, commercialized, and transformed by middlemen minority marketeers, many of them well educated. They would seize control of Hoodoo at a time when both African Americans and their folk spiritual traditions were most vulnerable to exploitation and racialized control. Marketeered Hoodoo will continue to misrepresent itself as a true rendering of the old Hoodoo system and tradition. Though the short-lived Hoodoo religion could not survive in North America, some practices of the old Hoodoo system are still alive in some southern-based African American churches. Knowledge of this led the shrewder marketeers of the past to attempt to corner the African American Hoodoo market by directly targeting black churches; contemporary marketeers appear to have not yet taken that approach.

In the fecund marketplace of cyberspace, self-styled Hoodoo marketeers who offer themselves up as arbiters and teachers of African American spiritual tradition abound. The courses on Hoodoo offer little substantive traditional information, but they do ensure both an immediate and long-range market and that the "student" spends a significant sum of money on the supplies sold by the "instructor" or the business partner. With the proliferation of Hoodoo marketeers and those seeking profit from it, Hoodoo as a national African American cultural product and spiritual tradition could disappear. Hoodoo currently occupies a less significant place than it once did in defining the African American psyche and national character.

Some contemporary Hoodoos and root workers, particularly those not formally educated and those divorced from the old tradition, have become dependent on profiteers while seeking outsider sources for both their supplies and information about their own tradition. This pattern revisits previously documented themes in the literature and studies of African American life, particularly the themes of racially targeted, economic, and cultural exploitation. This pattern replicates in microcosm those patterns that prevailed under colonialism and slavery: the dominance and exploitation of a people's culture, labor, and the materials necessary for the continuation of that culture and tradition.

Hoodoo marketeers profit during periods of high social distress. For African Americans, that social stress is largely underpinned by America's racial caste system and malfunctioning democracy. Black family destruction, mass incarceration, job discrimination, high unemployment, substandard education, and inferior housing are all part of America's posture toward African Americans. The American system of racial control has targeted blacks during their four-century-long sojourn here. In both interviews and conversations with old tradition hoodoos, as well as marketeers, both reveal experiencing an increase in the number of clients and frequency of visits around two key issues: black family destruction and mass incarceration.[1] These two issues reveal the long-standing and persistent attacks on African American family structure through exclusion from both jobs and education as well as from racially selective law enforcement and racially motivated mass incarceration of African American men.

While crafting sophisticated denials of their exploitative practices, marketeers capitalize on the social distress of African Americans. When interviewed, most of the white marketeers and Hoodoo exploiters claimed either racial or cultural solidarity with blacks. In an attempt to defend their exploitative practices, they claim authenticity by asserting that they either "were taught by blacks" or they "grew up around blacks." Still others assert that "race is not important" or "Hoodoo is about 'spirit,' not about race." Yet they play a game of deception covered by their sales pitch.

Hoodoo continued as the only African American spiritual system producing amulets for legal immunity, family stability, economic advancement, health concerns, as well as general protection for the black community until the infusion and exposure to African traditional religion in the latter half of the twentieth century. During the last three decades of the twentieth century, the updated Hoodoo bag amulet known as the "prayer cloth" offered by Rev. Frederick Eikerenkoetter, known to millions as Reverend Ike, made a renewed appearance. For many African Americans, the orthodoxy of marketeered Hoodoo is inaccessible and plagued by the themes of fear and cultural self-loathing, related to themes of assimilation and mainstream inclusion. This is highly problematic because, like other aspects of African American cultural tradition, Hoodoo is being seized upon and further diffused by a variety of both exploiters and legitimate spiritual practitioners.

Among the items that Hoodoo profiteers offer for sale are Hoodoo kits, probably not unlike those peddled by door-to-door Hoodoo salesmen in an earlier era. One can purchase do-it-yourself mojo bags and Hoodoo Internet books and courses by self-proclaimed experts, some who claim to have been "initiated by the Gullah." Having spent many years with my Gullah fiancé traveling to and staying in the Gullah community of "Buck Hall" Pineland outside of McClellanville, South Carolina, I know that one cannot be "initiated by the Gullah" as this marketeer has claimed.

Today, marketeers like those found at Internet Web sites such as luckymojo.com, oldstyleconjure.com, and conjuredoctor.com are typical of the marketeering effort but are by no means the only examples of marketeered Hoodoo. At this writing, by far the two best-marketeered sites were luckymojo.com and oldstyleconjure.com. Although she does not state it, the "hoodooist" at the latter site implies, through subtle misrepresentation, that the African ancestors who created Hoodoo are her own. This leads some clients to believe that she is African American, even though she is white. Her statements, as well as the write-up on the Web site, lead potential clients to believe that she is in fact African American. The owners of these and other sites were not raised in the black belt Hoodoo tradition; are not

African American; have undergone neither a Hoodoo initiation, an African traditional religion initiation, nor training in the old tradition; and have no connection with a Sanctified church. They have neither the authority nor the cultural knowledge to properly make the traditional African American amulet, the mojo bag, though they continue to do so and sell them and other Hoodoo items for their own profit.

This author was once confronted by a white participant at a meeting of the National African Religion Congress, who showed me a mojo bag he claimed was made for him by the "Hoodoo experts" at a well-known Web site; it in no way resembled the old tradition wrapped mojo bags of the plantation tradition. After speaking with the site owner, she explained that a number of people have been lying about being students of her course and that she creates "authentic" mojos, which are sewn closed.[2] Other sites were equally defensive and outright hostile to inquiries. All the sites viewed, except two African American sites, were practicing marketeered Hoodoo, some quite aggressively and with the zeal of religious fanaticism.

Oldstyleconjure.com offers fabricated "New Orleans–style" "voodoo dolls," which barely resemble either the amulets of the old tradition, the spiritual effigies created in certain types of work, or the Vodun *packette*. Instead, they resemble the tourist Voodoo dolls that anyone can buy in the tourist shops of New Orleans. The clever marketeers anticipate challenges from the African American community and many have issued statements intended to deflect and short-circuit charges of "cultural theft," "lack of authenticity," and "cultural exploitation by outsiders." The claims are intended as a cover by marketeers who have experienced or anticipate challenges to the legitimacy of their Hoodoo business. As a result, a large number of them have contradictory information in their postings and on their sites. An example of this can be found at a site that states, on one hand, that Hoodoo came to the United States with Africans; in another section, she states that Hoodoo is Christian. These contradictory claims are on different pages and difficult to observe by those not looking for inconsistencies in information. An average observer could ask the question, "Well, which way was it? Did Hoodoo come with Africans or did it originate in Christianity?" Some marketeers claim that Hoodoo is Jewish rather than Christian. Others claim that it is an amalgamation of numerous practices and traditions. The Hoodoo cyberspace universe often contributes to the obfuscation and confusion about the phenomenon known as Hoodoo.

When questioned about their background, ethnicity, or race, the whites who own the most successful sites and claim to "know Hoodoo" were all very defensive. All contacts that I spoke with issued some sort of claim intended to legitimate their "right" to make money from the sale of Hoodoo. One marketeer claimed to be "raised around blacks," another claimed to have "learned from blacks in the 1960s," another put a Negro client on the phone to validate her "right" to exploit the sale of Hoodoo recipes and supplies. All their responses indicate their own need to deflect challenges from the African American community to their authenticity, legitimacy, and intent.

To quote one of this author's informants, "To these people Hoodoo is nothing more than 'nigga wicca,' and it is not that."[3] Many vulnerable and ill-informed potential clients will see the false claim as legitimation and proof of authenticity. The outrageous claims are all designed to convey an air of legitimacy to the potential customer, who usually knows little if anything of the old plantation black belt Hoodoo system. At very best, the information that marketeers offer has been gleaned from an uncritically perused segment of scholarly literature on Hoodoo, such as the *Journal of American Folklore* or Harry Middleton Hyatt's five-volume work *Hoodoo-Conjuration-Witchcraft-Rootwork: Beliefs Accepted by Many Negroes and White Persons*. This generates concerns that need to be considered when using them as accurate Hoodoo documents. Much of the Hoodoo sold by marketeers is overlaid with fabrication. Items such as "war water," "death spells," "good luck powder," "lucky candles," and "money-drawing oil" in no way resemble the Hoodoo of the pre–World War I black community. And here is one dilemma for researchers who write about Hoodoo: The Hoodoo that some researchers write about is marketeered Hoodoo, which in few ways resembles the old African American Hoodoo system developed by and for African Americans.

African Americans' distrust, fear, and suspicion of whites led some blacks to fabricate interview information for money or to give inaccurate or limited information to white interviewers. One problem recognized by both Zora Neale Hurston and Hyatt was the possible "interviewer effect" in which an informant changes his or her answer to suit the expectations of the interviewer as perceived by the client. This was typical of black-white exchanges in the South at the time of Hyatt's work. By the time Hyatt started interviewing Hoodoo believers and practitioners, the old black belt Hoodoo system was already overshadowed by the marketeered versions of Hoodoo. This can account for consistencies in the interviews across time and region, which could be mistaken as indicators of authenticity. Some Internet marketeers publish these misinterpreted secondary sources for their own monetary benefit.

Today there is an extensive proliferation of Internet sites using the term *Hoodoo*; they number 1.5 million, and the number is growing. The movement by African Americans toward discarding black traditions to achieve racial integration and approval by mainstream arbiters threatens the remaining stability and possible rejuvenation of old tradition black belt Hoodoo. The old black belt Hoodoo system had been either completely driven underground or dissipated into Sanctified church ritual so that it was unrecognizable to most inside the African American Hoodoo community, or it had been completely taken over by marketeers.

On the other hand, there is hopeful evidence for the preservation and recuperation of old tradition Hoodoo. Several of this author's old tradition informants have witnessed an increase in the number of young people both turning to old tradition Hoodoo as a problem-solving paradigm and requesting training in the old tradition. A number of them are crossing over into African traditional religion, thus attesting to the need for alternative spirituality. As an Olorisha of Ogun in the Lukumi/Yoruba tradition, this author has personally observed an increase in the number of young people seeking assistance and support from, as well as conversion into, one of the New World Afrikan religious traditions, particularly Lukumi, Akan, Palo, and Voodoo. When questioned about their need to convert to an African traditional religion, some of them indicated that their first choice was Hoodoo, but since it is now controlled by whites, who sell the supplies and have limited access to the black community, they turned instead to African traditional religion.

In an earlier time, Hoodoo for African Americans was the only accessible African-derived alternative spiritual source. Certain African American churches, particularly those within the Sanctified church heritage, have kept the threadbare old tradition Hoodoo connection with the church alive and provide the much-needed institutional backdrop to African-styled alternative spiritual work. Within these sacred institutional contexts, one can still find elements from the African Religion Complex, the shout ritual, spirit possession, and water immersion baptism still intact. Unfortunately, many of the church-based root workers have few alternatives but to turn to marketeers as the black church becomes more assimilationist and continues to marginalize Hoodoo.

When one seeks spiritual help through Hoodoo in the context of the African American Sanctified church, one, more often than not, is seeking to have "roots" removed from rather than put on someone. Sanctified church members who engage in spirit work will promptly admit to being able to remove a Hoodoo fix but will readily claim to never have or even know how to put "roots" on anyone, though many will admit that they know someone who has or who currently can throw a fix. Perhaps Hoodoo will look to itself and its traditional African religious parents and New World cousins for its own rejuvenation and survival. And perhaps new workers in the old black belt Hoodoo tradition will help Hoodoo's threadbare bones put on the flesh of a healthy and rebounding supplemental spiritual system and continue to support African American psychic and cultural survival.

With respect to Hoodoo research, there are more than a few unexplored research paths, which, like "the road not taken," can make all the difference. The African American experience with Hoodoo must be researched and documented and should include a thorough investigation of Hoodoo's impact and influence on African American cultural life, particularly as it related to health care practices and health care decision making. The blues is full of references to Hoodoo, root work, conjuring, and fixing of enemies, rivals, mates, potential mates, and situations. But we must have more than a simple documenting of Hoodoo references as found in blues lyrics. Though largely absent from most research on Hoodoo, including this work, the role of power, class stratification, and race in the Hoodoo process should not be overlooked. Though present in the blues, content that references Hoodoo is for the most part absent from pre–Civil War African American musical forms,[4] as it is largely absent from, though not totally nonexistent, in post–World War II rhythm and blues. I cannot say that I have heard of any references to Hoodoo in hip-hop music that emerged at the end of the twentieth century. Future research on Hoodoo, as well as Hoodoo itself, must place the African American experience—rather than the interpretation of marketeers and exploiters—at the center of the investigation, squarely at the crossroads of the academic paradigm and the African American experience. Only then can we meet the devil at the crossroads and defeat him.

Notes

PRESCRIPT

1. The term *hoodooist* was used to describe the alleged practitioner.

2. Kuna, "Hoodoo."

3. The Ring Shout was the sacred circle dance performed by African American bondsmen and their descendants. The dance was always performed in a sacred context such as worship, death rituals, and other sacred occasions. It was observed from St. Louis to the Gullah Sea Islands, from Virginia to Mississippi, in Philadelphia, and in Maryland. The dance was always performed in a counterclockwise circling formation, with the center reserved for those who fell under the spirit and experienced possession. The ritual was modified with the introduction of church pews to the old "praise houses" and with the standard church pew formation in black churches. The ritual continues today as "shoutin'" or as "ketchin' the spirit." The Ring Shout can still, occasionally, be seen in its original circle formation along the Gullah Coast in older churches in communities like Awendaw, Buck Hall, and Pineland, South Carolina, on special occasions such as Mother's Day.

4. Kulii, "Hoodoo Tales Collected in Indiana." The informants in this study repeatedly stated that they learned about Hoodoo from the discussions of older family members.

5. Chireau, "Conjuring."

6. Mbiti, *Introduction to African Religion*, 25.

7. Thomas, "Working Class and Lower Class Origins of Black Culture."

8. Hyatt, *Hoodoo-Conjuration-Witchcraft-Rootwork.*

9. Puckett, *Folk Beliefs of the Southern Negro.*

10. Hurston, "High John De Conquer; Hurston, "Hoodoo in America."

11. Snow, *Walking Over Medicine;* Snow, "Sorcerers, Saints and Charlatans"; Snow, "Mail Order Magic"; Snow, "Folk Medical Beliefs and Their Implications for Care of Patients"; Mitchell, *Hoodoo Medicine;* Fontenot, *Secret Doctors;* Savage, "The Evolution of Hoodoo in Mississippi and Contemporary Black Health."

12. Cooley, "Root Doctors and Psychics in the Region"; Cooley, "Conversations About Hoodoo"; Cooley, "Root Stories"; Kulii, "A Look at Hoodoo in Three Urban Areas of Indiana."

13. Robinson, "Black Healers during the Colonial Period and Early 19th Century America," 81–86; Chireau, "Conjuring."

14. Chireau, *Black Magic.*

15. Bell, "Pattern, Structure and Logic in Afro-American Hoodoo Performance."

16. Anderson, *Conjure in African American Society.*

17. Most notably Luckymojo.com. The owner of the site was rude and off-putting, but only after I revealed both my status as an Olorisha/priestess of Ogun and that I was not interested in purchasing her wares. I found Ms. Yronwode to be very defensive, especially about the incorrect Hoodoo information she posts on the Internet. I found other Internet sites on Hoodoo, and the owners of the sites were even more defensive and hostile than Ms. Yronwode. Another site owner whom I contacted, calling herself "Starr," screamed and cursed into the phone that she was busy doing "readings" and that I better not "mess with her." Like the marketeers who advertise in black confessions magazines, few of the Internet marketeers were African American. Another site owner, who lists himself as both "Dr." and "PhD," became defensive and insulting when I asked about his credentials.

18. Whoopi Goldberg's portrayal of an African American psychic in the 1990 Hollywood movie *Ghost*, starring Patrick Swayze and Demi Moore, is reminiscent in certain scenes of Mantan Moreland's numerous portrayals in which he is fearful of "ghosts." These Hollywood attempts at humor ridicule African American deep spirituality.

19. See glossary for explanation of the term *called.*

20. Thomas, "Working-Class and Lower-Class Origins of Black Culture."

CHAPTER 1. TRADITIONAL RELIGION
IN WEST AFRICA AND IN THE NEW WORLD

1. Thornton, *The Kongolese Saint Anthony;* Thornton, "The Development of an African Catholic Church in the Kingdom of Kongo, 1491–1750." John Tucker places the conversion of the first Kongo ruler earlier than Thornton; Tucker, *Angola,* 29.

2. Schon and Crowther, *Journals of the Rev. James Frederick Schon and Mr. Samuel Crowther,* 33.

3. Mbiti, *African Religions and Philosophy,* 6.

4. Starobin, *Industrial Slavery in the Old South;* Bradford, "The Negro Ironworker in Ante-Bellum Virginia," *Journal of Southern History* 25 (May, 1959):194–206; Bromberg, "Slavery in the Virginia Tobacco Factories"; Green, "Georgia's Forgotten Industry"; Green, "Gold Mining"; Galloway, "Sugar Industry of Pernambuco during the Nineteenth Century"; Guthrie, "Colonial Economy"; Harrison, "The Evolution of Colombian Tobacco Trade to 1875."

5. An example is observed in the age-grade organizational unit that required that the youth, within a certain age range, be organized into mutual support

groups based on age or location in the life cycle. These groups, which influenced all societal members, helped maintain social order and enrich the meaning of the numerous transitional stages in African traditional life, while grounding and locating the individual in a multilayered obligatory network of guidance support and assistance. Traditionally these groups were responsible for members; they were their brother's keeper and were often assigned certain duties to be performed for the village community, herding, for example. This assigned obligation and responsibility extended into nearly all areas of life. For example, if a young man were interested in a young woman as a potential wife, a fellow age-grade group member might be expected to initiate the courtship and marriage process according to the traditionally required protocol. Group members who found themselves in foreign lands were expected to render assistance to age-grade group members from their community back home. In traditional times, the obligation to these groups was binding and presented the community with ready-made units for social action, change, or conservation, as these groups often moved as a unit, especially in village social and ritual activities. The principle of age-grade organization, with respect for elders, came to the North American mainland in the memories of African captives and was undoubtedly at least early on a small part of the way slaves attempted to organize their own lives, labor, and community.

6. Aimes, "African Institutions in America."

7. Sieber and Herreman, *Hair in African Art and Culture.*

8. Hall, *Africans in Colonial Louisiana,* 49.

9. Peek, *African Divination Systems;* Serpos, "Un Procède de Divination au Dahomey"; Hounwanou, *Le Fa,* 249; Dorjahn, "Some Aspects of Temne Divination"; Shaw, "An-bere"; Mendonsa, "Etiology and Divination among the Sisala of Northern Ghana"; Devisch, "Perspectives on Divination in Contemporary Sub-Saharan Africa"; Jackson, "An Approach to Kuranko Divination"; Bohannan, "Tiv Divination"; Gebauer, *Spider Divination in the Cameroons.*

10. Bascom, *Ifa Divination;* Bascom, *Sixteen Cowries.*

11. Mbiti, *Introduction to African Religion.*

12. Beecham, *Ashantee and the Gold Coast,* 239.

13. Ibid., 174–176.

14. Hall, *Africans in Colonial Louisiana,* 52; Imperato, *African Folk Medicine.*

15. Nassau, *Fetichism in West Africa,* 83.

16. Milligan, *The Fetish Folk of West Africa,* 39.

17. Ibid., 223–224.

18. Hall, *Africans in Colonial Louisiana,* 49.

19. Imperato, *African Folk Medicine,* 63; Marees, *Description and Historical Account of the Gold Kingdom of Guinea,* 73.

20. Schon and Crowther, *Journals of the Rev. James Frederick Schon and Mr. Samuel Crowther,* 30–31.

21. Beecham, *Ashantee and the Gold Coast,* 181–182.

22. Milligan, *The Fetish Folk of West Africa,* 150–151.

23. Beecham, *Ashantee and the Gold Coast,* 189.

24. Sofowora, *Medicinal Plants and Traditional Medicine in Africa,* 30–32.

25. Ibid., 30.

26. Ibid.

27. Mbiti, *Introduction to African Religion*, 192.

28. Thornton, *The Kongolese Saint Anthony*, 133.

29. Milligan, *The Fetish Folk of West Africa*, 220.

30. Beecham, *Ashantee and the Gold Coast*, 204.

31. Nassau, *Fetichism in West Africa*, 85.

32. Beecham, *Ashantee and the Gold Coast*, 49–50.

33. Ibid., 192.

34. Williams, "Development of Obeah in Jamaica."

35. Raboteau, *Slave Religion*.

36. Gebauer, *Spider Divination in the Cameroons*, 15.

CHAPTER 2. DISRUPTIVE INTERSECTION

1. Katz, *Black Indians*.

2. Professor Michael Gomez has done a brilliant job of exploring the possible influences and cultural significances in the development of African American identity and culture in the three areas and will not be repeated here. Rather, a brief and succinct overview of the major African groups and some of their influences will be given; Gomez, *Exchanging Our Country Marks*.

3. Hall, *Africans in Colonial Louisiana*, 162–164; see also Gomez, *Exchanging Our Country Marks*, 50–51.

4. Gomez, *Exchanging Our Country Marks*, 114.

5. Fu-Kiau, *African Cosmology of the Bantu-Kongo*; Stuckey, *Slave Culture*, 8–100; Thompson, *Flash of the Spirit*; MacGaffey, *Religion and Society in Central Africa*.

6. Georgia Writer's Project, *Drums and Shadows*, 62; Burwell, *A Girl's Life in Virginia before the War*, 163. For further descriptions of the Ring Shout, see Parrish, *Slave Songs of the Georgia Sea Islands*; Higginson, *Army Life in a Black Regiment*; Forten, *The Journal of Charlotte L. Forten*, 149, 151; Gannett, "The Freedmen at Port Royal," 10.

7. Morgan, *Slave Counterpoint*, 36.

8. See glossary for explanation of "track gathering," or "picking up tracks."

9. Morgan, *Slave Counterpoint*, 129.

10. For discussions of African ethnic identity in Louisiana, see Hall, *Africans in Colonial Louisiana*, 42–55.

11. Raboteau, *Slave Religion*, 43.

12. DuBois, *The Souls of Black Folk*, 196.

13. For an excellent analysis of the counterclockwise circle, see Stuckey, *Slave Culture*; Gaffney, *The Function and Form of the Ring Shout as a Religious Expression*.

14. For a source on the variety of Kongo *nkisi*, see MacGaffey, *Art and Healing of the Bakongo*.

15. Gomez, *Exchanging Our Country Marks*; Gomez discusses the major African ethnic groups that were brought to the United States during and after the colonial

period. These groups include, but are not limited to, Mande-speaking Bambara, Temne from Sierra Leone, Akhan, and Bakongo.

16. This date of 1807 marks the outlawing of the international slave trade.

17. Cooper, *Satanstoe;* in various places in the book, Cooper comments on the cultural relationship between African-born and American-born slaves. Apparently, African-born slaves were revered as cultural leaders and advisors in the slave community. Cooper describes scenes from a Pinkster festival in which African-born bondsmen advise American-born bondsmen on culture.

18. For a discussion of the diversity of the slave population in colonial South Carolina, see Higgins, "The Geographical Origins of Negro Slaves in Colonial South Carolina"; Higgins contends that a much higher percentage of American slaves than previously thought were imported directly from Africa through the Carolinas; see also Hall, *Africans in Colonial Louisiana,* 42–43.

19. Straight-line theory states that new immigrants discard their old ethnic identity for a new identity directly, with little regard for outside influences. Bumpy-line assimilation theory sees the assimilation of immigrants as a complex, multifaceted process with numerous political and social influences both encouraging and inhibiting ethnic transformation and assimilation.

20. Both Gwendolyn Midlo Hall and Walter Rodney discuss the process of interethnic assimilation in Africa; Hall, *Africans in Colonial Louisiana;* Rodney, *A History of the Upper Guinea Coast 1545–1800.*

21. For a discussion of this principle in action, see Thornton, *The Kongolese Saint Anthony;* see also Thornton, "The Development of an African Catholic Church in the Kingdom of the Congo, 1491–1750."

22. Parrish, *Slave Songs of the Georgia Sea Islands.*

23. Johnson, *Soul by Soul;* this work documents the high degree of fluidity in the American slave population resulting from sale and transportation from one region to another.

24. Emery, *Black Dance from 1619 to 1970.*

25. For a discussion of the possibilities of the Kongo cosmogram as a template for the Ring Shout, see Stuckey, *Slave Culture;* see also Gomez, *Exchanging Our Country Marks;* Thompson, *Flash of the Spirit.*

26. Parrish, *Slave Songs of the Georgia Sea Islands;* Stuckey, *Slave Culture;* Gaffney, "The Function and Form of the Ring Shout as a Religious Expression."

27. Melville Herskovits had this to say: "On the basis of such evidence from Africa and the New World as is available, then, a prima-facie case can be made that the slave population included a certain number of representatives from African governing and priestly classes"; Herskovits, *Myth of the Negro Past,* 107.

28. "Tatler On the Management of Negroes," 84–85.

29. Hall, "Negro Conjuring and Tricking," 241; Genovese, *Roll Jordan Roll,* 221; Jones, *The Religious Instruction of Negroes in the United States,* 128; Roberts, *From Trickster to Badman,* 65–107.

30. *South Carolina Gazette,* February 25–March 4, 1750; *South Carolina Gazette,* May 7–May 14, 1750; "The Negro Cesar's Cure for Poison," 103–104.

31. Robinson, "Black Healers during the Colonial Period and Early 19th Century America," 81–86.

32. Beecham, *Ashantee and the Gold Coast,* 192.

33. Ibid.

34. Glave, "Fetishism in Congo Land," 835.

35. Mather, *The Angel of Bethesda,* 107.

36. Report, June 29, 1729, to Board of Trades (CO 5) 1337:ff 132–133, British Public Record Office, Chancery Lane, London, WC2; Virginia State Library, Richmond, Virginia, Paul I. Chestnut; see also Headlam, *Calendar of State Papers,* 418–419.

37. Kuna, "Hoodoo," 273–275.

38. Lacy and Harrell, "Plantation Home Remedies."

39. Robinson, "Black Healers during the Colonial Period and Early 19th Century America," 92.

40. Ibid., 60.

41. Blanton, *Medicine in Virginia in the Eighteenth Century,* 45, 173, 212–213; Phillips, *Life and Labor in the Old South,* 165, 283.

42. Genovese, *Roll Jordan Roll,* 224; Yetman, *Life under the "Peculiar Institution,"* 286.

43. Patterson, *The Negro in Tennessee, 1790–1865,* 36.

44. Debien, *Plantations et esclaves à Sain-Domingue,* 60, 63, 68; James, *Black Jacobins,* 16–17; Naipaul, *Loss of El Dorado,* 112, 171, 326–327; Pope-Hennessy, *Sins of the Fathers,* 65, 227; Brackett, *Negro in Maryland,* 132–133; Phillips, "Slave Crime in Virginia," 337–338; Aptheker, *American Negro Slave Revolts,* 192, 197–198, 241–242; McDougle, *Slavery in Kentucky,* 38; Harriet Martineau, *Society in America,* vol. 2, 330; Scarborough, *The Overseer,* 172; Rawick, *The American Slave,* vol. 3, 158. According to Elenor Herron and Alice Mabel Bacon, writing in the late nineteenth century and referring to the frequency with which poisoning was used, "there was on the plantations in the old days a vast amount of just that sort of thing"; Herron and Bacon, "Conjuring and Conjure-Doctors in the Southern United States," 143–147, 224–226.

45. *The Pennsylvania Gazette,* November 23, 1749.

46. *The Pennsylvania Gazette,* February 19, 1751.

47. *The Pennsylvania Gazette,* July 24, 1755.

48. Chesnutt, "Superstitions and Folk Lore of the South," 233.

49. For a discussion of the use of African and Native American healing practices on the early frontier, see Wood, "People's Medicine in the Early South."

50. Leone and Fry, "Conjuring in the Big House Kitchen."

51. Glave, "Fetishism in Congo Land," 829–830.

52. Ibid., 829.

53. Stephen C. LaVere, *Robert Johnson: The Complete Recordings,* liner notes, Columbia Records, CBS Records, Inc., 1990, 18. In the mid-1950s, this author was taken into an after-hours joint in Cleveland, Ohio, in which patrons were discussing the ethic of never drinking from a bootlegged liquor bottle on which the seal was

already broken. In the more reputable jooks, honky-tonks, and after-hours joints, the seal on the bottle was broken at the table when the liquor was ordered. This was done so that the patrons at the ordering table could see the seal broken and know that the liquor was not tampered with.

54. Mbiti, *Introduction to African Religion*, 74, 77, 127, 139, 165, 170–173.

55. Mbiti, *African Religions and Philosophy*, 162–188.

56. DuBois, *The Souls of Black Folk*, 95.

57. *South Carolina Gazette*, September 17, 1772.

58. Johnson, *Soul by Soul*.

59. "Folk-Lore and Ethnology," *Southern Workman*, 315.

60. Achebe, *Things Fall Apart*, 79–81.

61. Torrey, *Witchdoctors and Psychiatrists*, 54–68. In this author's estimation, client expectation is especially significant in the curative process.

62. In several personal conversations with Sterling Stuckey concerning the Ring Shout, he mentioned that the linear organization of church pews prevents performance of the circular shout. I concluded that a linear shout is now performed, which uses the isles instead of the center of the floor as had previously been done in the old rural Ring Shout. For a description of how African American bondsmen handled church pews on the plantation, see Olmstead, *A Journey in the Seaboard Slave States*, 449.

63. Dubois, *The Souls of Black Folk*, 195.

64. Puckett, *Folk Beliefs of the Southern Negro*.

65. Conjure men in particular were known to be marked by unusual appearance or strange features, such as "blue gums" or "chicken breasted." They were also known to behave in an unorthodox fashion in their style of dress or language.

66. Thompson, "An Aesthetic of the Cool."

67. DuBois, *The Souls of Black Folk*, 195.

68. DuBois, *Black Folk: Then and Now*, 198.

69. Payne, *Recollections of Seventy Years*, 254.

70. Wood, "Peoples Medicine in the Early South."

71. Porteus, "The Gri-Gri Case"; Scott, "The Slave Insurrection in New York in 1712"; Davis, *A Rumor of Revolt;* Stuckey, *Slave Culture*, 50–51; Starobin, *Denmark Vesey;* Chase, "The 1741 Conspiracy to Burn New York."

72. Douglass, *The Life and Times of Frederick Douglass*, 130–141.

73. Hughes, *Thirty Years a Slave*, 108.

74. Owens, *Voodoo Tales*, 175.

75. With the loss of the old African traditional gods and the introduction of Christianity into the slave quarter, Psalms were substituted to invoke results and tailor intention. Examples include Psalms 4. This was used by slaves for wealth, chance, success, luck, and healing. Later this Psalm was used for winning at gambling, especially in the illegal lotteries known as the numbers. Special thanks to Cassandra Wimbs for sharing information on this aspect of Hoodoo.

CHAPTER 3. THE SEARCH FOR
HIGH JOHN THE CONQUER

1. Throughout this work, the spelling "Conquer" will be used. Though the assumption is that the correct term is "Conqueror," its pronunciation in southern African American communities in the United States was and is "Conquer." The term may or may not have anything to do with the term *conqueror*. John de Conquer could have originally been one word such as *jondekonka*, which eventually became Anglicized in its pronunciation. There is room for much linguistic and sociohistoric speculation.

2. Chireau, "Conjuring: An Analysis of African American Folk Beliefs and Practices."

3. One can find this ridiculous, racist interpretation of High John root's power discussed at the white-owned marketeering Web site luckymojo.com. This sexualized interpretation was developed and disseminated primarily by middlemen minority Ashkenazi Jewish merchants as they sought to take control of the Hoodoo trade and shut out blacks who served their own communities' spiritual needs. In the process, they destroyed the old Hoodoo system developed on the southern plantations by enslaved African Americans and further contributed to the racist ideology and deep-seated fear surrounding black male sexuality. European Jewish middlemen merchants were like Christians and all other whites in this respect.

4. Linajes, Rico-Gray, and Carrion, "Traditional Production System of the Root of Jalap, *Ipomoea purga* (Convolvulaceae), in Central Veracruz, Mexico," 85.

5. Carroll, *Blacks In Colonial Veracruz*, 4.

6. Linajes, "Traditional Production System of the Root of Jalap," 85.

7. Linajes, "Traditional Production System of the Root of Jalap," 85; Blanco, "El cultivo de las plantas medicinales en Mexico tiene gran porvenir; De Jauregui, "Estudios acerca de algunos purgantes indigenas"; Beaton, "Note on the Jalap Plant of Commerce"; Balfour, "Notice of Some Plants Which Flowered Recently in the Edinburgh Botanical Garden"; Hanbury, "On the Cultivation of Jalap."

8. Hurston, "High John De Conquer," 450.

9. Ibid., 452.

10. Ibid., 453.

11. Ibid.

12. Wimbs, "African American Theory, Belief and Practices," 52–55.

13. Hurston, "High John De Conquer," 452.

14. Oliver, *Blues Fell This Morning*, 125; Hurston, *Mules and Men*, 230.

15. Conversation with Babalawo Obalumi Ogunseye, Babalawo and Olorisha of Shango, October 1999, Philadelphia, Pennsylvania.

16. For a discussion of "balance" as a universal African aesthetic and organizing principle, see Thompson, "An Aesthetic of the Cool."

17. The term *incremental repetition* is borrowed from Hurston's essay "Characteristics of Negro Expression," 44.

18. This John story was told to a group of us by James Peterson after a bid whist card game at his home in Fort Lauderdale, Florida, in November 1964.

19. Johnson, *The Fabled Doctor Jim Jordan,* 39.

20. McTeer, *Fifty Years as a Low Country Witch Doctor,* 24.

21. Ibid.

22. Schmalleger, "The Root Doctor and the Courtroom."

23. Johnson, *The Fabled Doctor Jim Jordan,* 83.

24. Personal email communication with border control agent and botanist William Graves at Laredo, Texas.

25. Aptheker, "Maroons within the Present Limits of the United States."

26. Johnson, *Soul by Soul,* 76–77.

27. Ibid., 71.

28. Brown, *The Narrative of William Wells Brown,* 193, 210.

29. Johnson, *Soul by Soul,* 41.

30. Ibid., 71.

31. Ibid., 72.

32. Hall, *Databases for the Study of Afro-Louisiana History and Genealogy.*

33. Guillot, *Negros rebeledes y negros cimarrones,* 80–85.

34. Bowser, *The African Slave in Colonial Peru,* 187–188; Lockhart, *Spanish Peru,* 189.

35. Arcaya, *Insurrecion de los negros de la Serrania de Coro,* 23–49.

36. Interview with Dr. Thomas Morton, professor at Temple University, author and expert on Palenque San Basilio, Philadelphia, Pa., March 15, 2010.

37. Aptheker, "Maroons within the Present Limits of the United States."

38. Carroll, "Mandinga."

39. Kent, "Palmares," 55; Diggs, "Zumbi and the Republic of Os Palmares"; Ennes, "The Palmares 'Republic' of Pernambuco," 208.

40. Hall, *Africans in Colonial Louisiana,* 203.

41. Ibid., 226.

42. Ibid.; chapter 7 outlines valuable details of the relationship between Maroons, slaves, and people outside the slave community.

43. Ibid., 232.

44. Dieterien, *Essai sur la religion Bambara,* 87, 94, 147.

45. Both the Creole French and English translation are taken from Cable, "Creole Slave Songs." There is a slightly different version in Hall's *Africans in Colonial Louisiana* that challenges Cable's translation of the opening line of the song. *Zeinzens,* according to Hall, is a Bambara and Creole word referring to an amulet created from human remains for protection. Since the slave population of New Orleans and parts of Louisiana contained a significant Bambara presence, Hall's interpretation may be closer to the mark than Cable's translation. Among the Bambara, *Sinzin* is deeply associated with the birth of twins, particularly when one twin has died; see Imperato, *African Folk Medicine,* 118; see also Imperato, "Twins among the Bambara and Malinke of Mali," Imperato, "Bamana and Maninka Twin Figures"; Imperato and Imperato, "Twins, Hermaphrodites, and an Androgynous Albino Deity."

46. For a more detailed discussion of Maroons within the limits of the United States, see Aptheker, "Maroons within the Present Limits of the United States."

47. Hurston, "High John De Conquer," 455.

48. Ibid.

49. Ibid., 458.

CHAPTER 4. CRISIS AT THE CROSSROADS

1. Henri, *Black Migration, Movement North, 1900–1920,* 60–62, 135–136.

2. Pendleton, "Notes on Negro Folk-Lore and Witchcraft in the South," 203–204.

3. Parrish, *Slave Songs of the Georgia Sea Islands;* Bailey with Bledsoe, *God, Dr. Buzzard and the Bolito Man.*

4. Szwed and Marks, "The Afro-American Transformation of European Set Dances and Dance Suites"; Hazzard-Donald, "The Circle and the Line."

5. Twain, *The Adventures of Huckleberry Finn,* 3–4.

6. Bailey with Bledsoe, *God, Dr. Buzzard, and the Bolito Man,* 87.

7. Chesnutt, *The Conjure Woman and Other Conjure Tales,* 112.

8. Ibid., 113.

9. Ibid., 112.

10. Neal, *Ju-Ju in My Life,* 20–24.

11. Faulkner, *The Sound and the Fury,* 69.

12. DuBose Heyward, "The Half Pint Flask," in Hutchisson, *A DuBose Heyward Reader.*

13. Berendt, *Midnight in the Garden of Good and Evil.*

14. *Ju-Ju: Research Papers in Afro-American Studies* (Spring 1975): iii.

15. Owen-Workman, Phillips, and Stout, *Readers, Advisors, and Storefront Churches.*

16. Special thanks to Cassandra Wimbs, who supplied me with a list of Psalms used by Hoodoo practitioners.

17. Hutchisson, *A DuBose Heyward Reader,* 186; "Mortuary Customs and Beliefs of South Carolina Negroes," 318–319.

18. Rucker, *Black Herman's Secrets of Magic, Mystery, and Legerdemain.*

19. Haskell, "Sacrificial Offerings among North Carolina Negroes," 267–268.

20. Zora Neale Hurston probably was among the last generation to undergo an actual Hoodoo initiation. She describes these initiations in *Mules and Men.*

21. For a partial accounting of the relationship between the black church and Hoodoo, see Chireau, *Black Magic.*

22. Puckett, *Folk Beliefs of the Southern Negro,* 168–169; Puckett interview with informant no. 124, Alf Goodman, Columbus, Mississippi.

23. Bailey with Bledsoe, *God, Dr. Buzzard and the Bolito Man,* 87.

24. Bell, "Pattern, Structure and Logic in Afro-American Hoodoo Performance," 8.

25. Pendleton, "Notes on Negro Folk-Lore and Witchcraft in the South," 203–204.

26. DuBois, *The Souls of Black Folk,* 96.

27. Ibid., 195–197.

28. Hurston, *The Sanctified Church;* Baer, "An Anthropological View of Black

Spiritual Churches in Nashville, Tennessee"; Drake and Cayton, *Black Metropolis;* Jacobs and Kaslow, *The Spiritual Churches of New Orleans.*

29. Payne, *Recollections of Seventy Years,* 254.

30. Henry Brown, quoted in Raboteau, *Slave Religion,* 73.

31. Hurston, *Mules and Men,* 277.

32. Cross, "Witchcraft in North Carolina."

33. Dr. John Brickell, *The Natural History of North Carolina* (Dublin, 1737), 370–374, quoted in Cross, "Witchcraft in North Carolina," 219.

34. "Tail Dragger," by Willie Dixon (Hoochie Coochie Music, Admin. by Bug/Arc Music Corp., BMI), recorded by Howlin' Wolf on August 14, 1963.

35. Moore, "Superstitions from Georgia," 226–228.

36. Cross, "Witchcraft in North Carolina," 255.

37. "Aunt Memory," in "The Florida Negro" Collection, Florida State Archives, Tallahassee, Florida, series 1585, carton 1, Folder no. 35.

38. Bailey with Bledsoe, *God, Dr. Buzzard and the Bolito Man,* 65.

39. Conversation with Willis James "Buck" Jones, July 1977, Leesburg, Texas. According to Jones, his sister, and his wife, Vera, the victim would walk down the road past Jones's house. Most people in the area knew that he had been rooted.

40. Willis "Buck" Jones conversation, July 1977, Leesburg, Texas.

41. Hyatt, *Hoodoo-Conjuration-Witchcraft-Rootwork,* 4:2818–2936.

42. Parsons, *Folklore of the Sea Islands, South Carolina,* 198.

43. *The Cleveland Gazette,* Saturday, September 8, 1883.

44. Hurston, *Mules and Men,* 130.

45. DuBois, *The Philadelphia Negro,* 102.

46. Nye, *The Unembarrassed Muse,* 162; Anderson, *Snake Oil, Hustlers, and Hambones,* 78.

47. Anderson, *Snake Oil, Hustlers, and Hambones,* 78.

48. Owens, *Voodoo Tales,* 169, 170, 171.

49. Anderson, *Snake Oil, Hustlers, and Hambones,* 101; Hoyt, *Town Hall Tonight,* 245–246.

50. Banks, *First Person America,* 186–187.

51. Kiser, *Sea Island to City,* 37.

52. *Pittsburgh Courier,* April 6, 1912, 4.

53. Puckett, *Folk Beliefs of the Southern Negro,* 168–169.

54. Still, *Early Recollections and Life of Dr. James Still.*

55. Parsons, *Folklore of the Sea Islands, South Carolina,* 199.

56. Puckett, *Folk Beliefs of the Southern Negro;* Fontenot, *Secret Doctors.*

57. Moore, "Superstitions from Georgia" (1892), 230–231.

58. Parsons, *Folklore of the Sea Islands, South Carolina,* 206, note 1.

CHAPTER 5. THE DEMISE OF DR. BUZZARD

1. Long, *Spiritual Merchants, Religion, Magic and Commerce;* Long gives a thorough history and description of the major manufacturers and suppliers in the Hoodoo spiritual trade.

2. In urban areas such as Philadelphia, New York, Pittsburgh, and Cleveland, root and herb peddlers walked the streets crying out their fresh and newly dried products. They belong to a cultural tradition of African American street-crying peddlers such as the Arabbers of Baltimore, Maryland; see Roland Freeman, *The Arabbers of Baltimore.*

3. Ross, *How Rabbit Tricked Otter and Other Cherokee Trickster Stories,* 6–7.

4. *St. Helena Island Cemetery Survey,* October 15, 1999, 6; see also letter from Grace Morris Cordial, South Carolina Resources Librarian in Beaufort County Public Library Vertical File, Beaufort, South Carolina.

5. McTeer, *High Sheriff of the Low Country;* McTeer, *Fifty Years as a Low Country Witch Doctor.*

6. Personal interview with Brother A. B. Gregory, great-grandson of Stepheney Robinson, Dr. Buzzard, St. Helena Island, South Carolina, August 2000.

7. McTeer, *High Sheriff of the Low Country;* McTeer, *Fifty Years as a Low Country Witch Doctor;* this fact is mentioned in both books by McTeer.

8. Personal interview with Gullah speaker Frances Nesbitt, age sixty-four, August 2003, Buck Hall community, Awendaw, South Carolina.

9. Adams, "Dr. Bug, Dr. Buzzard, and the U.S.A."

10. The phrase *chew the root* here refers to a type of courtroom ritual performed on the defendants behalf, in which a magical root is chewed and the saliva is spit discreetly in the courtroom. It is believed that the defendant will win the case or receive much lighter punishment if the root is chewed for them or by them on their own behalf. In most instances, the root is galanga root, a relative of the ginger plant, known in Hoodoo work as "little John," "low John," or "chewing John."

11. Adams, "Dr. Bug, Dr. Buzzard, and the U.S.A." 71.

12. Ibid.

13. The use of bones, hair, and graveyard dirt is an indication of Kongo origins. Hoodoo shares the use of these items with the practice of Palo in the United States.

14. Interview and conversation with Albert Hampton, longtime employee of Philadelphia's well-known Hoodoo supply store Lady Dale's Curio Shop, April 1996, Philadelphia.

15. Long, *Spiritual Merchants, Religion, Magic and Commerce,* 187.

16. Ibid.

17. Ibid., 189–190.

18. Henri, *Black Migration, Movement North 1900–1920.*

19. Long, *Spiritual Merchants, Religion, Magic and Commerce,* 189.

20. The term *race records* refers to a time when the music world was racially segregated. It designated music that was recorded by and sold primarily to African Americans. Dream books were pamphlets containing the numerical interpretation of dreams. These books were used by numbers gamblers to recommend a number to be played based on a dream and sometimes on a vision.

21. Long, *Spiritual Merchants, Religion, Magic and Commerce,* 199.

22. Ibid., 193–194.

23. Ibid., 198.

24. Ibid., 199.

25. Hurston, *The Sanctified Church*, 103.

26. Baer, "An Anthropological View of Black Spiritual Churches in Nashville, Tennessee," 61; Hurston, "Hoodoo in America"; see also Chireau, *Black Magic*.

27. Drake and Cayton, *Black Metropolis*, 613.

28. Ibid., 642.

29. Long, *Spiritual Merchants, Religion, Magic and Commerce*, 200–201.

30. Ibid.; Hyatt, *Hoodoo-Conjuration-Witchcraft-Rootwork*, 2:10075–10088; Georgia Writers Project, *Drums and Shadows*, interview with Mattie Sampson, Brownsville, Georgia, 55–56.

31. Long, *Spiritual Merchants, Religion, Magic and Commerce*, 201.

32. Wimbs, "African-American Theory, Beliefs and Practices," 6.

33. Hughes, *Thirty Years a Slave*, 26.

34. Wimbs, "African-American Theory, Beliefs and Practices," 20.

35. Ibid.

36. Conversation with Mrs. Austin, age eighty-two, August 1998, Philadelphia.

37. Interview with Stonewall Hazzard, age ninety-three, October 1987, Cleveland, Ohio.

38. Numbers, also known as policy, were the illegal lotteries that proliferated in many urban black communities during this period.

39. To hit a number is to win at the lottery.

40. Carlson, "Numbers Gambling," 114.

41. Harry B. Weiss, "Oneirocritica Americana," 522.

42. Ibid., 528–529.

43. Gardner, "The Complete Fortune Teller and Dream Book."

44. Weiss, "Oneirocritica Americana," 530.

45. Long, *Spiritual Merchants, Religion, Magic and Commerce*, 163–165.

46. Ibid., 31–32.

47. Ibid., 32.

48. "Negro Superstitions: Bolita," Florida State Archives, Tallahassee, Florida, Florida Negro Collection, Series 1585, carton no. 1, folder 35, 1–16.

49. Egen, *Plainclothesman*, 60–64.

50. Carlson, "Numbers Gambling," 12.

51. Ibid., 125.

CHAPTER 6. HEALIN' DA SICK, RAISIN DA DAID

1. Kulii, "A Look at Hoodoo in Three Urban Areas of Indiana," 140.

2. In July 1983 while vacationing near Negril, Jamaica, this author had the opportunity to converse with an apprentice bush doctor, or traditional herbalist. I queried him about treatments for a chest cold, for a fever blister, and to stem bleeding. I was familiar with treatments for several ailments because they had been used on me by my maternal grandmother, who was from the black belt southern town of Mount Meigs, Alabama. When we discussed treatment for a chest cold or a cold involving chest congestion, he prescribed exactly the same treatment that had been administered to me circa 1955: nine drops of coal oil (highly refined

kerosene) on a teaspoon of white sugar and swallowed by the patient. I was surprised that the treatment the apprentice learned from an upcountry bush doctor was exactly the same one used by many blacks in the United States; the treatment was administered to me in Cleveland, Ohio. We also knew other treatments, such as certain cobwebs with styptic properties applied to cuts to stem blood flow and ear wax as a treatment for cold sores and fever blisters. On a recent trip to Pretoria, South Africa, in March 2012, I interviewed a traditional healer, a South African Ndebele Sangoma, who also knew the exact same treatments.

The words to the song by Bill Withers in the epigraph illustrate the role of the black midwife as healer in the African American community. There are additional references that fill out the picture of Withers's "Grandma," particularly the verse that states:

Grandma's hands used to clap in church on Sunday
Grandma's hands shook a tambourine so well

As a member of the Sanctified Church (Sanctified churches are known for the use of tambourines), Grandma would have been familiar with the root worker/midwife tradition. There are indicators in the lyrics that signal and support this. Grandma's description as outlined in the lyrics informs us of the values, behaviors, and role of the granny midwife from a particular era. The popularity of the song in the African American community was informed by the cultural familiarity with the values expressed in the song. Black grandmothers, often the maternal grandmothers, are legendary among African Americans, particularly those blacks with strong and more recent southern black belt roots.

3. Robinson, "Black Healers during the Colonial Period and Early 19th Century America," 69.

4. Ibid., 80.

5. Ibid., 84.

6. Ibid.

7. *Pennsylvania Gazette*, November 23, 1749.

8. Robinson, "Black Healers during the Colonial Period and Early 19th Century America," 85; Morals, *International Library of Negro Life and History*, 12.

9. Robinson, "Black Healers during the Colonial Period and Early 19th Century America," 80–81.

10. Rayburn, "The 'Granny Woman' in the Ozarks," 147–148.

11. The term *nature* (pronounced "naitcha") in this context refers to male sexual potency or impotence. An impotent man or a man with erection problems was said to have "lost his nature."

12. Mathews, "Killing the Medical Self-Help Tradition among African Americans," 62.

13. Parsons, *Folklore of the Sea Islands, South Carolina*, 198.

14. Johnson, *The Fabled Doctor Jim Jordan*, 48.

15. Clayton, *Mother Wit*, 113.

16. Jessie L. Marriner, "Midwifery in Alabama," 3, private manuscript in this author's collection.

17. Dougherty, "Southern Lay Midwives as Ritual Specialists," 162.

18. Van Blarcom, "Rat Pie," 324.

19. Neimark, *Way of the Orisha;* Neimark discusses his encounter with *abiku* both in the introduction and in early chapters.

20. Van Blarcom, "Rat Pie," 322, 328; Dougherty, "Southern Lay Midwives as Ritual Specialists," 152–154.

21. For an example of this inaccuracy and mislabeling, see www.luckymojo .com/nationsack.html (accessed April 26, 2012).

22. In only one of Hyatt's interviews, an informant equates the so-called nation sack to tobies. This is a direct indication that she was speaking of nature sacks. I believe there is confusion there and that the informant was familiar with the nature sack and her account was of a traditional Hoodoo nature sack. She may even have corrected her English in an attempt to give what she thought was a "proper" pronunciation while talking to a white man; African Americans still frequently do this. The nation sacks that are offered for sale online through Web sites like luckymojo.com are imitations of the original and should in no way be confused with old black belt Hoodoo nature sacks. Old tradition nature sacks contained no commercial marketeered supplies. They contained no dragon's blood, magnetic sand, heart charms, or anything purchased from outsiders; see "Scott Ainslie's Blues Notes" at http://cattailmusic.com/Blues/BluesNotes/NationSacks.htm (accessed March 15, 2012). This Web site gives an account of the tent preacher's donation sack but does not address the long-standing confusion. Given that uneducated African Americans of the period did not pronounce their final consonants, it is not likely that they would have said "nation" or explicitly pronounced the final consonant. This pronunciation falls well outside of black American linguistic patterns. Whites hearing this would assume that the Negroes were attempting to pronounce "nation" and conflated the tent preacher's donation sack/nation sack with the African American Hoodoo amulet nature sack.

23. Mathews, "Killing the Medical Self-Help Tradition among African Americans," 62.

24. Reeb, "Granny Midwives in Mississippi," 18.

25. Herbalist Tommie Bass, quoted in Smith and Holmes, *Listen to Me Good*, 40.

26. Ibid., 53.

27. Rayburn, "The 'Granny Woman' in the Ozarks," 145–148.

28. Van Blarcom, "Rat Pie," 327.

29. Bailey with Bledsoe, *God, Dr. Buzzard, and the Bolito Man*, 76.

30. Linda Janet Holmes, "African American Midwives in the South," in Eakins, *The American Way of Birth*, 282.

31. Ibid.; see also Dougherty, "Southern Lay Midwives as Ritual Specialists," 282–283.

32. Smith and Holmes, *Listen to Me Good*, 51.

33. Mathews, "Killing the Medical Self-Help Tradition among African Americans," 61.

34. Ibid.

35. Ibid., 67.

36. Ibid.

37. Fontenot, *Secret Doctors,* 35–36.

38. Robinson, "Black Healers during the Colonial Period and Early 19th Century America," 87.

39. Onstott, *Drum,* 225, 226–227.

40. Sofowora, *Medicinal Plants and Traditional Medicine In Africa,* 52.

41. Puckett, *Folk Beliefs of the Southern Negro,* 332.

42. Ibid., 379.

43. Ibid., 185.

44. Ibid., 365.

45. Fontenot, *Secret Doctors,* 114–118.

46. Ibid., 114.

47. Ibid., 114–115.

48. Ibid., 115.

49. Genovese, *Roll Jordan Roll,* 224.

50. Bailey with Bledsoe, *God, Dr. Buzzard, and the Bolito Man,* 202.

51. Ibid., 204.

52. Interviews and conversations with Darlene Curry and Susie Isaac, John Isaac's daughters, age eighty-four and eighty-two years, respectively, Cleveland and Ravenna, Ohio, October 1990.

53. Still, *Early Recollections and Life of Dr. James Still 1812–1885,* 41.

54. Ibid., 70–71.

55. African slaves and their descendants were frequently experimented on by the white medical profession. The infamous Tuskegee syphilis study further supported black belief that they were frequently used in medical studies and experiments.

56. Both the night doctor and the needle doctor (as opposed to the root doctor) were believed to kidnap blacks who were out walking alone at night in isolated areas, particularly those surrounding large research hospitals like Johns Hopkins in Baltimore, Maryland; see Skloot, *The Immortal Life of Henrietta Lacks;* see also Washington, *Medical Apartheid.*

57. Results from a questionnaire distributed by this author in September 2002 in Arlington, Virginia.

58. American Social Hygiene Association, *Preliminary Report of a Survey of Medical and Educational Aspects of Social Hygiene in the City of New Orleans,* 99–100.

59. Ibid., 99.

60. Ibid., 101.

61. Long, *Spiritual Merchants, Religion, Magic and Commerce,* 143–144.

62. Ibid., 145–146.

CHAPTER 7. BLACK BELT HOODOO IN THE
POST–WORLD WAR II CULTURAL ENVIRONMENT

1. Jones-Jackson, *When Roots Die.*

2. Snow, "Mail Order Magic."

3. Torrey, *The Mind Game.*

4. Interview with Brother A. B. Gregory, St. Helena Island, South Carolina, July 20 and 21, 2005.

5. Telephone conversation with Dr. Wilbert Jordan, Los Angeles, April 2001.

6. For an account of the legacy of distrust resulting from medical experimentation on blacks, see Washington, *Medical Apartheid.*

7. Interview with Ms. Mary Russell, Sheffield, Alabama, July 2003.

8. Interview and conversation with Honi Coles and Sandman Simms, October 1980, Ithaca, New York; Peters, "Passing On."

9. For more on the term *social dislocation,* see Wilson, *When Work Disappears.*

10. Myrdal, *An American Dilemma,* 1242, n. 64.

11. Fontenot, *Secret Doctors,* 115–116.

12. Personal interview with Ms. Mary Russell, root worker, Sheffield, Alabama, July 20 and 21, 2002.

13. Ibid.

14. Personal interview with Brother A. B. Gregory, St. Helena Island, South Carolina, July 2004.

15. Personal telephone interviews with Chukwunyere Eze Ndubuisi, also known as Papa Ce, November 2005, Philadelphia, and April 10, 2009, Chicago.

16. Email from Djenra Windwalker, November 30, 2005.

17. Ibid.

18. Telephone interview with root worker Arthur Flowers, Syracuse, New York, December 20, 2005.

19. Telephone interview with root worker Arthur Flowers, Syracuse, New York, January 11, 2006.

20. Personal interview with Phoenix Savage, Philadelphia, October 2004; telephone interview with Phoenix Savage, January 13, 2006.

21. His legs had suddenly become so weak that he couldn't walk, and doctors could neither explain the malady nor help him, so family members made one final attempt. John was put on a bus and sent to his sister's home in Mobile, Alabama. After performing the preliminary spiritual preparations, she and other Hoodoos buried John up to a little above his waist, standing straight up in the sand as described in chapter 6. When the ritual was completed and John was pulled from the sand, he was able to both walk and to return to his home free from crutches.

22. Telephone interview with Hougan Dafusky Jones, Philadelphia, August 4, 2010.

23. Personal discussions and conversations with Dr. Abba Barden, physician at the Penn Center for Primary Care in Philadelphia, June and August 2005 and October 2006. Dr. Barden revealed that older African American patients, particularly those over age fifty, often raise the possibility that their illness could have been caused by someone working roots on them. Because Dr. Barden is Ghanaian, she is familiar with and often more understanding and tolerant of these patient responses than are white physicians trained in the Western medical tradition. She revealed that she has seen similar responses at home in Ghana, West Africa.

POSTSCRIPT

1. Interviews with Mary Russell, Sheffield, Alabama, 2002, 2003, and Papa Ce, Chicago, Illinois, April 1, 2010.

2. Email from luckymojo.com's Cat Yronwode, September 1, 2010.

3. Interview with Papa Ce, old tradition Hoodoo practitioner, April 1, 2010, Chicago, Illinois.

4. Epstein, *Sinful Tunes and Spirituals.*

Glossary

This glossary is by no means comprehensive; rather, it is both an overview of and an introduction to some Hoodoo terminology and concepts.

Born with a veil—Children who are born with a caul or a piece of amniotic sack covering their faces are said to be born with the veil and are believed to have heightened spiritual power and were often recruited into the root worker tradition.

Bottle tree—A dead tree on which numerous colored bottles (some people prefer blue or blue-green bottles, but all colors are used) have been placed on the ends of branches or hung from the branches. It is believed that the brightly colored bottles, gleaming as the sun shines through them, attract potentially evil spirits and keep them from getting into the house and causing problems.

Burn bread on—Essentially this phrase has a meaning similar to the expression "put the bad mouth on." When and how it entered the Hoodoo phraseology and lexicon is uncertain. It is not widely used but heard occasionally. The more frequently heard phrase "burn a candle on" is more widely known.

Called—Being "called" is one way to legitimately enter Hoodoo practice. The ritual of being called involves some unusual or supernatural event that signals the God-given ordination of a potential conjure doctor. The unusual event attending the calling may be at birth, such as being born with a veil, or it may happen later in life, signaled by some unusual event, like the clapping of thunder or lightening striking a tree. Or it may be signaled by the appearance of a birthmark or any unusual aspect of the called person's life.

Chew the root—Term used to refer to part of the once well-known "court case ritual" in which a conjurer, after other ritual preparations, attends the court hearing of his client and chews galanga root (chewing John), recites secret words of power, and spits in the courtroom, spreading the spiritual protection of the root and turning the entire court proceeding in favor of his client. In some cases, the client can chew the root on his own behalf.

Conja (conjure)—Another name for either the Hoodoo tradition or a conjurer/root worker.

Cross—Means the same as "to trick," "to gopher," "to hoodoo," or "to root" someone. May refer to the sacredness of crossed or intersecting places, such as the crossroads, or the sacred cross of the Kongo cosmogram.

Dancing dime—A Hoodoo divination device used to diagnose a malady caused by Hoodoo. A root doctor usually boils a silver dime in water; if the coin moves around, jiggling and flipping, it has a meaning, which is read by the root doctor. This ritual has been performed with coins or metal slugs resembling coins or even with metal buttons as a substitute for the silver dime. Silver dimes were difficult for slaves to acquire, so the ritual substituted other coins or coinlike objects.

Doctor—Usually meaning a "root doctor."

Dodywood—A powdery substance taken from the stump of dead or decaying pine trees. This dust was used to treat cuts and was used by midwives to seal and heal the umbilicus.

Dress—In the context of Hoodoo, this simply means "to prepare." To dress a candle means to prepare it to be burned for a specific purpose. This term also means to put a certain type of Hoodoo on someone. A woman, for example, can dress a man so that he cannot achieve an erection, so that he will lose his job, or so that he will have a long streak of bad luck. The same can be done to a woman to prevent her from leaving or for any other purpose. Oftentimes when protective powders are spread around a room, such as a courtroom, that room is said to be dressed. Almost anything can be dressed, such as beds, pillows, articles of clothing, as well as locations.

Feed the hand—This phrase refers to the practices necessary to refresh and maintain the power and potency of the amulet/mojo. This is usually done with some kind of alcohol, such as corn liquor, gin, whisky, or perfume or cologne. When ingestible liquid such as wine or liquor is used, it is taken into the mouth and sprayed onto the mojo bag. When perfume or cologne is used, it is simply dripped or sprayed from an atomizer onto the mojo.

Fix—To put roots on, to hex, or to dress.

Goober dust—Goobers are peanuts (*pindas*); goober dust was ground peanut hulls used in traditional West African and Kongo religion and in old tradition black belt Hoodoo. The severe reaction to goober dust was undoubtedly due to peanut allergy, unrecognized then, unlike today where we guard against such a reaction that could possibly cause death. The two terms goopher dust and goober dust have shifting meanings and are often used interchangeably today.

Goopher, goopher pack—A type of amulet that often but not always contains graveyard dirt. Those packs that contain graveyard dirt sometimes have to be returned to the root worker that made it so that the power will not reach out and harm the client. When used as a verb, to goopher means the same as to Hoodoo.

Goopher dust, goofy dust—Has a range of meanings; as a verb, to goopher means "to fix." It also is another name for graveyard dirt.

Haint, hant—Another name for an evil witchlike supernatural being that is believed to chase its victims to their death or to mount them during sleep and ride them like a horse until exhaustion sets in or sunrise appears. Haints are sometimes referred to as witches.

Haint blue—A deep, rich sky blue color believed to repel haints. Believers used this color paint to protect their windows and doors from entry by a haint. It can still be seen on St. Helena Island, South Carolina, today.

Hand—A name for a mojo bag. Often referred to as "lucky hand," hands come in different types, just as all mojoes do. A mojo/hand prepared for luck in gambling is a gambling hand. Originally a hand was made specifically for a client's needs—each hand was different. A special type of hand was wrapped or prepared for left-handed people. The label *hand* is used because originally certain types of mojos were tailored to the size and shape of the client's left palm.

High John the Conquer root—A tuberous type of morning glory root native to the area around Xalapa, Vera Cruz, Mexico. Known botanically as *Ipomoea jalapa*, it is probably the most sacred and powerful root in contemporary Hoodoo work.

Hoodoo—The traditional black belt African American folk healing and spiritual controlling system. This system draws most heavily from African traditional religion but later, as a result of enslavement, integrates elements of Native American traditional religion and beliefs and some Old World European folk beliefs. The term also is used to designate a root worker, conjurer, two-head, or root doctor, as in that person is a Hoodoo.

Hot foot—A term probably devised by snake oil hoodoo marketeers. This term refers to the old tradition Hoodoo fix, known in some regions as "the walking foot" (pronounced without the final *g*, walkin' foot), and the traditional African and African American practice of picking up tracks. The medical malady known today as restless leg syndrome (RLS) could be judged to be a variety of the walking foot.

Jack—Another name for a type of Hoodoo amulet or mojo bag.

Jack ball—This term has two usages: one for the divination device similar to the walking boy in which a weighted mojo ball was suspended from a string about eighteen to twenty inches long and used the same way as the walking boy. The other use for the term is to designate a type of amulet carried for protection and luck. As in I got my jack ball with me tonight. The African American dance known as Ballin' the Jack is a Hoodoo reference.

Juju—A generic term referring to any and all types of traditional and alternative African religious practices. This term is recognizable to, and means the same thing to, anyone who knows of the controlling aspect of African traditional religion. When terms such as Santeria, Hoodoo, or Vodun fail to register, the term Juju means the same to blacks in both Africa and the African diaspora.

Jump the broom—A Hoodoo marriage ritual in which the woman was required to jump over the broom to prove to her new spouse that she was not a witch. It was believed that a witch could not jump over the broom until she counted each straw. By jumping the broom, the new bride proved that she was not a haint or witch disguised as a woman.

Lightening dust—Dust used in Hoodoo rituals that has been gathered from a decomposing tree that has been struck by lightning.

Long head—Another name for a conjurer or root doctor.

Mojo—A traditional African American amulet. A genuine mojo or mojo bag can only be wrapped properly by an old tradition root worker.

Nature sack, nation sack—A type of mojo originally controlled only by midwife conjurer women. There is some confusion about this type of mojo. The use of the term *nation sack* is a mispronunciation by whites who are "correcting" black English. The term used among southern black belt African Americans was and is *nature sack,* referring to male sexual potency, virility as nature. To say that a man has lost his nature means that he either cannot achieve an erection or has difficulty with such. The term nature (pronounced "naitcha" the final consonant *r* is never pronounced) sack was used by women who wanted to control their man's sexuality and virility and keep him from infidelity. The sack had to be tied during coitus, with the final knot tied upon the man's sexual climax. It could prove to be a complex and dangerous ritual, especially if the woman was discovered while doing it. A woman who had tied a nature sack on a man hid and protected the amulet. The location was considered so secret that many men feared even touching a nature sack; some even feared mentioning it. For an explanation of how it becomes confused with the tent show preacher's donation sack, see note 22 in chapter 6.

Numbers—The illegal lotteries that flourished in African American communities from around World War I until state-operated lotteries displaced them across America beginning in the late 1960s and early 1970s.

Package—Another name for an old tradition mojo bag, amulet, or charm.

Pick up tracks, gathered track—Though rarely performed today, this old tradition Hoodoo practice was once one of the most feared. As the victim walked along and left footprints, the dust forming the footprints was picked up and used to fix that particular individual. This practice is long standing and largely unchanged, performed today as it was on the plantation and in West and West Central Africa before the enslavement of Africans in the United States. Each use was tailored to the individual, and any attempt to use the marketeered hot foot powders would pollute the ritual and could even prove harmful to the client.

Plat-eye—An evil spirit that changes form or shape-shifts in order to lure its victims into danger or into the woods, where they are left to die. Matches and sulfur taken from matches were used to repel Plat-eye. This spirit may have derived from Native American influences or sources.

Possum bone reading—A divination system in which seven or nine opossum ver-tebrae are use to divine information for the client. This was one of the primary divination systems used on the plantation. Believed to be close to the ancestors, the opossum was chosen because it was often seen in the cemetery. Today, all the intermediary forces known as New World Orisha are said to enjoy eating possum, and they are "fed" possum for a variety of purposes.

Put the bad mouth on—This phrase refers to the traditional West African and Hoo-doo belief in the power of the spoken word. Putting the bad mouth on someone is the same as forecasting negative occurrences for that person. Only the spoken forecast has the potency to bring the occurrence into existence. An example: If someone says to you, "I hope you don't get into trouble on your job," a response might be, "Don't put the bad mouth on me and make that happen."

Root doctor, rootman, root woman, root worker—A traditional African American community lay Hoodoo practitioner, folk herbalist, and healer.

Roots, put roots on, to be rooted—To cast a spell, usually negative, on someone in the Hoodoo tradition is to root them.

Seer—A root worker with power to predict the future or to see unrevealed phe-nomena. Sometimes incorrectly referred to as "psychics," this title, almost always urban, updates and legitimizes root workers who use it. The term is most fre-quently used by non–African Americans who practice other traditions such as palm reading.

Spiritualist—A title adopted by some old tradition workers who may be closely associated with a spiritualist church. The title is most often used by palm readers and crystal ball and tarot card readers and may or may not have anything to do with old tradition Hoodoo.

Swamper—An old tradition black belt conjurer or root worker who goes out and harvests his or her own plants, roots, and supplies.

Throw at—To put a fix on. If someone is throwing at you, he or she is trying to put Hoodoo on you somehow. Ritual objects are used, including roots, stones, iron, alligator teeth, dried and pulverized peanut shells, animal hair, and chicken feet, when throwing at someone.

Tie—A term describing part of the preparation process of a traditional, personal-ized mojo amulet. This term also refers to the general use of tied knots in both medicinal and spiritual work. Tying is an important gesture in and of itself. Incanta-tion of sacred words or prayer is used to sanctify each knot as it is tightened. When stitches are used instead of tied knots, each stitch, or series of stitches, receives an incantation or verse. The infamous nature sack (mistakenly dubbed nation sack) is tied with the final knot tied during coitus. Someone seeking an old tradition mojo might ask the root worker, "Can you tie the bag for me?" This process must include the proper prayers to activate the power in the amulet.

Toby—Another name for a mojo bag, perhaps from a medicine show or snake oil Hoodoo.

Trick—Another term for Hoodoo used as a verb. To trick someone is to Hoodoo them. Laying a trick means depositing a Hoodoo amulet or powders or goopher pack so as to harm or change the behavior of the person targeted. The term *trick* has multiple meanings and is widely used in several contexts in African American culture, such as tricking or turning a trick, meaning prostitution, and trick bag, literally and figuratively referring to spiritual and physical connections to important people or beings and objects. The ability to make things happen. The tools, skill, and connections necessary to make things happen.

Trick bag—A conjure pack or root pack designed usually to bring harm or to ward off a certain individual. Used also to mean spiritual and medicinal resources, as in "I have a few items in my trick bag that will help."

Two-head—An old tradition black belt Hoodoo name for a conjurer, root doctor, root worker, or Hoodoo practitioner. The term refers to the belief that the root worker can see into two worlds: the corporeal world of everyday existence and the invisible spirit world.

Walking boy—A traditional divination device used by African American conjurers working in the old black belt tradition. This device was used on plantations throughout the Deep South. A small bottle was attached to a string or cord about two feet long. The bottle was then allowed to swing freely like a pendulum. This device was also used to locate conjure packets or negative mojoes that had been buried near the home of or in the potential pathway of an individual.

Walking foot—A type of old tradition Hoodoo charm and ritual used to make the target walk constantly and in an unconventional and unusual manner. This may be the source or origin of the snake oil Hoodoo hot foot powders and sprays. It appears that this is what the snake oil or marketeered Hoodoo is attempting to imitate.

Wrap—A term that means the same as "to tie." Mojoes are either wrapped or tied. A client might ask, "Can you wrap the package for me?"

Glossary

Bibliography

Achebe, Chinua. *Things Fall Apart.* Greenwich, Conn.: Fawcett, 1959.

Adams, George C. S. "Rattlesnake Eye." *Southern Folklore Quarterly* 2 (1938): 37–38.

Adams, Samuel Hopkins. "Dr. Bug, Dr. Buzzard, and the U.S.A." *True* (July 1949): 36, 69–71.

Aimes, Hubert H. S. "African Institutions in America." *Journal of American Folklore* 18, no. 68 (January–March 1905): 15–32.

American Social Hygiene Association. *Preliminary Report of a Survey of Medical and Educational Aspects of Social Hygiene in the City of New Orleans.* New York: ASHA, 1931. (Manuscript in the Amistad Collection, Tulane University, New Orleans, Louisiana.)

Anderson, Ann. *Snake Oil, Hustlers and Hambones.* Jefferson, N.C.: McFarland, 2000.

Anderson, Jeffery. *Conjure in African American Society.* Baton Rouge: Louisiana State University Press, 2005.

Aptheker, Herbert. *American Negro Slave Revolts.* New York: International, 1969.

Aptheker, Herbert. "Maroons within the Present Limits of the United States." *Journal of Negro History* 24, no. 2 (April 1939): 167–184.

Arcaya, Pedro M. *Insurrecion de los negros de la Serrania de Coro.* Caracas, Venezuela: Instituto Panamericano de Geografia e Historia, publ. no. 7, 1930.

Backus, E. M., and Ethel Hatton Leitner. "Negro Tales from Georgia." *Journal of American Folklore* 25 (1912): 125–135.

Bacon, Alice Mabel. "Work and Methods of the Hampton Folklore Society." *Journal of American Folklore* 11, no. 40 (January–March 1897): 17–21.

Baer, Hans. "An Anthropological View of Black Spiritual Churches in Nashville, Tennessee." *Central Issues in Anthropology,* vol. 2, no. 2 (1980): 53–68.

Baer, Hans, and Yvonne Jones, eds. *African Americans in the South.* Athens: University of Georgia Press, 1992.

Bailey, Cornelia Walker, with Christena Bledsoe. *God, Dr. Buzzard, and the Bolito Man.* New York: Doubleday, 2000.

Balfour, J. H. "Notice of Some Plants Which Flowered Recently in the Edinburgh Botanical Garden." *Edinburgh New Philosophical Journal* 44 (1848): 200–205.

Banks, Ann. *First Person America*. New York: Vintage Books, 1981.

Barnes, Sandra. *Africa's Ogun: Old World and New*. Bloomington: Indiana University Press, 1997.

Barrows, Julie. "Herb Cures in an Isolated Black Community in the Florida Parishes." *Louisiana Folklore Miscellany* 3, no. 1 (1970): 25–27.

Bascom, William R. *Ifa Divination: Communication between Gods and Men in West Africa*. Bloomington: Indiana University Press, 1969.

Bascom, William R. *Sixteen Cowries: Yoruba Divination from Africa to the New World*. Bloomington: Indiana University Press, 1993.

Bastide, Roger. *The African Religions of Brazil*. Baltimore: Johns Hopkins University Press, 1978.

Beaton, D. "Note on the Jalap Plant of Commerce." *Garden Management* 15 (1839): 328–329.

Beecham, John. *Ashantee and the Gold Coast*. London: Dawsons of Pall Mall, 1968.

"Beliefs and Customs Connected with Death and Burial." *Southern Workman* 26 (1897): 18–19.

Bell, Michael Edward. "Harry Middleton Hyatt's Quest for the Essence of the Human Spirit." *Journal of American Folklore* 19 (1979): 1–27.

Bell, Michael Edward. "Pattern, Structure and Logic in Afro-American Hoodoo Performance." PhD diss., Indiana University, 1980.

Berendt, John. *Midnight in the Garden of Good and Evil*. New York: Vintage Books, 1999.

Blanco, M. G. "El cultivo de las plantas medicinales en Mexico tiene gran porvenir." *Tierra* 4:81–83.

Blanton, Wyndham B. *Medicine in Virginia in the Eighteenth Century*. Richmond, Va.: Garrett and Massie, 1931.

Bohannan, Paul. "Tiv Divination." In *Studies in Social Anthropology*, edited by J. H. M. Beattie and R. G. Lienhards, 149–166. Oxford: Clarendon Press, 1975.

Bolton, H. Carrington. "The Decoration of Graves of Negroes in South Carolina." *Journal of American Folklore* 4 (1891): 214.

Bowser, Frederick P. *The African Slave in Colonial Peru, 1524–1650*. Stanford, Calif.: Stanford University Press, 1974.

Brackett, Jeffrey Richardson. *Negro in Maryland: A Study of the Institution of Slavery*. Baltimore: N. Murray, Johns Hopkins University, 1889.

Bradford, Sydney S. "The Negro Ironworker in Ante-Bellum Virginia." *Journal of Southern History* 25 (May 1959): 194–206.

Brady, C. M. "The Negro as a Patient in General Practice." *New Orleans Surgical Journal* 56 (1903–4): 431–445.

Bromberg, Alan B. "Slavery in the Virginia Tobacco Factories, 1800–1860." Master's thesis, University of Virginia, 1968.

Brown, William Wells. *The Narrative of William Wells Brown, A Fugitive Slave*. New York: Johnson Reprint, 1970.

Burwell, Letitia M. *A Girl's Life in Virginia before the War.* New York: Frederick A. Stokes, 1895.

Cable, George W. "Creole Slave Songs." *The Century Magazine* 31, no. 6 (April 1886): 814–815.

Cannon, Walter B. "Voodoo Death." *Psychosomatic Medicine* 19 (1957): 182–191.

Carlson, Gustav G. "Numbers Gambling: A Study of a Culture Complex." PhD diss., University of Michigan, 1940.

Carroll, Patrick J. *Blacks in Colonial Veracruz.* Austin: University of Texas Press, 1991.

Carroll, Patrick J. "Mandinga: The Evolution of a Mexican Runaway Slave Community, 1735–1827." *Comparative Studies in Society and History* 19, no. 4 (October 1977): 488–505.

Chase, Jeanne. "The 1741 Conspiracy to Burn New York: Black Plot or Black Magic?" *Social Science Information* 22, no. 6 (1983): 969–981.

Chatelain, Heli. "Angolan Customs." *Journal of American Folklore* 9, no. 32 (January–March 1896): 13–18.

Chesnutt, Charles W. *The Conjure Woman and Other Conjure Tales.* Durham, N.C.: Duke University Press, 1993.

Chesnutt, Charles W. "Superstitions and Folklore of the South." *Modern Culture* (1901): 231–235.

Chireau, Yvonne. *Black Magic.* Berkeley: University of California Press, 2003.

Chireau, Yvonne. "Conjuring: An Analysis of African American Folk Beliefs and Practices." PhD diss., Princeton University, 1994.

Clar, Mimi. "Negro Beliefs." *Western Folklore* 18 (1959): 332–334.

Clark, Joseph D. "North Carolina Popular Beliefs and Superstitions." *North Carolina Folklore Journal* 18, no. 1 (1970): 1–68.

Clayton, Edward T. "The Truth About Voodoo: Despite Claims That Cult Is Dead, Voodoo Practices Still Flourish as Lucrative Racket in New Orleans." *Ebony* (April 1951): 54–56.

Clayton, Ronnie W. *Mother Wit: The Ex-Slave Narratives of the Louisiana Writers Project.* New York: Peter Lang, 1990.

Cohen, Hennig. "Burial of the Drowned among the Gullah Negroes." *Southern Folklore Quarterly* 22, no. 2 (June 1958): 93–97.

"Conjuring in Arkansas." *Journal of American Folklore,* "Folklore and Ethnology" 1 (1888): 83.

Contributor's Club. "A Negro Witch Story." *Atlantic Monthly* 75 (1895): 715–717.

Contributor's Club. "Some Negro Superstitions." *Atlantic Monthly* 75 (1895): 136–139.

Cooley, Gilbert. "Conversations About Hoodoo." *Indiana Folklore* 10, no. 2 (1977): 201–215.

Cooley, Gilbert. "Root Doctors and Psychics in the Region." *Indiana Folklore* 10, no. 2 (1977): 191–200.

Cooley, Gilbert. "Root Stories." *North Carolina Folklore Journal* 23, no. 2 (May 1975): 35–43.

Cooper, James Fennimore. *Satanstoe: A Tale of the Colony.* Garden City, N.Y.: Dolphin Books, 1962.

Cross, Tom Peete. "Witchcraft in North Carolina." *Studies in Philology* 16 (1919): 217–287.

Cunard, Nancy, ed. *Negro Anthology.* New York: Negro Universities Press, 1969.

Cunningham, Eloise. "The Negro Storefront Church in Cleveland." Manuscript in Cleveland Public Library, John G. White Collection, Newbell Niles Puckett Collection, "Religious Beliefs of Southern Negroes," Box 1, item II (May 1947): 1–33b.

Davenport, Fredrick Morgan. "The Religions of the American Negro." *Contemporary Review* 88 (September 1905): 369–375.

Davis, Daniel W. "Conjuration." *Southern Workman* 27 (December 1898): 251–252.

Davis, Thomas. *A Rumor of Revolt: The Great Negro Plot in Colonial New York.* New York: Free Press, 1985.

Debien, Gabriel. *Plantations et esclaves à St. Domingue.* Dakar, Senegal: Université de Dakar, 1962.

De Jauregui, M. F. "Estudios acerca de algunos purgantes indigenas." *La Naturaleza* 7 (1887): 104–113.

Devisch, R. "Perspectives on Divination in Contemporary Sub-Saharan Africa." In *Theoretical Explorations in African Religion,* edited by W. Van Binsbergen and M. Schoffeleers, 50–83. London: Kegan Paul, 1985.

Dieterien, Germaine. *Essai sur la religion Bambara.* Paris: Presses Universitaires de France, 1950.

Diggs, Irene. "Zumbi and the Republic of Os Palmares." *Phylon* 14, no. 1 (1953): 62–70.

Dorjahn, Vernon. "Some Aspects of Temne Divination." *Sierra Leone Bulletin of Religion* 4, no. 1 (June 1962): 1–9.

Dorson, Richard M. "Hoodoos and Two-Heads." *American Negro Folktales,* 186–212. Greenwich, Conn.: Fawcett, 1958.

Dougherty, Molly C. "Southern Lay Midwives as Ritual Specialists." In *Women in Ritual and Symbolic Roles,* edited by Judith Hoch-Smith and Anita Spring. New York: Plenum Press, 1978.

Douglas, S. W. "Difficulties and Superstitions Encountered in Practice among the Negro." *The Journal of the Arkansas Medical Society* 18, no. 8 (January 1922): 155–158.

Douglass, Frederick. *The Life and Times of Frederick Douglass.* New York: Collier, 1962.

Drake, St. Clair, and Horace Cayton. *Black Metropolis.* New York: Harper and Row, 1962.

Drolet, Patricia Lund. "The Congo Ritual of Northeastern Panama: An Afro-American Expressive Structure of Cultural Adaptation." PhD diss., University of Illinois at Urbana-Champaign, 1980.

DuBois, W. E. B. *Black Folk: Then and Now.* Millwood, N.Y.: Kraus-Thomson, 1975.

DuBois, W. E. B. *The Philadelphia Negro.* Philadelphia: University of Pennsylvania Press, 1996.

DuBois, W. E. B. *The Souls of Black Folk.* Millwood, N.Y.: Kraus-Thomson, 1973.

Dutton, Wendy. "The Problem of Invisibility: Voodoo and Zora Neale Hurston." *Frontiers: A Journal of Women Studies* 13, no. 2 (1993): 131–153.

Eakins, Pamela S., ed. *The American Way of Birth.* Philadelphia: Temple University Press, 1986.

Egen, Capt. Frederick W. *Plainclothesman: A Handbook of Vice and Gambling Investigation.* New York: Arco, 1959.

Emery, Lynn F. *Black Dance from 1619 to 1970.* Palo Alto, Calif.: National Press Books, 1972.

Ennes, Ernesto. "The Palmares 'Republic' of Pernambuco." *The Americas,* 5, no. 2 (October 1948): 200–216.

Epstein, Dena. *Sinful Tunes and Spirituals: Black Folk Music to the Civil War.* Urbana: University of Illinois Press, 1977.

Evans, David, Don Stephen Rice, and Joanne Kline Partin. "Parallels in West African, West Indian and North Carolina Folklore." *North Carolina Folklore Journal* 17, no. 2 (1969): 77–84.

Faulkner, William. *The Sound and the Fury.* New York: Random House, 1984.

Fitchett, E. Horace. "Superstitions in South Carolina." *The Crisis* 43 (1936): 360–361, 370.

Florida Negro. "Aunt Memory" and "Negro Superstitions: Bolita." Florida State Archives, Tallahassee, Florida, Series 1585, carton no. 1, folder no. 35.

"Folk-Lore and Ethnology." *Southern Workman* 28 (1899): 315.

Fontenot, Wanda. *Secret Doctors.* Westport, Conn.: Bergin and Garvey, 1994.

Forten, Charlotte. *The Journal of Charlotte L. Forten.* New York: Dryden Press, 1953.

Fortier, Alcee. "Customs and Superstitions in Louisiana." *Journal of American Folklore* 1 (1888): 136–140.

Freeman, Roland. *The Arabbers of Baltimore.* Centreville, Md.: Tidewater, 1989.

Fu-Kiau, Kimbwandende Kia Bunseki. *African Cosmology of the Bantu-Kongo,* 2nd ed. Brooklyn, N.Y.: Athelia Henrietta Press, 2001.

Gaffney, Floyd. "The Function and Form of the Ring Shout as a Religious Expression: From West African Origins through the Era of Slavery in America." Master's thesis, Adelphi University, 1962.

Galloway, J. H. "Sugar Industry of Pernambuco during the Nineteenth Century." *Annals of the Association of American Geographers* 58 (June 1968): 285–303.

Gannett, Edward Channing. "The Freedmen at Port Royal." *North American Review* 101 (July 1865): 1–28.

Gardner, Eric. "The Complete Fortune Teller and Dream Book: An Antebellum Text by Chloe Russel, A Woman of Colour." *New England Quarterly* 78, no. 2 (June 2005): 259–288.

Gebauer, Paul. *Spider Divination in the Cameroons.* Milwaukee, Wis.: Milwaukee Public Museum Publication in Anthropology, no. 10, 1964.

Genovese, Eugene. *Roll Jordan Roll: The World the Slaves Made.* New York: Vintage Books, 1976.

Georgia Writer's Project. *Drums and Shadows.* Athens: University of Georgia Press, 1940.

Gibb, Eleanor. "Conjure and 'Suasion: Plantation Chronicles." *Atlantic Monthly* 128 (1921): 761–770.

Gibson, H. E. "Folk Medicine among the Gullahs: African Legacy." *Negro Digest* 11 (August 1962): 77–80.

Glave, E. J. "Fetishism in Congo Land." *Century Magazine* 41, no. 6 (April 1891): 835.

Gomez, Michael A. *Exchanging Our Country Marks.* Chapel Hill: University of North Carolina Press, 1998.

Granberry, E. "Black Jupiter: A Voodoo King in Florida's Jungle." *Travel* (April 1932): 32–35, 54.

Green, Fletcher M. "Georgia's Forgotten Industry: Gold Mining." *Georgia Historical Quarterly* 19 (June–September 1935): 93–111, 210–228.

Green, Fletcher M. "Gold Mining: A Forgotten Industry of Antebellum North Carolina." *North Carolina Historical Review* 14 (January–October 1937): 1–19.

Guillot, Carlos Federico. *Negros rebeledes y negros cimarrones.* Buenos Aires, Argentina: Farina Editores, 1961.

Guthrie, Chester L. "Colonial Economy: Trade, Industry and Labor in Seventeenth Century Mexico City." *Revista de Historia de America* 7 (December 1939): 103–134.

Hall, Arthur L., and Peter G. Bourne. "Indigenous Therapist in a Southern Black Urban Community." *Archives of General Psychiatry* 28, no. 1 (January 1973): 137–142.

Hall, Gwendolyn Midlo. *Africans in Colonial Louisiana.* Baton Rouge: Louisiana State University Press, 1992.

Hall, Gwendolyn Midlo. *Databases for the Study of Afro-Louisiana History and Genealogy, 1699–1869: Computerized Information from Original Manuscript Sources.* Baton Rouge: Louisiana State University Press: CD-Rom Edition, March 1, 2000.

Hall, Julien A. "Negro Conjuring and Tricking." *Journal of American Folklore* 10, no. 36 (January–March 1897): 241–243.

Hanbury, D. "On the Cultivation of Jalap." *London Pharmaceutical Journal* 39 (1867): 352–356.

Hand, Wayland. "Physical Harm, Sickness, and Death by Conjury." *Acta Ethnographica Academiae Scientiarum Hungaricae* (1970): 169–177.

Hand, Wayland D. "The Folkhealer: Calling and Endowment." *Journal of the History of Medicine* 26 (1971): 263–275.

Handy, Sara M. "Negro Superstitions." *Lippincott's Magazine* 48 (1891): 735–739.

Harrison, John P. "The Evolution of Colombian Tobacco Trade to 1875." *Hispanic American Historical Review* 32 (May 1952): 163–174.

Haskell, Joseph A., "Sacrificial Offerings among North Carolina Negroes." *Journal of American Folklore* 4 (1891): 267–269.

Hazzard-Donald, Katrina. "The Circle and the Line: Speculations on the Development of African American Vernacular Dancing." *Western Journal of Black Studies* 20, no. 1 (Spring 1996): 28–38.

Headlam, Cecil, ed. *Calendar of State Papers: Colonial Series: American and West Indies 1728–1729,* vol. 35. Vaduz, Liechtenstein: Kraus Reprint, 1964.

Hearn, Lafcadio. "Jot—The Haunt of the Obi-Man." In *Children of the Levee*, edited by O. W. Frost, 49–53. Lexington: University of Kentucky Press, 1957.

Hendricks, George D. "Voodoo Powder." *Western Folklore* 17 (1958): 132.

Henri, Florette. *Black Migration, Movement North 1900–1920.* Garden City, N.Y.: Anchor Books, 1976.

Herron, Elenor, and Alice Mabel Bacon. "Conjuring and Conjure-Doctors in the Southern United States." *Journal of American Folklore* 9, no. 33 (1896): 143–147, 224–226.

Herron, Lenora, and Alice M. Bacon. "Conjuring and Conjure Doctors." *Southern Workman* 24 (1895):117–118, 193–194, 209–211.

Herskovits, Melville. "Folklore After a Hundred Years: A Problem in Redefinition." *Journal of American Folklore* 59, no. 232 (1946): 89–101.

Herskovits, Melville J. "Letter to the Editor concerning the Review of Zora Neale Hurston's "Mules and Men (#5467) by Joseph J. Williams." *Folk-Lore* 48 (1937): 219–221.

Herskovits, Melville J. *Myth of the Negro Past.* Boston: Beacon Press, 1951.

Higgins, Robert. "The Geographical Origin of Negro Slaves in Colonial South Carolina." *South Atlantic Quarterly* 70 (1971): 34–47.

Higginson, Thomas Wentworth. *Army Life in a Black Regiment.* Boston: Fields, Osgood, 1870.

Hill, Carole E. "Black Healing Practices in the Rural South." *Journal of Popular Culture* 6, no. 4 (Spring 1973): 849–853.

Hounwanou, Remy. *Le Fa: Une Geomancie Divinatoire du Golfe du Benin: Pratiques et Technique.* Lomé, Togo: Les Nouvelles Editions Africaines, 1984.

Hoyt, Harlowe R. *Town Hall Tonight.* Englewood Cliffs, N.J.: Prentice-Hall, 1995.

Hughes, Louis. *Thirty Years a Slave.* 1897. Reprint, New York: Negro Universities Press, 1969.

Hurston, Zora Neale. "Characteristics of Negro Expression." In *Negro Anthology*, edited by Nancy Cunard. New York: Negro Universities Press, 1969.

Hurston, Zora Neale. "High John De Conquer." *American Mercury* 57 (1943): 450–458.

Hurston, Zora Neale. "Hoodoo in America." *Journal of American Folklore* 44 (October–December 1931): 317–418.

Hurston, Zora Neale. *Mules and Men.* New York: Perennial Library, 1935.

Hurston, Zora Neale. *The Sanctified Church.* Berkeley, Calif.: Turtle Island, 1984.

Hutchisson, James, ed. *A DuBose Heyward Reader.* Athens: University of Georgia Press, 2003.

Hyatt, Harry Middleton. *Hoodoo-Conjuration-Witchcraft-Rootwork: Beliefs Accepted by Many Negroes and White Persons, These Being Orally Recorded among Blacks and Whites,* 5 vols. Memoirs of the Alma Egan Hyatt Foundation. Hannibal, Mo.: Western, 1970–78.

Imperato, Pascal James. *African Folk Medicine.* Baltimore: York Press, 1977.

Imperato, P. J. "Bamana and Maninka Twin Figures." *African Arts* 8, no. 4 (1975): 52–60.

Imperato, P. J. "Twins among the Bambara and Malinke of Mali." *Journal of Tropical Medicine and Hygiene* 74, no. 7 (1971): 154–159.

Imperato, Pascal James, and Gavin H. Imperato. "Twins, Hermaphrodites, and an Androgynous Albino Deity: Twins and Sculpted Twin Figures among the Bamana and Maninka of Mali." *African Arts* 41 no. 1 (Spring 2008): 40.

Ingersoll, Ernest. "Decoration of Negro Graves." *Journal of American Folklore* 5 (1892): 68.

Jackson, L. P. "Religious Development of the Negro in Virginia from 1760–1860." *Journal of Negro History* 16 (1931): 168–239.

Jackson, Michael. "An Approach to Kuranko Divination." *Human Relations* 31, no. 2 (1978): 117–138.

Jacobs, Claude F., and Andrew J. Kaslow. *The Spiritual Churches of New Orleans.* Knoxville: University of Tennessee Press, 1991.

James, C. L. R. *Black Jacobins: Toussaint l'Ouverture and the San Domingo Revolution.* New York: Vintage Books, 1963.

Johnson, F. Roy. *The Fabled Doctor Jim Jordan: A Story of Conjure.* Murfreesboro, N.C.: Johnson, 1963.

Johnson, Walter. *Soul by Soul.* Cambridge, Mass.: Harvard University Press, 1999.

Jones, Rev. Charles C. *The Religious Instruction of Negroes in the United States.* Savannah, Ga.: Thomas Purse, 1842.

Jones-Jackson, Patricia. *When Roots Die: Endangered Traditions on the Sea Islands.* Athens: University of Georgia Press, 1987.

Katz, William Loren. *Black Indians.* New York: Ethrac, 1986.

Kennedy, Stetson. "Naningo in Florida." *Southern Folklore Quarterly* 4, no. 3 (September 1940): 153–156.

Kent, R. "Palmares: An African State in Brazil." In *Maroon Societies,* edited by Richard Price. New York: Anchor/Doubleday, 1973.

Kiser, Clyde Vernon. *Sea Island to City.* New York: Antheneum, 1969.

Kulii, Elon. "Hoodoo Tales Collected in Indiana." *Journal of American Folklore* 16 (1979): 75–96.

Kulii, Elon Ali. "A Look at Hoodoo in Three Urban Areas of Indiana: Folklore and Change." PhD diss., Indiana University, June 1982.

Kuna, Ralph R. "Hoodoo: The Indigenous Medicine and Psychiatry of the Black American." *Ethnomedizin* 3 (1974/75): 273–294.

Lacy, Virginia Jane, and David Edwin Harrell Jr. "Plantation Home Remedies: Medicinal Recipes from the Diary of John Pope." *Tennessee Historical Quarterly* 22 (September 1963): 259–265.

Lauer, Roger M. "Urban Shamans: The Influence of Folk-Healers on Medical Care in Our Cities." *New Physician* 32 (1973): 486–489.

Lea, M. S. "Two-Head Doctors." *The American Mercury* (October 1927): 236–240.

Lee, Collins. "Some Negro Lore from Baltimore." *Journal of American Folklore* 5, no. 17 (April–June 1892): 110–12.

Leone, Mark P., and Gladys-Marie Fry. "Conjuring in the Big House Kitchen." *Journal of American Folklore* 112, no. 445 (1999): 372–403.

Letcher, James H. "The Treatment of Some Diseases by the Old Time Negro." *The Railway Surgical Journal* 17 (1910/11): 170–175.

Lett, Anna. "Some West Tennessee Superstitions about Conjurers, Witches, Ghosts and the Devil." *Tennessee Folklore Society Bulletin* 36, no. 2 (1970): 37–45.

Lex, Barbara W. "Voodoo Death: New Thoughts on an Old Explanation." *American Anthropologist* 76 (1974): 818–823.

Linajes, Alberto, Victor Rico-Gray, and Gloria Carrion. "Traditional Production System of the Root of Jalap, *Ipomoea purga* (Convolvulaceae), in Central Veracruz, Mexico." *Economic Botany* 48, no. 1 (1994): 85.

Lockhart, James. *Spanish Peru, 1532–1560*. Madison: University of Wisconsin Press, 1974.

Long, Carolyn Morrow. *Spiritual Merchants, Religion, Magic and Commerce*. Knoxville: University of Tennessee Press, 2001.

MacGaffey, Wyatt, trans. and ed. *Art and Healing of the Bakongo, Commented by Themselves: Minkisi from the Laman Collection*. Bloomington: Indiana University Press, 1991.

MacGaffey, Wyatt. *Religion and Society in Central Africa*. Chicago: University of Chicago Press, 1986.

Maddox, John L. "Modern Voodooism." *Hygeia* 12 (February 1934): 153–156.

Marees, Pieter de. *Description and Historical Account of the Gold Kingdom of Guinea*. New York: Oxford University Press, 1987.

Martineau, Harriet. *Society in America*, vol. 2. New York: Saunders and Otley, 1837.

Mason, John, and Gary Edwards. *Black Gods: Orisha Studies in the New World*. Brooklyn, N.Y.: Yoruba Theological Archministry, 1998.

Mather, Cotton. *The Angel of Bethesda*. Edited by Gordon W. Jones. Borre, Mass.: Barr and American Antiquarian Society, 1972.

Mathews, Holly F. "Killing the Medical Self-Help Tradition among African Americans: The Case of Lay Midwifery in North Carolina, 1912–1983." In *African Americans in the South*, edited by Hans A. Baer and Yvonne Jones. Athens: University of Georgia Press, 1992.

Mathis, James L. "A Sophisticated Version of Voodoo Death." *Psychosomatic Medicine* 26 (1964): 104–107.

Mayer, Phillip. "Gusii Initiation Ceremonies." *Journal of the Royal Anthropological Institute* 83 (January–June 1953): 9–36.

Mbiti, John S. *African Religions and Philosophy*, 2nd ed. Portsmouth, N.H.: Heinemann Educational Books, 1990.

Mbiti, John S., *Introduction to African Religion*, 2nd ed. Portsmouth, N.H.: Heinemann Educational Books, 1975.

McCall, George J. "Symbiosis: The Case of Hoodoo and the Numbers Racket." *Social Problems* 10 (Spring 1963): 361–371.

McDougle, Ivan E. *Slavery in Kentucky*. Westport, Conn.: Negro Universities Press, 1970.

McTeer, J. E. *Fifty Years as a Low Country Witch Doctor*. Columbia, S.C.: R. L. Bryan, 1976.

McTeer, J. E. *High Sheriff of the Low Country.* Beaufort, S.C.: Beaufort Book, 1970.

McWillie, Judith. "Writing in an Unknown Tongue." In *Cultural Perspectives on the American South*, vol. 5, "Religion," edited by Charles Reagan Wilson. New York: Gordon and Breach, 1991.

Mendonsa, Eugene L. "Etiology and Divination among the Sisala of Northern Ghana." *Journal of Religion in Africa* 9 (1978): 33–50.

Michaelson, Mike. "Can a Root Doctor Actually Put the Hex on You or Is It a Great Put-on?" *Today's Health* (March 1972).

Miller, Kelley. "The Historic Background of the Negro Physician." *Journal of Negro History* 1, no. 2 (April 1916): 99–109.

Milligan, Robert H. *The Fetish Folk of West Africa.* New York: AMS Press, 1970.

Mitchell, Faith. *Hoodoo Medicine: Sea Island Herbal Remedies.* New York: Reed, Cannon, and Johnson, 1978.

Moore, Ruby Andrews. "Superstitions from Georgia." *Journal of American Folklore* 5 (1892): 230–231.

Moore, Ruby Andrews. "Superstitions from Georgia." *Journal of American Folklore* 7 (1894): 305–306.

Moore, Ruby Andrews. "Superstitions from Georgia." *Journal of American Folklore* 9, no. 2 (1896): 226–228.

Morals, Herbert M. *International Library of Negro Life and History: The History of the Negro in Medicine.* New York: Publishers Company, 1967.

Morgan, Philip D. *Slave Counterpoint.* Chapel Hill: University of North Carolina Press, 1998.

"Mortuary Customs and Beliefs of South Carolina Negroes." *Journal of American Folklore* 7, no. 27 (1894): 318–319.

Mullen, Patrick. "The Function of Folk Belief among Negro Fishermen of the Texas Coast." *Southern Folklore Quarterly* 33 (1969): 80–91.

Munoz, Nelida A. "Haitian Voodoo: Social Control of the Unconscious." *Caribbean Review* 4 (1972): 6–10.

Murchinson, Carl, and Ralph Gilbert. "The Religion of the Negro Male Criminal." *Pedagogical Seminary and Journal of Genetic Psychology* 32 (1932): 447–454.

Myrdal, Gunnar. *An American Dilemma: The Negro Problem and Modern Democracy.* New York: Harper and Row, 1944.

Naipaul, V. S. *Loss of El Dorado: A History.* New York: A. A. Knopf, 1970.

Nassau, Robert Hamill. *Fetichism in West Africa.* New York: Charles Scribner's Sons, 1904.

Neal, James H. *Ju-ju in My Life.* London: George G. Harrap, 1966.

"The Negro Cesar's Cure for Poison." *Massachusetts Magazine* 4 (1792): 103–104.

"Negro Superstitions in South Carolina." *Journal of American Folklore* 8 (1895): 251–252.

Neimark, Philip John. *Way of the Orisha: Empowering Your Life through the Ancient African Religion of Ifa.* New York: Harper Collins, 1993.

Norris, Thaddeus. "Negro Superstitions." *Lippincott's Magazine* 6 (July 1870): 90–95.

Nye, Russel B. *The Unembarrassed Muse: The Popular Arts in America.* New York: Dial Press, 1970.

Oliver, Paul. *Blues Fell This Morning: Meaning in the Blues.* Cambridge: Cambridge University Press, 1960.

Olmstead, Frederick Law. *A Journey in the Seaboard Slave States.* New York: Dix and Edwards, 1856.

Omari, Mikell Smith. "The Role of the Gods in Afro-Brazilian Ancestral Ritual." *African Arts* 23 (November 1989): 54–61, 103–104.

Onstott, Kyle. *Drum.* Greenwich, Conn.: Fawcett, 1962.

Orr, Ellen. "The Bottle Tree." *Mississippi Folklore Register* 4 (Winter 1969): 109–111.

Osofsky, Gilbert, ed. *Puttin' on Ole Massa.* New York: Harper and Row, 1969.

Owen-Workman, Michelle A., Stephen Bennett Phillips, and Renee Stout. *Readers, Advisors, and Storefront Churches: Renee Stout, A Mid-career Retrospective.* Kansas City, Mo.: UMKC, Belger Arts Center, 2002.

Owens, Mary A. "Among the Voodoos," In *Proceedings of the Second International Folk-lore Congress, 1891,* edited by Joseph Jacobs and Alfred Nutt. (London: David Nutt, 1892): 230–248.

Owens, Mary A. *Voodoo Tales.* New York: Negro Universities Press, 1969.

Parrish, Lydia. *Slave Songs of the Georgia Sea Islands.* New York: Creative Age Press, 1942.

Parsons, Elsie Clews. *Folklore of the Sea Islands, South Carolina (Memoirs of the American Folk-Lore Society, vol. XVI).* Cambridge, Mass.: American Folk-Lore Society, 1923.

Parsons, Elsie Clews. "Tales from Guilford County, North Carolina." *Journal of American Folklore* 30 (1917): 168- 200.

Patterson, Caleb Perry. *The Negro in Tennessee, 1790–1865.* New York: Negro Universities Press, 1968.

Payne, Daniel Alexander. *Recollections of Seventy Years,* 2nd ed. New York: Arno Press and the New York Times, 1968; originally published in Nashville Tenn.: A.M.E. Sunday School Union, 1888.

Peek, Philip M., ed. *African Divination Systems.* Bloomington: Indiana University Press, 1991.

Pendleton, Louis. "Notes on Negro Folk-Lore and Witchcraft in the South." *Journal of American Folklore* 3, no. 10 (1890): 201–207.

Peters, Donna Marie. "Passing On." PhD diss., New School for Social Research, New York, 2002.

Phillips, U. B. *Life and Labor in the Old South.* Boston: Little, Brown, 1929.

Phillips, U. B. "Slave Crime in Virginia." *American Historical Review* 20 (January 1915): 326–327.

Pitts, Walter F. *Old Ship of Zion: The Afro-Baptist Ritual in the African Diaspora.* New York: Oxford University Press, 1993.

Pope-Hennessy, James. *Sins of the Fathers: A Study of the Atlantic Slave Traders 1441–1807.* London: Weidenfeld and Nicolson, 1967.

Porteous, Laura. "The Gri-Gri Case." *Louisiana Historical Quarterly* 17 (January 1934): 48–63.

Price, Richard, ed. *Maroon Societies.* New York: Anchor Press/Doubleday, 1973.

Puckett, Newbell Niles. *Folk Beliefs of the Southern Negro.* Montclair, N.J.: Patterson Smith, 1968.

Raboteau, Albert J. *Slave Religion.* New York: Oxford University Press, 1978.

Rawick, George, ed. *The American Slave: South Carolina Narratives,* vol. 3. Westport, Conn.: Greenwood Press, 1972.

Rayburn, Otto Ernest. "The 'Granny Woman' in the Ozarks." *Midwest Folklore* 9 (1959): 145–148.

Reeb, Rene M. "Granny Midwives in Mississippi: Career and Birthing Practices." *Journal of Transcultural Nursing* 4, no. 2 (Winter 1992): 18–27.

Richardson, Clement. "Some Slave Superstitions." *Southern Workman* 41 (1912): 246–248.

Richter, Curt P. "On the Phenomenon of Sudden Death in Animals and Man." *Psychosomatic Medicine* 19 (1957): 191–198.

Roberts, Hilda. "Louisiana Superstitions." *Journal of American Folklore* 40 (1927): 144–208.

Roberts, John. *From Trickster to Badman: The Black Folk Hero in Slavery and Freedom.* Philadelphia: University of Pennsylvania Press, 1989.

Robinson, Jean. "Black Healers during the Colonial Period and Early 19th Century America." PhD diss., Southern Illinois University at Carbondale, 1979.

Rodney, Walter. *A History of the Upper Guinea Coast 1545–1800.* New York: Monthly Review Press, 1982.

Ross, Gayle. *How Rabbit Tricked Otter and Other Cherokee Trickster Stories.* New York: Harper Collins, 1994.

Rucker, Herman. *Black Herman's Secrets of Magic, Mystery and Legerdemain,* 15th ed. Dallas: Dorene, 1938.

Savage, Phoenix. "The Evolution of Hoodoo in Mississippi and Contemporary Black Health." Master's thesis, University of Mississippi, 2001.

Scarborough, William Kauffman. *The Overseer: Plantation Management in the Old South.* Baton Rouge: Louisiana State University Press, 1966.

Schmalleger, Frank. "The Root Doctor and the Courtroom." *North Carolina Folklore* 29 (1981): 102–105.

Schon, James Frederick, and Samuel Crowther. *Journals of the Rev. James Frederick Schon and Mr. Samuel Crowther, Who with the Sanction of Her Majesty's Government Accompanied the Expedition up the Niger in 1841 on Behalf of the Church Missionary Society,* 2nd ed. London: Frank Cass, 1970.

Scott, Kenneth. "The Slave Insurrection in New York in 1712." *New York Historical Society Quarterly* 45 (1961): 43–74.

Serpos, Abdou. "Un Procède de Divination au Dahomey: La Gourde-Pendule." *Bulletin de IIFAN* 5, no. 1–4 (1943): 122–135.

Shaw, Rosalind. "An-bere: A Traditional Form of Temne Divination." *African Research Bulletin* 9, no. 12 (1978): 3–24.

Sieber, Roy, and Frank Herreman, eds. *Hair in African Art and Culture.* New York: Museum for African Art, 2000.

Simpson, George Eaton. "Four Vodun Ceremonies." *Journal of American Folklore* 59, no. 232 (April–June 1946): 154–167.

Sisk, Glenn. "Funeral Customs in the Alabama Black Belt, 1870–1910." *Southern Folklore Quarterly* 23, no. 3 (September 1959): 169–171.

Skloot, Rebecca. *The Immortal Life of Henrietta Lacks*. New York: Crown, 2010.

Smith, Margaret Charles, and Linda Janet Holmes. *Listen to Me Good*. Columbus: Ohio State University Press, 1996.

S. M. P. "Voodooism in Tennessee." *Atlantic Monthly* 64 (1889): 376–380.

Snow, Loudell F. "Folk Medical Beliefs and Their Implications for Care of Patients: A Review Based on Studies among Black Americans." *Annals of Internal Medicine* 81, no. 1 (1974): 82–96.

Snow, Loudell F. "Mail Order Magic: The Commercial Exploitation of Folk Belief." *Journal of the Folklore Institute* 16 (1979): 44–74.

Snow, Loudell F. "Sorcerers, Saints and Charlatans: Black Folk Healers in Urban America." *Culture, Medicine and Psychiatry* 2 (1978): 69–106.

Snow, Loudell F. *Walking Over Medicine*. Boulder, Colo.: Westview Press, 1993.

Sofowora, Abayomi. *Medicinal Plants and Traditional Medicine in Africa*. New York: John Wiley and Sons, 1982.

Starobin, Robert. *Denmark Vesey: The Slave Conspiracy of 1822*. Englewood Cliffs, N.J.: Prentice Hall, 1970.

Starobin, Robert. *Industrial Slavery in the Old South*. New York: Oxford University Press, 1970.

Steagill, Archie. "The Voodoo Man of the Brazos." *Publication of the Texas Folklore Society* no. 17 (1941): 113–114.

Steiner, Roland. "Brasiel Robinson Possessed of Two Spirits." *Journal of American Folklore* 13 (1900): 226–228.

Steiner, Roland. "Observations on the Practice of Conjuring in Georgia." *Journal of American Folklore* 14 (1901): 173–180.

Steiner, Roland. "Superstitions and Beliefs from Central Georgia." *Journal of American Folklore* 12 (1899): 261–271.

Still, James. *Early Recollections and Life of Dr. James Still 1812–1885*. New Brunswick, N.J., 1973; Medford, N.J.: Medford Historical Society, 1971.

Stuckey, Sterling. *Slave Culture*. New York: Oxford University Press, 1987.

Szwed, John, and Morton Marks. "The Afro-American Transformation of European Set Dances and Dance Suites." *Dance Research Journal* 20, no. 1 (Summer 1988): 29–36.

"Tatler On the Management of Negroes." *Southern Cultivator* 9 (June 1851): 84–85.

Thanet, Octave. "Folklore in Arkansas." *Journal of American Folklore* 5, no. 18 (April–June 1892): 121–125.

Thomas, Richard W. "Working-Class and Lower-Class Origins of Black Culture: Class Formation and the Division of Black Cultural Labor." *Minority Voices* 1, no. 2 (Fall 1977): 81–103.

Thompson, Robert Farris. "An Aesthetic of the Cool: West African Dance." *African Forum* 2, no. 2 (Fall 1966): 13.

Thompson, Robert Farris. *Flash of the Spirit.* New York, 1983.

Thornton, John. "The Development of an African Catholic Church in the Kingdom of Kongo, 1491–1750." *Journal of African History* 25, no. 2 (1984): 147–167.

Thornton, John. *The Kongolese Saint Anthony.* Cambridge: Cambridge University Press, 1998.

Tinling, David C. "Voodoo, Root Work and Medicine." *Psychosomatic Medicine* 29 (1967): 483–490.

Torrey, E. Fuller. *The Mind Game: Witchdoctors and Psychiatrists.* New York: Emerson Hall, Bantam, 1973.

Truesdell, Seneca E. "Buffalo Chips as a Remedy." *Journal of American Folklore* 12, no. 47 (October–December 1899): 295.

Tucker, John. *Angola: The Land of the Blacksmith Prince.* London: World Dominion Press, 1933.

Twain, Mark. *The Adventures of Huckleberry Finn.* New York: Penguin Books USA, 1985.

Tyler, Varro. "The Elusive History of High John the Conqueror Root." *Pharmacy in History* 33, no. 4 (1991): 164–166.

Van Blarcom, Carolyn Conant. "Rat Pie: Among the Black Midwives of the South." *Harpers Monthly Magazine* 160 (1930): 322–332.

Waring, Mary A. "Negro Superstitions in South Carolina." *Journal of American Folklore* 8 (1895): 251–252.

Warner, H. E. "Folk Medicine of Pension Claimants." *Journal of American Folklore* 2, no. 4 (1889): 238–239.

Washington, Harriet A. *Medical Apartheid: The Dark History of Medical Experimentation on African Americans from Colonial Times to the Present.* New York: Doubleday, 2007.

Webb, Bernice Larson. "A Study of Voodoo Mail-Order Advertising in Louisiana." *Louisiana Review* 2 (Summer 1973): 65–71.

Webb, Julie Yvonne. "Louisiana Voodoo and Superstitions Related to Health." *H.S.M.H.A. Health Reports* 86, no. 4 (1971): 241–301.

Weiss, Harry B. "Oneirocritica Americana." *Bulletin of the New York Public Library* 48, no. 6 (June 1944): 519–541.

Whitney, Anne. "Items of Maryland Belief and Custom." *Journal of American Folklore* 12, no. 47 (October–December 1899): 273–274.

Whitten, Norman E. Jr. "Contemporary Patterns of Malign Occultism among Negroes in North Carolina." *Journal of American Folklore* 75 (October–December 1962): 311–325.

Williams, Joseph J. "Development of Obeah in Jamaica." *Voodoos and Obeahs: Phases of West Indian Witchcraft.* New York: Lincoln MacVeagh Dial Press, 1932).

Wilson, David J. "Bishop E. E. Everett and Some Aspects of Occultism and Folk Religion in Negro Philadelphia." *Keystone Folklore* 14 (1969): 59–80.

Wilson, William Julius. *When Work Disappears: The World of the New Urban Poor.* New York: Knopf, 1996.

Wimbs, Cassandra. "African-American Theory, Beliefs and Practices: Candle Shops." Master's thesis, University of California at Berkeley, 1989.

Wintrob, Roland M. "The Influence of Others: Witchcraft and Rootwork as Explanations of Behavior Disturbances." *Journal of Nervous and Mental Disease* 156 (1973): 318–326.

Wood, Peter. "People's Medicine in the Early South." *Southern Exposure* 6 (Summer 1978): 50–53.

Work, Monroe. "Some Geechee Folklore." *Southern Workman* 35 (1905): 633–639.

Yetman, Norman R., ed. *Life under the "Peculiar Institution."* New York: Holt, Rinehart, and Winston, 1970.

Index

Crowther, Samuel, 25, 26
crystal ball gazers, 103
Cuba: religion in, 31, 42–43; slavery
    abolished in, 30
curses, protection against, 44

dance: African American core culture,
    6, 14, 16, 119; Big Apple, 61, 86; Buz-
    zard Lope, 44; counterclockwise sa-
    cred circle, 37, 44, 45–48, 58, 60–61,
    86, 89, 94, 97, 145; distinguishing
    qualities of, 46; Eagle Rock, 86; exotic
    themes of, 103; and muscle memory,
    46; "picking up or harvesting leaves,"
    44; Ring Shout, 6, 44, 60–62, 85–86;
    social, 44, 60, 86; tap, 168; West Afri-
    can, 5–6
Dancingtree Moonwater, 172, 177–78
deamon spirits, 92
"death of the Gods," 41, 42
death rituals, 37, 61
de Laurence Company, Chicago, 124
devil's work, 4, 91
dice, 92
diggers, 165
dime: amulet, *148*, 150; dancing, 92
divination systems, 22–24, 27, 30, 31,
    55–56, 92, 129
Dixon, Willie, "Tail Dragger," 100
DNA or life code, 25
dominoes, 92
Donahue, Phil, 1
donation sacks, 140–41
Douglass, Frederick, 64
Drake, St. Clair, 125
Dr. Bug, 92, 121
Dr. Buzzard (Robinson), 74, 89, 92,
    117, 119–22, 134, 153, 166, 173
Dr. Duke, 98
dream books, 130–32, *132*
dream interpretation, 128, 129, 131
Dr. John of New Orleans, 92
DuBois, W. E. B., 39, 57, 61, 63, 95–96;
    The Philadelphia Negro, 105
Dunbar, Paul Laurence, "We Wear the
    Mask," 51

Eagle Rock (dance), 86
Eikerenkoetter, Rev. Frederick (Rever-
    end Ike), 170, 181
Elfe, Willie, 137

Ellis, Charles and William, 152
emancipation, 53–54, 60, 63, 67; and
    black belt tradition, 84–90; and vul-
    nerability, 179
Esu/Elegba, 13
Ewe culture, 37

faith healing, 94, 167
Fang people, 25, 26
Fantee people, 23, 26
Faulkner, William, 86, 88, 89
Ferdon, Jim, 108
fetish, 27, 63–64
fictive kinship, 117–18
fingernails, safeguarding, 102
fix (spell), 99
flashpoints, 24–25
Flowers, Arthur, 172, 175–76
folk magic, 98, 99
Fon culture, 23, 30, 31, 37
Fontenot, Wanda, 11, 147, 149
fortune-tellers, 103

GaGa, 30
galanga root, 74, 120
Garrison, Ann, 78
Gentile, Benedetto, 131
Glave, E. J., 51
glory hand, 81
Goldberg, Whoopi, 14
Gomez, Michael, 41
Gooch, William, 51–52
Granny Ya, 143
gravediggers, 104
grave site decoration, 26
graveyard dirt, 26, 31
great migration, 85, 91–92, 97–99,
    109–12, 124, 157, 167, 179
Gregory, Brother A. B., 165, 166, 172,
    173
gris-gris, 37
Gullah church, 11–12
Gullah Coast, 121, 173, 181
Gypsies, 103, 119

haints, 44, 60, 92
hair trimmings, 102 3
Haiti: revolution in, 30; Vodun in, 5, 6,
    31, 127
Hall, Gwendolyn Midlo, 79, 80
Hall, Julien A., 50

Hallam, Lewis, 106
Hampshire's Horse, 92
Hampton Institute, *Southern Workman*, 59
Harris, Hattie, 147
harvest grounds, loss of, 122, 157, 158, 165, 166
Harvey, Brantley, 121
head shaving, 94, 97
healing ritual, 56–57
healing symbol, 114–15, *114*
herbal healing: and conjurers, 150; and knowledge of plants, 29, 51–52, 91, 137, 150–51; and medicine, 53, 91, 135–36, 137, 153; and midwives, 137, 146; Native American influence in, 7, 39, 52; and poisons, 29, 52, 53–54, 56, 152; and religious traditions, 31, 44; and root doctors, 52, 91, 114, 135; and slavery, 50–54, 64, 136–37; and spiritual forces, 27–30, 51–52, 64, 135
herbs, harvesting of, 104–5
Herron, Leonora, 9
Herskovits, Melville, 10
Heyward, DuBose, 86; "The Half-Pint Flask," 88–89; *Porgy*, 88
High John the Conquer, 44, 68–83; and Gaspar Yanga, 75–80, *76*; Hurston on, 10, 70, 83; and John the Prophet, 3, 96; legacy of, 83; low John, 74; middle John, 74; "Mr. Jim's Bawdy John Tale," 73–74; myth of, 67, 69–71, 72–74, 75, 81, 92; running John, 74; and St. Malo, 80–83
High John the Conquer root, 8, 68–69, 126, 128, 141, 150; chewing, and courtroom work, 74–75, 120, 121; names of, 69, 74; significance of, 68, 71–72, 74; sources of, 69, 75, 104
Hippocrates, 130
Hobley, N. H., 138
home remedies, negative effects of, 154
Hoodoo: adaptability of, 49, 54, 60, 67, 84, 97–98, 126; artifacts of, 54–56, *55*; and black nationalists, 90; evolving, 5, 6–7, 13, 14–15, 39, 41, 45, 50, 60–62, 67, 89–90, 91, 122, 126, 168–72, 179–85; false claims of, 181–84; golden age of, 93, 97; harm caused by, 136, 154; healing symbol, 114–15,

114; influence on literature of, 86; as intergenerational, 15, 61; labels of, 4; legends and myths, 70–71, 75, 80–83, 92; national identity of, 92, 94–95; opposition to, 9, 109, 119; recruitment and training in, 92; regional clusters of, 36–38; and Ring Shout, 6, 44, 45–48, 60–62; scope of, 3–4, 9, 64, 90, 179; signs and gestures, 60, 128–29; and slavery, 35–37, 39–41, 49–50, 54–56, 57–61, 67, 90; snake-oil or marketeered, 4–5, 15, 16–17, 90–91, 107–12, 116–19, 122–28, 131, 163–65, 179–83; sources of, 30, 34–37, 47, 98–99; supplies and paraphernalia of, 4–5, 98, 119, 122–28, 131, 157, 162; survival of, 14–15, 60, 62, 85, 184–85; uses of the term, 1–3, 4, 14, 32. *See also* religion
"Hoodoo clergy," 55
Hoodoo drugstore, 154–55, 157, 162
horse races, betting on, 132–33
hot foot powder, 102, 163
Howlin' Wolf (Burnett), 100
Hughes, Louis, 65, 126–27
Hurston, Zora Neale, 10–11, 70, 83, 94, 98, 183
husbands, women seeking, 167, 171–72
Hyatt, Harry Middleton, 10, 11, 94, 102, 141, 183

idol worship, 20
Ifa divination, 22, 147
Igbo society, 22, 30, 31, 37
illness, spiritual origins of, 9, 56–57, 59, 135–36
incantations, 92, 113, 144, 146, 163
inclusive-integrative principle, 43–44, 54
Internet: advertising on, 160–61, 162–63, 181; exploitation on, 164, 169, 180, 181–84
internment soil, 26, 31
interviewer effect, 10, 183
Isaac, John, 151
Islam, 90, 162
Iyalorichas/Iyalorishas, 31, 168

jalap root, 69, 75, 76, 104, 122
James, U. P., 130
Jesus of Nazareth, 71
Jewish merchants, 90, 106, 123

36, 43, 45, 48, 99; and herbal healing, 7, 39, 52; and slaves, 36, 58; spiritual traditions of, 12, 30, 31, 120

nature: elements of, 44, 47; forces of, 60; signs in, 92

nature/nation sacks, 140–42

naturopathy. *See* herbal healing

Neal, James H., 88

Neal, Larry, 89

Neimark, Philip John, 139

Nesbitt, Frances, 121

New Orleans: Hoodoo in, 36, 37, 39, 85; slave pens of, 58, 77–78, 79; Voodoo in, 6, 39, 95, 126–27, 162

New World Pan-Africanism, 168–69

Nganga (priest), 51

numbers, 128, 129–34

Obasi, Myra, 1

Obeah, 30, 32, 170

occult, 103, 111, 123–24

Onesimus (servant), 51

oracles, 27

Orisha tradition, 23, 31, 126; and *abiku*, 139; author's initiation into, 12–13, 56; healing practices in, 29–30; survival of, 43, 168, 184

Otto, David, 1

Owens, Mary Alicia, 67, 107–8

palm readers, 103, 119

palms, rubbing, 102

Palo Mayombe/Palo Monte, 13, 30, 31, 184

Papa Ce, 172, 173–74

paradigm of silence, 54

Parrish, Lydia, 44

Parsons, Elsie Clews, 115

Payne, Bishop Daniel, 97

Pendleton, Louis, 95

perception, 39

Perry, Lincoln "Stepin Fetchit," 14

placentas, 117, 140, 144

Plat-eye, 44, 92

playing cards, 92

poisons, knowledge of, 29, 52, 53–54, 56, 152

Porgy and Bess (Broadway), 88

prayers, healing, 28

Primus (slave), 137

protection from whites, 117, 179, 181

protective medicine, 137

protective objects, 56

Protestantism, and African American spirituality, 5, 33, 36, 45, 64

Pryor, Richard, 89

Psalms, 92, 140, 177

Puckett, Newbell Niles, 10, 94, 113, 147

Quarra St. Malo/Dirge of St. Malo, 81–82

Raboteau, Albert, 32, 39

race: delimitations of the term, 8; marginalization through, 85, 106; stereotypes of, 14, 165

"race betterment," 157, 168

racial terrorism, 85, 95, 109, 179

racism, white supremacy, 63, 85, 169

railroad tracks, as power site, 44

rattlesnake, power of, 164

reciprocity, 87

Reconstruction, 43, 85; end of, 110; and Hoodoo's second stage, 90–115

Regla de Ocha, 31

Regla de Orisha, 13

religion: and adaptation, 47, 49, 60; ARC, 40, 41, 43, 44, 125, 171, 184; and artistic creation, 22; belief in supreme being, 21; black church tradition, 5, 15, 61, 112–13; and dance, 6, 61; definitions of, 3; functions of, 3, 21; fundamentalist, 60, 171; and lay helpers, 170–71; and ritual, 21; and slavery, 3, 21, 30, 42, 43, 44–45, 49, 56–59, 61–64; and superstition, 3, 4, 20; syncretic transfer of, 2–3, 30, 33, 45, 63, 94

Reverend Ike, 170, 181

Reynolds, John P., 52

Rice, Thomas "Daddy," 106

rice plantations, 38

Richmond, Hoodoo in, 36, 38

Ring Shout, 3, 11; commercial secularization of, 85–86; and counterclockwise sacred dance circle, 37, 45–48, 60–61, 145; and Hoodoo, 6, 44, 45–48, 60–62; possession ritual, 86; worship services, 58, 125

rites of passage, 94

Robination Horse, 44, 92

Robinson, Jean, 11

Robinson, Stepheney (Dr. Buzzard), 119–22, 153, 173

Roediger, David R., 8

root chewing, 74–75, 120, 121

root doctors, 105–6, 135, 153; adaptation of, 112, 162; and conjurers, 52, 63, 91, 150; conjurers separated from, 91, 113–14; networks of, 93, 104, 169; and poisons, 52, 53–54; roles of, 91, 107, 136

roots, harvesting of, 104–5

root work, 4, 32, 55, 103, 110, 112

Ross, Gayle, 120

Russel, Chloe, 130

sacred days, 92

Sanctified Church, 5, 96, 125, 184

sand, healing, 151

Santeria, 5, 6, 11, 13, 30, 31, 71, 126, 162, 166

Sapelo Island, Georgia, 86–87, 94

Savage, Phoenix, 11, 172, 176–77

Schmalliger, Frank, 74

Schon, Rev. James Frederick, 25, 26

secret societies, 22, 54, 60

Seven Sisters of Algiers, 92

shaman, 27, 29, 50

Shango, 71

Shango Baptist, 30, 31, 168, 169

shape-shifting, 92

sharecropping, 63

shoes, 38

Shout. *See* Ring Shout

sign interpretation, 128–29

Silverberg, Alex, 122, 123, 131

Sixth and Seventh Books of Moses, 111–12

slave doctors, 52–53, 90

slavery, 34–67; African-based culture of, 41, 57–58; codependence in, 50; and cotton, 38, 42, 43; end of, 53–54, 60, 63, 67; historic memory of, 39, 44–45; and Hoodoo, 35–37, 39–41, 49–50, 54–56, 57–61, 67, 90; paradigm of silence, 54; on plantations, 38, 58, 85, 110; and religion, 3, 21, 30, 42, 43, 44–45, 49, 56–59, 61–64; and role structuring, 48–50

slaves: assimilation of, 41–43, 49; as conjure doctors, 63, 91; cultural exchanges among, 58–59, 85; ethnicity of, 12, 57; families disrupted, 41; healing practices of, 50–54, 57, 136–38, 146, 152; and inclusive-integrative principle, 43–44; involuntary transfer of, 21, 36, 42; labor of, 12, 16, 42, 63;

mojo bags of, 41, 65–67, *65, 66*; and Native Americans, 36, 58; networks of, 78–79; poison plants known to, 52, 53–54, 152; rebellions of, 64, 69–70, 80; runaway, 80; sacred dances of, 44, 45–48; sales of, 41, 58, 78, 79; and spirit possession, 47, 48, 57

slave stewards, 78–79

snakebite cures, 50

snake-oil Hoodoo: advertising, 110–12, 117–18, 125; limitations of, 127–28; marketeered, 4–5, 15, 16–17, 90–91, 103, 107–12, 116–19, 122–28, 131, 163–65, 179–83; use of term, 15

Snow, Loudell F., 11, 157

Sofowora, Abayomi, 147

southern style, use of term, 16

speaking in tongues, 125

spells, 99

spiders, sacred, 32

spirit healing, 94

spirit plant, 83, 88

spirit possession, 27, 30, 47, 48, 57, 94, 125

spirit realm, 23–24

spiritualism, 4, 51–52, 124

Spiritualist Church, 5, 125

spirit work, 4, 112, 184

spit, 31

Steiner, Roland, 9

St. Helena Island, 120–21, 166

Still, Dr. James of the Pine Barrens, 114, 152

St. Malo, 80–83

Stout, Renee, 90

string: in healing, 28–29, 114, 147–50, *148, 149;* in mojo bags, 67

Stuckey, Sterling, 45, 48

supernatural phenomena, 9, 23, 60, 62, 99, 105, 135–36

superstition, 3, 4, 20

swampers, 98, 103, 119, 124, 157

Tarzan, 20–21

Temne society, 22

Thomas, George A., 155

threshold, as power site, 44

tobacco plantations, 38

Torrey, E. Fuller, 160

track gathering, 38, 75, 99–102

treaters, 63, 91, 92, 135–36, 146–47

trickster deity, 13, 87

Turner, James, 151–52
Twain, Mark, 86, 89
twitching eye, 128–29
two-head (conjurer), 62, 63, 102, 104, 106, 107, 114, 125

umbilical cords, 104, 117, 138, 140
Uncle Nero, 151
undertakers, 104, 122, 124
universal balance, 63
urbanization, 85, 97–98, 110–12, 118, 124, 125, 127, 156–57, 167–68

Valmor Company, 124–25
Vaugn, Jim, 75
vocalization, 113
Vodu, 23
Vodun, 5, 6, 13, 14, 30, 31, 44, 127, 166
Voodoo, 184; in New Orleans, 6, 39, 95, 126–27, 162; use of the term, 1–2, 14

Walker, Alice, 89; *The Color Purple*, 60
Walker, Madam C. J., 124
walkin' foot, 102, 163
walking boy, 92, 128
wanga amulets, 37
water: baptism in the river, 115; flowing, 102; from the foundry, 115, 163; healing, 151; immersion in, 30, 35,

94, 125; sacred water, 163; war water, 163, 183
Welsing, Frances Cress, 8
West Africa: breakdown of religion in, 39; healing rituals of, 56–57; religious leader's roles in, 57; secret societies of, 22; status hierarchy in, 21–22, 49; tradition of, 5–6, 166
Wimbs, Cassandra, 11, 71, 126–27
Windwalker, Djenra, 172, 174–75
witchcraft, 4, 31, 60, 92, 99
witch doctors, 103
words: mystical power of, 28; pronunciation of, 113
World War II, 90; postwar environment, 156–78
World Wars: and national identity, 117; period between, 116–34

Xalapa, Mexico, 69, 71

Yanga, Gaspar, 75–80, 76
Yoruba tradition, 37, 166; and *abiku*, 139; healing practices in, 147; High John the Conquer myth, 72; and Orisha, 12, 13, 23, 29, 31, 126, 184; religion in, 22, 24, 30

zinzin amulets, 37

Katrina Hazzard-Donald
is an associate professor of sociology,
anthropology, and criminal justice at
Rutgers University-Camden and the
author of *Jookin': The Rise of Social Dance
Formations in African American Culture.*

The University of Illinois Press
is a founding member of the
Association of American University Presses.

———————————————

University of Illinois Press
1325 South Oak Street
Champaign, IL 61820-6903
www.press.uillinois.edu